A History of Presteigne

Radnorshire's
Old County Town:
A History of Presteigne

by

Keith Parker

Logaston Press 1997

LOGASTON PRESS
Little Logaston Woonton Almeley
Herefordshire HR3 6QH

First published by Logaston Press 1997
Copyright © Keith Parker 1997

All rights reserved. No part of this publication
may be reproduced, stored in a retrieval system,
or transmitted, in any form or by any means,
electronic, mechanical, photocopying, recording
or otherwise, without the prior permission,
in writing of the publisher.

ISBN 1 873827 79 2

Set in Times 11 on 13 pt
by Logaston Press and printed in Great Britain
by The Cromwell Press

Contents

		Page
	Foreword	*vii*
	Introduction	*ix*
I	The Early History of the Area	1
II	The Middle Ages	13
III	Tudor Presteigne	29
IV	Plague, War and Fire	53
V	Stagnation and Recovery	83
VI	From the French Wars to Victoria	107
VII	High Victorian Presteigne	135
VIII	The Struggle for a Future	173
IX	Towards the 21st Century	225
	Bibliography	231

*For Abigail and Hannah
Harris*

Foreword

More than fifty years have elapsed since W.H. Howse wrote his well-received *Presteigne Past and Present* and during that time perspectives have changed, whilst many more sources have become available to historians. As a result our understanding of the history of the town has been considerably enhanced by Lord Rennell's *Valley on the March* (1958) and many articles published in the *Transactions* of the Radnorshire Society and of the Woolhope Naturalists' Field Club and in other journals.

However, such publications are not always readily accessible to the general reader, nor do all relevant articles, books and theses have the history of Presteigne as a central theme. Thus, the major task undertaken by the writer has been one of synthesis: to update Mr Howse's conclusions of 1945 in light of recent research. To this extent, this book is based not only on the writer's own research, but also leans heavily upon the scholarship and hard work of many others, though the responsibility for the conclusions reached, and for any errors in fact or interpretation, rests with him.

In the interests of the general reader, footnotes have been largely avoided, though by way of acknowledgement and to assist those who may wish to research some aspect of Presteigne's history in greater detail, a list of sources used for each chapter is given at the end of the text.

Place names invariably pose a problem, particularly on the Welsh border, for in addition to English place names changing over time, Welsh place names have sometimes been modified as a result of anglicisation. The course adopted in the text has been to use the spelling followed on current Ordnance Survey maps, which may irritate the purist, but has the virtue of following current local usage. Somewhat inconsistently, Imperial units of weights, measures and mensuration have been used in preference to the metric, along with pre-decimal monetary units.

This book could not have been written without the help of the staff of record offices and libraries, who dealt with my innumerable requests and enquiries with unfailing patience and courtesy. The writer is grateful in this respect to the staff of the National Library of Wales at Aberystwyth, Powys County Archives Office, Hereford and Worcester County Record Office, Hereford City Library Reference Section, Hereford Cathedral Library, the Leominster branch of Hereford County Library, the Llandrindod Wells and Presteigne branches of Powys County Library, Presteigne Museum and to the Honorary Librarians of the Radnorshire Society. His thanks are also due to Ms Elizabeth Stuart for her careful transcription of many documents at the Public Record Office at Chancery Lane and at Kew.

Many people have assisted by providing information on particular aspects of the town's history, notably Mrs Glenys Lister, Mrs Eve Rendle, and Messrs Colin Barrett, Stuart Bennett, Ian Creed, Paul Davidson, Harry Hatfield, Kurt Ockert and Geoffrey Ridyard. Mr Christopher Harley also kindly allowed me to consult the detailed card index to the Brampton Bryan Estate Papers at the Hereford and Worcester County Record Office. The writer also wishes to thank Mrs Cherry Leversedge, Mrs Eve Rendle, Mr Colin Barrett, Mr John Crowe, Mr Gwyn John and Mr Kurt Ockert for permission to use photographs in their possession as illustrations. Many of these were first published as postcards by Percy B. Yates. I must also thank the Radnorshire Society for allowing me to use two of A.M. Wilson's photographs, the Clwyd-Powys Archaeological Trust for the aerial photograph of Hindwell Fort and the Hereford and Worcester Record Office and Powys County Archives Office for their permission to reproduce documents as illustrations.

Thanks are also due to Andy Johnson and Ron Shoesmith of Logaston Press for their advice on the text and its preparation for publication, also for the index; to Brian Byron for redrawing my very inadequate sketch maps, charts and diagrams; and to Paul Remfry for his valuable comments on an early draft of the first two chapters. Lastly, but by no means least, I must acknowledge with gratitude the patience and forebearance of my wife in coping with my sometimes unsociable preoccupation with local history over so many years.

Introduction

Presteigne, the old county town of Radnorshire, is an archetypal border town, for it is situated on the south bank of the river Lugg, which at this point serves as the boundary between England and Wales, and much of the ecclesiastical parish lies over the border in Herefordshire.

By virtue of its position the town looks eastwards into England, for it lies at the point where the Lugg begins to broaden out towards the Hereford plain. The farming pattern in the area, like the local accent, has much more in common with north-west Herefordshire than with the Welsh uplands. To the west, its links with Wales are hampered by the mass of Radnor Forest and relative ease of communication to the east has ensured that Presteigne's commercial links have always been with its English neighbours, notably Ludlow, Leominster, Hereford and Shrewsbury.

Though English influences have always been strong, for until the formation of Radnorshire in 1536 the area lay in Herefordshire, Shropshire or the Marches, it cannot be regarded as essentially English in character, even if its vernacular architecture conveys this impression, for it has always been subject to strong countervailing Welsh influences. Initial Anglo-Saxon penetration was largely by a process of assimilation, thus even at the outset Celtic influences were far from negligible. Again, though probably reconverted by priests of the Hereford diocese, within whose jurisdiction Presteigne has always been, the influence of Celtic christianity, particularly of St David, remained strong in the Arrow and Lugg valleys, stretching as far as Leominster, even in the medieval period.

Its role as the local market centre and later as county town of Radnorshire and the venue for Quarter Sessions and Great Sessions also thrust it into closer contact with its far more Welsh hinterland, thus ensuring a continuing Welsh influence. However, the most effective factor in ensuring the survival of Welsh influence in the locality has been the continuous migration into the area from the Welsh uplands. This was on a relatively large scale between the fourteenth and seventeenth centuries after the ravages of the plague epidemics, but on a lesser scale thereafter, through marriage and through the migration of successful and enterprising hill farmers to the more fertile land of the Lugg valley, trends encapsulated in the old Radnorshire tradition of going 'down country for a farm and up country for a wife'.

Neither wholly English nor Welsh, the town has always shown a dogged capacity to withstand sometimes dramatic reversals in its fortunes by adapting to new circumstances and exploiting fresh opportunities as they have arisen. It is this sheer tenacity, rather than its brief moments of national prominence which makes Presteigne's history both interesting and so typical of the small towns of the Welsh Marches.

CHAPTER I

The Early History of the Area

Although the present settlement of Presteigne can trace its origins back to the Anglo-Saxon period, in order to place the town fully in its historical perspective, it is necessary to trace, in broad outline, the earlier history of the area, though since the evidence is so scanty any such survey must be highly tentative.

    The relief and drainage patterns of the locality were profoundly influenced by the later phases of the Ice Age. The lateral moraine of the Arrow glacier blocked the Hindwell Brook at Roddhurst, diverting it away from the Arrow towards the Lugg which was itself blocked by moraine at the Woodhouse, near Shobdon, thus creating a lake in the valley which extended approximately to the present 500 foot contour line. Ultimately the water level rose to the point where an overflow channel was created through what was to become Kinsham Gorge and beyond Kinsham the Lugg took over what had been the original channel of the river Teme. As the water level dropped and the Lugg glacier retreated, transverse mounds of debris were deposited along the valley floor, hampering the flow of the Lugg, creating lakes and ultimately marshland, remnants of which survive today to the north-west of Clatterbrune, at Byton and Combe and, in the Hindwell valley, at Knill.

The Late Neolithic and Bronze Ages
For most of the prehistoric period much of the Presteigne area was thus largely marshland which drained only slowly. The accepted view is that the first permanent settlement occurred relatively late, probably not much earlier than 1200 BC, and was restricted to narrow strips of land on each

side of the valley, sandwiched between the marshy flood plain of the Lugg and the clay belt around the valley at 500-600 feet where thick woodland began. The habitable area had a fairly shallow layer of soil overlying gravel and was probably covered by light scrub which could be cleared fairly easily. On the evidence of the few remains of ancient settlement, it has been generally accepted that the population it sustained was probably small.

Standing stones have been identified at Combe and Lower Kinsham, that at the latter location and known as the Devil Stone having seven possible cup marks on what were the upper and north faces. Close to the Devil Stone there are two tumuli. The larger is forty-five yards in diameter and some six feet in height, and surrounded by a ditch nearly ten yards wide. The smaller is thirty-five yards in diameter, five feet high and surrounded by a ditch ten yards in width. On the opposite side of the valley, close to Upper Heath, there may have once been another standing stone, for this point, where two footpaths cross, was known in the sixteenth century as 'Herston Cross', a name which has survived today in the form of the nearby Hoarstone Cottage.

Again, relatively few artefacts of the period have been found in the locality except at the Upper Heath where a possible chipping centre was identified in 1954. Other recorded finds include a few convex scrapers and a number of flint flakes at Home Farm, Norton; a flint arrowhead at Discoed; a few scrapers and flakes at Stapleton; and one scraper found in a garden in Scottleton Street. Though W.H. Howse postulates the existence of a number of ridgeway tracks in the Presteigne area, there are no indications of a trade route along the Teme-Lugg watershed to compare with that between the Teme and the Clun.

However, in the absence of aerial surveys or any systematic and detailed archaeological work, any conclusions concerning the area in the period under discussion can only be provisional. The conventional view that the area was thinly populated certainly seems open to question following C.J. Dunn's fieldwork in the nearby Radnor Basin during the 1960s, which suggests that the population of that area in the later prehistoric period may have been greater than had been previously believed, while the Clwyd-Powys Archaeological Trust's current fieldwork in the Walton area provides evidence, not only of a larger population, but also of a highly developed socio-political system in the borderlands.

The Iron Age Hill Forts
Two major hillforts are to be found in the locality, at Burfa and Wapley.

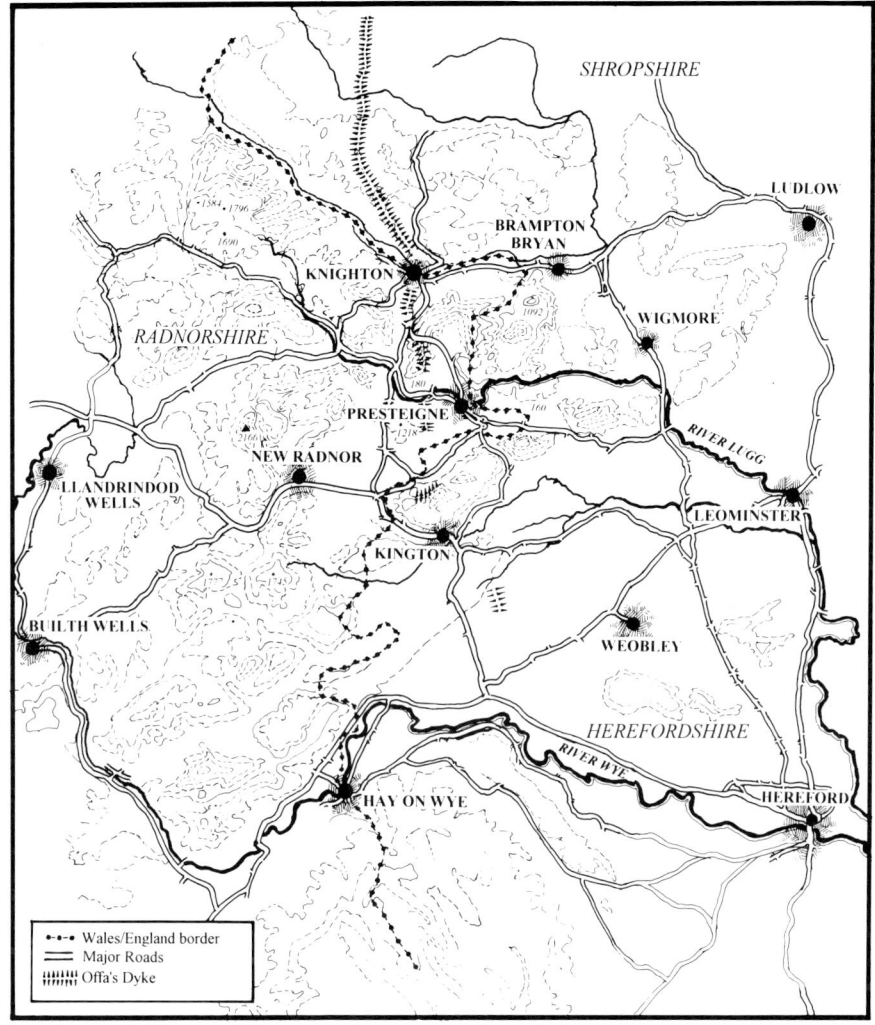

Fig. 1: Map showing Presteigne and surrounding area

Both may have been permanent settlements, though since neither have been excavated, little can be said with any certainty. In their present form both probably date from about 400 BC, the date attributed to the Croft Ambrey hillfort by S.C. Stanford in the 1960s.

At Wapley, just over two miles to the south-east of Presteigne, the hilltop enclosure is protected by five banks and ditches to the east where the slope is negligible, and by four banks and ditches on the steeper slope to the west of the south gate. At their widest the defences extend over nearly 100 yards. The habitable area within the enclosure is rather more than seven acres and the defences around it occupy a further fifteen acres.

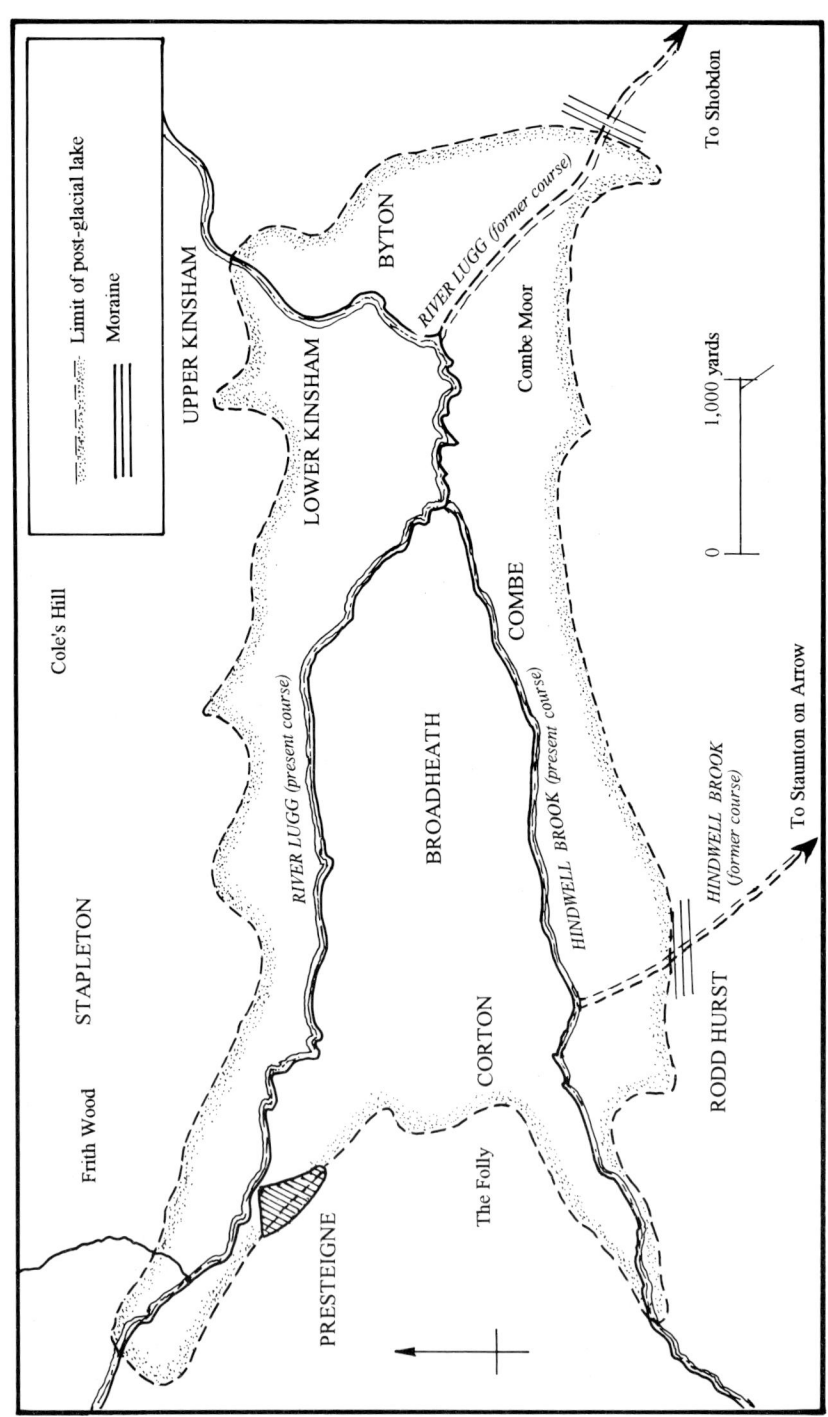

Fig. 2: The Presteigne area after the Ice Age (c.8,000 BC)

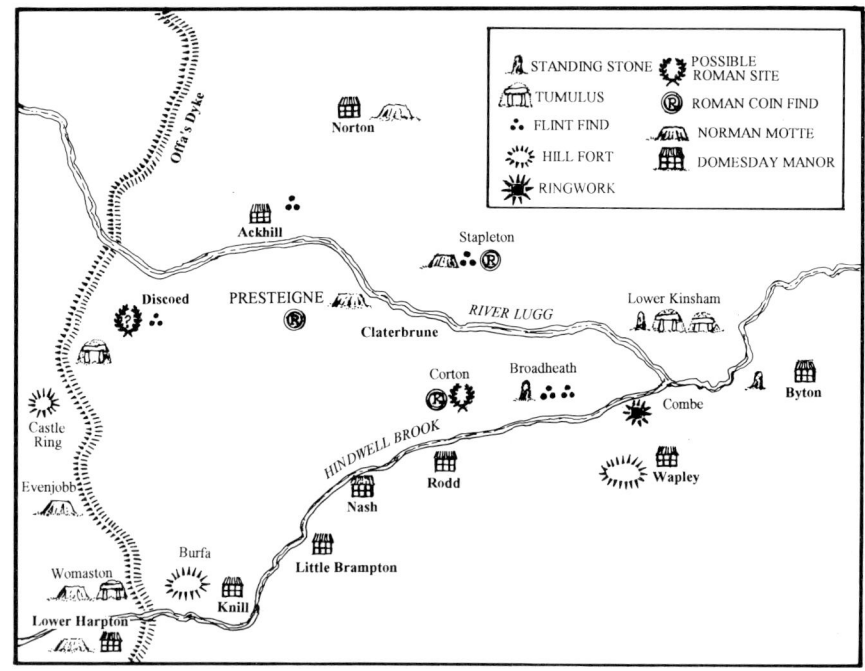

Fig. 3: The archaeology of the Presteigne area

Without excavation any estimate of its population can only be tentative, but using Dr Stanford's estimate of Croft Ambrey's population as a standard (236 persons per hectare, equivalent to 94 persons per acre), Wapley, if a permanent settlement, may have had a population of about 660. Given the convention that a medieval settlement occupied 7% of its cultivable area, it would seem that the inhabitants of Wapley would have required about 285 acres of cultivable land to support themselves. The most likely location of this would have been on the dip slope towards Weobley's Ash and Stansbatch, for the area below the scarp to the east of the Lugg was not easily accessible from the camp.

Nearly three miles S.S.W. of Presteigne, overlooking the Hindwell Brook, lies the equally formidable Burfa Camp, occupying about twenty acres. On the summit of a hill, more than 1,000 feet above sea level, it is defended on the steeper side of the hill by a low embankment and a shallow ditch, but elsewhere the defences consist of two walls each twelve feet in height, each with an exterior ditch with falls of twenty feet. As at Wapley, the entrance was by means of a deeply recessed passageway. On the basis of Dr Stanford's estimate of Croft Ambrey's population and allowing for some of the enclosed area serving only a defensive function, Burfa could have accommodated a permanent population of about that suggested for Wapley and would have required a similar amount of arable land.

The area around Presteigne probably lay outside the direct sphere of influence of either hillfort—neither was oriented towards the Presteigne locality for both overlooked more favoured areas to the south; in the case of Wapley—Staunton and Stansbatch, and in the case of Burfa—Harpton and Knill. Moreover, even if it possessed land with some potential as arable or pasture, it was not easily accessible due to distance. Not for the last time the Presteigne area found itself a border region, its marshes and brushwood uneasily shared by the hunters, wild fowlers and fishermen of both forts, with control of possible outpost sites such as the Warden and Stapleton mounds and their dependent settlements, passing from one fort to the other as their respective military powers fluctuated.

As was the case with Croft Ambrey, Wapley and Burfa forts were probably forcibly cleared by the Romans, though their defensive potential may have led to their use as temporary refuges in the following centuries. There is certainly a tradition that Wapley was utilised by Caradoc during his campaign against the Romans and by Glyndwr's forces in the early fifteenth century.

The Roman Period
Following his flight to the west in 47 AD Caradoc continued his struggle against the Romans with the aid of the Silures and Ordovices. Local tradition maintains that his final campaign was mounted from Wapley, one half of his forces crossing the Lugg to march over Stonewall Hill to Knighton, while the other half followed down the Lugg valley, the two forces joining up in the Teme valley to be defeated by Scapula in 51 AD at Coxall Knoll. However this tradition is discounted by recent authorities who locate the scene of Caradoc's defeat further to the north and west, on the upper reaches of the Severn.

Even so, the wider locality was the scene of Roman operations during the first decades of the Roman penetration of Wales; near Leintwardine the Jay Lane fort was occupied by a force of 500 auxiliaries from 47 to 61 AD, whilst in $c.$51-58 AD a fort was built at Hindwell near Walton where several marching camps have been identified. By 75-76 AD, in the course of their final campaign against the Silures, the Romans had established a fort at Castell Collen. As the area became pacified the Jay Lane fort was abandoned in favour of nearby Buckton, $c.$80-90 AD, whilst the Hindwell fort may have been replaced by a fort at Discoed at about the same time.

The site of Hindwell Fort in front of the farm buildings

By the middle of the second century, garrisons in Wales were substantially reduced and in the area of the Marches Roman authority was maintained by a quadrilateral of forts at Caersws, Castell Collen, Forden and Leintwardine, all manned by auxiliary cavalry. Though no Roman remains have been identified in Presteigne, it lies on a natural line of communication between Leintwardine, Hindwell and Castell Collen, a route which may well have been used by Roman troops and officials. This would account for the scattering of isolated Roman coins found in the locality, which date in the main from the second and third centuries.

However, the discovery of the 'Corton hoard' suggests that the Roman presence in the Presteigne locality may have been less transitory than has been envisaged previously. The initial discovery was made at Corton House in 1940-41 when a tennis court was dug up and thirty or so coins were found in or near an earthenware or metal pot which was subsequently thrown away. The pot had been covered with a small stone tile and was found at a depth of eighteen inches below the surface. In the following years further coins were found on the site and it is believed that the hoard amounted to at least eighty coins, about half of which have not been recorded, having been lost, given away, or in the possession of people who have moved away from the area. All the coins which have been recorded date from the period 79-169 AD.

The finding of the hoard during years of national crisis, the time span over which the coins were found and the interval of some ten years which elapsed before reports of the original find appeared in local historical journals, may all have tended to lessen its impact and the possible significance seems to have been overlooked. One report stated that the first coins were found 'beneath a number of stones of various sizes, some of them large slabs' and that six cartloads of such stones were removed to the nearby Nash quarry. This would suggest the presence of a building or buildings on the site during the later second century AD, possibly a small Romano-British villa or a military installation. The site would have been well suited to either purpose for it lies on the south-facing lower slopes of a ridge separating the Hindwell and Lugg valleys. However, in the absence of definite archaeological evidence, the existence of a Roman settlement on the site must remain hypothetical.

The Dark Ages
The collapse of Roman authority in Britain in the fifth century led to the establishment of small Romano-British kingdoms, with the Presteigne area, like the bulk of Radnorshire, forming part of the mid-Wales kingdom of Powys and then a component of one of the subsequent principalities which disintegrated either prior to, or as a result of Anglo-Saxon penetration in the mid-seventh century. Castle Ring near Evenjobb possibly dates from this sub-Roman period, though with the lack of any evidence such an attribution can only be speculative.

More recently the Anglo-Saxon penetration of the Welsh borderland has been viewed as occurring through a process of assimilation rather than by conquest and this has led to an emphasis upon the continuation of a strong Celtic influence in the region. Thus, whilst many of the small nucleated settlements have typically early Anglo-Saxon 'ton' endings— Byton, Norton, Little Brampton, Harpton, Walton and Kinnerton, the rivers retained their Celtic names, the Lugg and Teme being typical examples. Again, the influence of the Welsh Church, particularly of St David, clearly stretched down from the Radnor uplands with church dedications to the saint at Glascwm, Colva, Cregina and Rhulen, along the Arrow and Lugg valleys towards Leominster. Here he may have founded a monastery and his feast was regarded as one of the principal festivals in the church year in the Middle Ages. J. Hillaby also argues that the Mercian sub-kingdom of the Western Hecani, later known as the

Offa's Dyke almost due west of Presteigne

Magonsaetan, centred initially on Leominster and after 693 on Hereford, consisted in the main of a Celtic speaking people, at least partly Christian, occupying the Arrow and Lugg valleys since the sub-Roman period, who had preserved their identity by a process of accommodation with Mercia.

Offa's Dyke

Anglo-Saxon penetration into the Welsh borderland in the seventh century and the rise of Mercia into a powerful kingdom led to a definition of boundaries in order to avoid border disputes and to act as a forward defence against the Welsh. The best known and most extensive of the dykes constructed to fulfil such purposes is Offa's Dyke, eighty miles of earthwork stretching discontinuously between the Severn and the Dee, the construction of which began in 784. In Radnorshire the alignment followed by the dyke left Anglo-Saxon settlements such as Walton, Kinnerton and Harpton in the Radnor valley under Welsh control. The dyke runs three miles west of Presteigne, towards Kington to the south and Knighton to the north, the most accessible section from Presteigne being the stretch near Yew Tree Farm, half a mile beyond Discoed. In the upper Lugg valley the dyke marks the boundary of the diocese of Hereford, which Hillaby identifies as the limits of Magonsaetan influence, leaving Presteigne within Mercian control and thus, by implication, just within the Magonsaetan kingdom since the sub-Roman period.

In his study of the Dyke, F. Noble sees its construction as not serving any pre-eminently military purpose, but rather as marking the boundary between two peoples with markedly different legal codes and social structures, thus defining the sphere of influence of the two competing jurisdictions and social systems and providing a basis for the settlement of any disputes occurring along the border. In the uplands the more massive stretches of the Dyke served to deter raiders and to channel traffic through the recognised crossing points such as existed at Knighton.

Presteigne's Origins

In view of the lack of documentary evidence, a suitable point for any discussion of the town's origins is that afforded by place-name evidence. Writing in 1818, Jonathan Williams disposed of a suggested Welsh origin of the name, *prysg-duon* or 'the place of the black copses', not least on etymological grounds, going on to claim a Norman origin with its name derived from *presa*, the Norman Latin word for the fee for depasturing cattle on the royal waste, and *teigni*, meaning royal officers. Certainly the earliest reference to the town comes in the twelfth century, in a folio attached to the Balliol Domesday, dating from 1170 and describing Osbern fitzRichard le Scrope's lands in the locality *c.*1137-39. However, Williams' explanation is untenable on two grounds: the folio refers to Osbern holding seven hides at or near 'Presthemede', a very early form of the town's name, and one to which Williams' derivation is inappropriate; and the presence of late tenth or early eleventh century elements in the fabric of the church, discussed later, suggests that the settlement has pre-Norman origins.

More recent studies suggest an ecclesiastical origin for the town. Professor Ekwall sees Presthemede as derived from *preost haemed*, translated broadly as 'the household of priests'; while B.G. Charles views it as deriving from *preost hem maed* or 'the border meadow of the priests', a view supported by Domesday evidence. Taken in conjunction with the pre-Conquest elements in the parish church, these interpretations suggest that the town's origins can be traced back to a small community of priests and their servants, who settled above the flood line near a ford over the Lugg during the later Anglo-Saxon period in order to serve the small communities settled in the area.

This view accords with current thinking on the re-conversion of the Herefordshire/Welsh borderlands between the seventh and tenth centuries, and with the structure of the ecclesiastical parish of Presteigne. Thus Hillaby sees the re-conversion of the lower Lugg valley, possibly as far as Wapley, taking place in the seventh century through the efforts of priests from the royal minster of Leominster. This pattern was continued after the establishment of the bishopric of Hereford in 676, when other minster churches were set up at Bromyard and Bromfield in the following century or so, staffed by priests from the bishop's household. Hence the founding of the church at Presteigne may have marked the establishment of such a minster there to serve the upper Lugg valley.

Each minster had spiritual responsibility for its locality or *parochia*, which later, in more populated areas, would be divided into parishes, each of which would have its own church. In more sparsely populated areas, the area served by the mother church itself became the parish. Large sprawling parishes containing many townships, all served by one central church thus became a characteristic of the Marches. Clun is frequently cited as an example, but Presteigne would serve just as well, for the ecclesiastical parish covers 11,248 acres and includes Presteigne, Litton, Stapleton, Willey, Lower Kinsham, Combe, Rodd, Nash and Little Brampton, all served by the parish church, together with the chapelry of Discoed.

The date of the original settlement is far from clear. It is tempting to see the dedication of the parish church to St. Andrew as proof of a link with the original minster at Leominster, which in pre-Norman times consisted of two churches, that dedicated to SS Peter and Paul and the other, later destroyed, dedicated to St Andrew. However, there is no evidence to suggest that Presteigne ever formed part of the ecclesiastical endowment connected with Leominster minster, which Domesday records as being in the hands of Queen Edith, the wife of Edward the Confessor, in 1066. Even so, the presence of a well-established and valuable settlement by the time of Domesday, with a pre-Conquest stone rather than timber church, suggests that it had been in existence for some time prior to the Conquest. However, the original minster foundation seems never to have developed beyond its embryonic form, probably because of the political uncertainties and military conflict which bedevilled the Welsh borderland for much of the eleventh and twelfth centuries.

CHAPTER II

The Middle Ages

The Settlement Pattern
Since there was no reference to Presthemede in that section of the Domesday Survey relating to Herefordshire, Lord Rennell assumed that its exclusion was because the settlement lay outside the local manorial system. Both he and W.H. Howse concluded that the most local Domesday reference was that to the two hide manor of Claterbrune, (a hide consisted of 120 acres on average, but variable according to the quality of the land), included in a list of eleven manors in the neighbourhood belonging to Osbern fitz Richard le Scrope. Lord Rennell believed that its arable land lay each side of the present Broadheath road from the Cat and Fiddle to Broadaxe, with the home farm at Whitewall or Hoarstone Cottage, and the manor house at Clatterbrune. He also suggested that Osbern's one hide manor of Querentune, which most authorities of the time identified as Kinnerton, was also located in the vicinity of Presteigne. His attribution was based on the order in which Osbern's manors in the locality were listed, with Querentune named between Claterbrune, and Discoed and Cascob. Taking Querentune as 'the ton of the quern', Lord Rennell supported his attribution by the presence, west of Presteigne, of the later St Mary's Mill.

However, such conclusions are no longer accepted, for Bruce Coplestone-Crow has identified Querentune with Combe and Presteigne with Humet, a previously unidentified manor lying in the Leintwardine Hundred of Shropshire. He sees 'Humet' as a contracted form of *hem maed*, the 'border meadow', a triangular area of flat land near Kinsham at the confluence of the Lugg and the Hindwell Brook. He suggests that later part of the *hem maed* came into the hands of the community of priests, hence 'Presthemede', while the rest remained with, or passed into the hands of the crown, by 1216 becoming 'Kingeshemede' or Kinsham.

Humet, like his other manors in the locality, had been held by Osbern since the reign of Edward the Confessor, but was easily the largest, at five hides (Discoed, Harpton and Titley were each of three hides), with land for twenty ploughs and probably extending into other townships served by St Andrew's church. The manor included two men at arms with one plough and, with three ploughs between them, five villagers, five smallholders and a radman or rider, a freeman who originally served as a messenger and mounted escort. The manor had been waste in 1066 and was still so in 1086, except for the lordship, which was valued at ten shillings.

In the Domesday Survey Humet is noted as lying in Shropshire, along with Lingen, Willey, Cascob, Ackhill and Norton. This might seem surprising, but in the eleventh century the boundaries between Herefordshire, Shropshire and Wales appear to have been unusually fluid, possibly as a result of the mid-eleventh century raids and counter raids across the border.

The Local Political and Military Situation in the Eleventh Century
For much of the eleventh century the situation along the Welsh borderland was far from settled. Godwin of Wessex and Leofric of Mercia were both seeking to extend their influence in the region and the frequent and dramatic reversals in the fortunes of the two rival noble houses tended to create a sustained atmosphere of tension and instability. Thus the appointment of Swein Godwinsson as Earl of Hereford in 1043 seemed to seal Godwin's control of the region, but his triumph was shortlived, for in 1047 Swein was disgraced and exiled.

Swein was succeeded as Earl of Hereford by Edward the Confessor's Norman nephew Ralf and it was possibly at this time that other Normans were granted lands along the border so as to counter Welsh aggression and to build up royal authority in the region in order to contain the bitter rivalry between the two noble Saxon families. Among these Normans were Richard le Scrope, whose local base was Richard's Castle, and his son Osbern. The le Scropes' grants included a block of manors in the locality including Milton, Byton, Wapley, Rodd, Titley, Little Brampton, Knill, Nash, Discoed and Cascob in addition to the two Presteigne manors of Humet and Claterbrune. These grants were probably made at the expense of local magnates and must have provoked some resentment.

Earl Godwin and his son, Harold, their influence on the wane, went into exile in 1051.

Gruffydd ap Llewelyn sought to exploit these divisions, launching a series of raids on the area, most notably those of 1052 and 1055 when he penetrated as far as Hereford, inflicting a humiliating defeat on Earl Ralf's forces. Presteigne may well have suffered in these incursions, for investigations carried out in the parish church in the early 1960s suggests extensive damage to the fabric of the earlier church on the site may date from $c.1050$. By 1055 much of north-west Herefordshire and east Radnorshire had been devastated. The civil settlements had been largely abandoned and who controlled or lived there is unknown.

Returning to England in 1052, Harold Godwinsson seized his father's earldom of Wessex in 1053 and was appointed Earl of Hereford in 1057 on the death of Ralf. Harold defeated and drove back the Welsh in 1063 and reasserted English control over north-west Herefordshire and the Radnor and Lugg valleys, securing for himself some forty-five manors in the region, totalling at least 190 hides.

Nor did the Conquest bring peace to the area, for between 1067 and 1070, when he made his peace with the Norman regime, Eadric the Savage, with the aid of the Welsh, launched a series of destructive raids along the borderland. Not surprisingly Domesday described Osbern's block of manors on the Hereford-Radnor border as 'was and is waste', adding tersely: 'On these waste lands have grown woods in which this Osbern goes hunting and he has from them what he can catch. Nothing else.' However, the situation must not be exaggerated, for 'waste' does not imply wholesale de-population and devastation, with all the land left uncultivated; the term simply signifies that these communities were functioning well below their productive capacity and that the manorial organisation had ceased to operate effectively.

Lord Rennell takes the statement in the Balliol Domesday that Osbern held seven hides 'at' or 'near' Presthemede to be the first, indirect statement to the lordship of Stapleton which had not been mentioned in 1086, but which had risen into prominence by the reign of Henry II (1154-89). It is now clear that that statement refers to the manors of Humet and Claterbrune from which the local power and influence of the lords of Richard's Castle was obtained. However, by the opening decades of the twelfth century Presthemede had clearly established a dominant position over the nearby settlements. It was the centre of the Marcher lordship of Presteigne, held under the Burford barony in Shropshire, and was the religious focus of the locality, for it was to St Andrew's church that the people of the neighbouring communities brought their tithes and church dues and where their dead were buried. In such circumstances Presteigne probably soon developed administrative, judicial and commercial functions.

The Mortimer Connection
In 1137-39 Presteigne belonged to Osbern's grandson, Osbern fitz Hugh, who like most of the local magnates such as the Mortimers, Braoses and Lacys, supported Stephen against Matilda in the struggle for the throne following the death of Henry I. In 1144 Roger Port of Kington, a supporter of Matilda, seized Presteigne, placing it under the control of Thomas de Fraxino (de Fresne) who, in 1145, gave the church in Presteigne to St Guthlac's Priory in Hereford. The settlement, in the barony and lordship of Kington (or of Huntington after 1149), remained in the hands of the Port family until 1172 when Adam Port was banished by Henry II for rebellion. For the remainder of the twelfth century the barony of Kington/Huntington, including Presteigne, was administered on behalf of the crown by the sheriff of Hereford. For most of the 1190s this post was held by William de Braose of Radnor who steadily increased his personal control over the Huntington lordship, formalising the position by purchasing it from the crown in 1203.

Presteigne itself seems to have remained in the hands of the de Fraxino family as sub-tenants throughout the period and when William Braose rebelled in 1208, Thomas Fraxino was able to withdraw his lands around Presteigne into a barony which he held directly of King John until 1218, when Reginald Braose resumed his loyalty to the crown. Fraxino's barony then returned to the lordship of Huntington, once more under Braose control.

That the Fraxino family were able to establish such a barony, even temporarily, suggests that that they enjoyed the favour of King John who, according to local tradition, was a frequent visitor to the area, using Barland as his hunting lodge on such occasions. However, the tradition should be treated with scepticism, for it is not supported by any evidence. Nor were all local magnates closely identified with John, for it is claimed that Sir Roger de Knill and Hugh Rodd accompanied Richard I on the third crusade, Rodd being knighted at Ascalon in 1191.

In 1230 William Braose, who had succeeded his father, Reginald Braose in 1228, was executed by Llewelyn ap Iowerth (Llewelyn the Great), leaving his four infant daughters to inherit his estates in the absence of a male heir, a situation which the Mortimer family of Wigmore sought to exploit to the full. The Mortimers had acquired Wigmore by 1086, after the

The ruined and debris-filled gateway to Wigmore Castle

rebellion of the son of William fitz Osbern, Earl of Hereford. In addition to Wigmore, at the time of the Domesday Survey the Mortimers held sixteen other manors in Herefordshire together with fifty in Shropshire, as well as estates in several other counties. Between the eleventh and thirteenth centuries the Mortimers also built up a substantial, if somewhat insecure, Marcher lordship in mid-Wales.

In 1230 Ralph Mortimer married Gwladys Ddu, the daughter of Llewelyn the Great and the widow of Reginald Braose, securing through her a claim to the Braose lands in mid-Wales, including Presteigne. The Mortimer grip was tightened by the marriage of Ralph's son, Roger Mortimer, to Maud, one of the heiresses of William Braose, in the early 1240s, though the division of the Braose estates between the heiresses was not finally agreed until 1259 and then only grudgingly. The Mortimers gained only the lordships of Radnor and Presteigne, while Humphrey Bohun, Earl of Hereford, secured the lion's share of the Braose estates in Brecon, Huntington and Hay through his marriage to Eleanor, another of the Braose heiresses.

The Warden Castle
W.H. Howse suggested that the Mortimers built a motte and bailey castle on the Warden, a strategic site overlooking the town, probably *c.*1180-

1200 to counter the earlier Stapleton Castle built by the lords of Richard's Castle and to tighten the Mortimer grip on the upper Lugg valley. Certainly the first documentary reference to its existence comes in the Mortimer confirmation in 1249 of a 1244 charter, which describes the castle as being held of the Mortimers by Thomas de Fraxino. However, Paul Remfry maintains that it was built by Osbern fitz Richard, probably by 1086 and possibly before 1066, citing the valuation of the lordship of Humet at ten shillings in the Domesday Survey in justification. Thus he regards Stapleton Castle as built sometime after 1144 by Osbern fitz Hugh to counter Presteigne Castle as part of his campaign to regain control of Presteigne from Roger Port of Kington. When this failed, the castle served as the centre of the lordship of Stapleton, within the barony of Burford, created from surrounding manors held by Osbern fitz Richard in 1086.

Most authorities accept that, unlike its Stapleton neighbour, the Warden castle was never rebuilt in stone, but throughout its existence consisted of a wooden tower surrounded by an earthen wall topped by a palisade. Certainly there are no signs of masonry foundations. However, given that the site was landscaped twice in the late eighteenth and early nineteenth centuries, well after its destruction by Llewelyn ap Gruffydd in 1262 when the town surrendered the castle to him without a struggle, it is possible that the castle contained some masonry elements. In the absence of any tangible evidence any such suggestion remains highly speculative.

The site passed eventually into the hands of the Harley family, who had been military retainers of the Mortimers since at least 1309, and in the late eighteenth century it was laid out as a public pleasure ground with flower beds, promenades and a bowling green. In 1805 the fifth Earl of Oxford formally presented the Warden to the town, a gift challenged unsuccessfully by his daughter, Lady Langdale, in 1870.

The Development of the Town
As the settlement spread up the slope from the vicinity of the church along what was to become Great Street and later Broad Street, it merged with settlement spreading eastwards from around the castle along the King's Highway, as the High Street and Hereford Street were first called, thus creating a straggling two street settlement. The growth of the settlement was probably encouraged by the Mortimers, for the creation of a town would bring income from the tolls levied on sales at the weekly market.

Possible clues as to Presteigne's growth in the later thirteenth century, may be traced from existing property boundaries in the present town centre. These are clearly observable on a large scale map, thus enabling a very tentative guess to be made as to the town's extent at this period. Many of the houses on each side of Broad Street, High Street and St David's Street stand, usually gable end on to the street, on long, narrow strips of land, reminiscent of medieval burgages and possibly overlying the remains of the old Saxon and Domesday settlement. On the east side of Broad Street and the west side of St David's Street, the thirteenth century holdings were bisected, probably in the later fifteenth or early sixteenth century by Harper's Lane and Pound Lane respectively. In the High Street, particularly on the north side and the west side of Broad Street the original pattern has been obscured, probably in the sixteenth or early seventeenth centuries, by the construction of courtyards, some linked by narrow alleyways. West Street, now Scottleton Street, also probably dates from the late fifteenth or earlier sixteenth century.

The boundary of the town to the north may have been Canon's Lane, which probably stretched as far as St David's Street originally, which would have separated the secular town from the older ecclesiastical settlement, and West Wall. To the south-west and south the boundary may have run along Wherby Lane which originally might have run as far as the present Station Road, then no more than a track, which, with the Back Lane, marked the eastern limit of the town.

Such a settlement pattern would have left the castle on the Warden to the south-west overlooking the town and with a clear field of fire. The area within the boundaries suggested would have been sufficient for eighty burgages, each of about 850 square yards, together with craftsmen's premises, workshops and warehouses along the High Street and Hereford Street.

It is not clear when Presteigne's market began. A charter in 1225 granting William fitz Warin, the castellan of Hereford, the right to hold a weekly market on Wednesdays in Presteigne, together with a fair on 29-30 November, the eve and feast day of St Andrew was clearly an error, and the fee of five marks was returned to him in 1229 with a gift of five bucks by way of apology. Most authorities accept that the grant of a market occurred in the period between 1230 and 1250 and it may have followed the marriage of Roger Mortimer to Maud Braose *c.*1246 or the rather earlier acquisition of the lordship of Huntington by the Bohuns through a similar marriage to a Braose co-heiress. Whenever the grant was secured, a second fair on 24 June, the Nativity of St John, was added

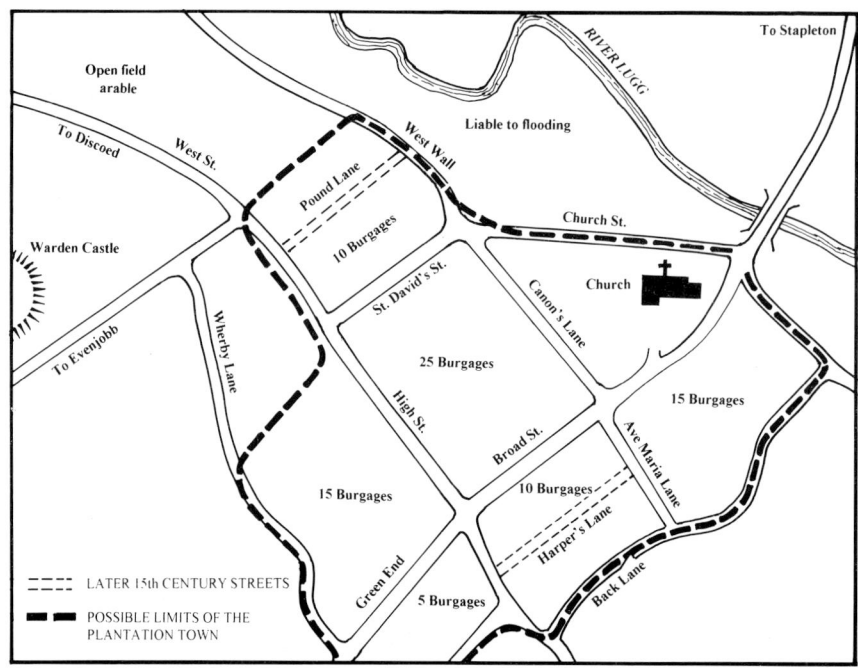

Fig. 4: The possible plantation town of the early fourteenth century. The estimated number of burgages is based on present property boundaries and the assumption that each burgage consisted of c.850 square yards

to that of the eve and feast day of St Andrew and the market day transferred to Saturday.

By the end of the thirteenth century the town had developed into one of the most prosperous in the locality. M.A. Faraday's analysis of the assessment for the Fifteenth of 1293 shows Presteigne as having seventy taxpayers, paying an average of 31d., compared with 34d. in Stapleton and New Radnor, 29d. in Norton, 28d. in Knighton and 17d. in Bleddfa. Lord Rennell gives details of an inquisition of 1304 which lists seventy-three tenants in Presteigne and fragments of a manorial roll listing eighty tenants, though the latter includes twenty-three tenements in Froege Strete (now Ford Street) over the Lugg and therefore outside the confines of the town. Using the conventional multiplier of five, for the family size of the times, these three more or less contemporary sources suggest a population of about 350 for the town at the beginning of the fourteenth century.

The Decline of the Later Fourteenth Century

By the second half of the fourteenth century, if not before, the town's future seemed less secure. In part this stemmed from the deterioration in climatic conditions from the optimum of $c.1300$, which led to the limit of cereal cultivation in the uplands falling by as much as two hundred feet or so over a few decades and some adjustment in farming patterns in more favoured areas. This was bound to have a harmful effect upon the economies of towns such as Presteigne, which was almost completely dependent upon its rural hinterland.

However, the principal cause of the decline was the series of plague epidemics in the second half of the fourteenth century. The initial epidemic of 1349-50, the 'Black Death', probably killed some 25-35% of the population of England and Wales and this was followed by further widespread outbreaks of plague in 1360-62, 1368-69, 1373-75, 1382 and 1390. Of the impact of such epidemics upon Presteigne itself there is no direct evidence, though inferences may be drawn from Hereford diocesan records and those of other Mortimer and Bohun manors in the locality.

The diocese of Hereford was hit hard by the epidemic of 1349-50, the episcopal register recording: 'it swept away over half the population; land was untilled and the supply of clergy was lamentably reduced.' There was certainly a sharp fall in the number of ordinations in the diocese, with an average of thirty-four ordinations per annum in the five years after 1349 compared with an average of seventy-two per annum in the five years preceding 1349. The death rate amongst the clergy was also high, with 48% of the livings falling vacant in 1349, though some of these vacancies stemmed from exchange. J.F.D. Shrewsbury estimates that Leominster deanery, which included Presteigne, suffered less severely than most with 26% of the livings falling vacant in 1349, which includes two vacancies recorded for Knill.

Though there were heavy arrears of rent and some leasing of demesnes (lands farmed directly by the lord) along the central Marches after the 1349-50 outbreak, the Kington-New Radnor-Presteigne area seems to have been harder hit by the epidemic of 1368-69. W.J. Rees noted a significant number of customary tenements falling vacant at Rushock and Hergest, while in 1372 the demesne at Pilleth was let, which suggests that the customary labour used to work the demesne was no longer available in sufficient quantity. The marked extension of sheep farming along the central Marches, a product of climatic change in the main, may also have been a response to depopulation produced by relatively high mortality or by migration to more favoured areas hard hit by the plague, where good land was readily available and wage rates were higher.

Economic dislocation was carried a stage further by Glyndwr's attack on the area in 1401 when the town was sacked, the rentals of the lordship of Presteigne falling to £3 7s. 'because the tenements were destroyed and burnt by the rebels'. In 1406 it was reported that the parish church and the vicar's glebeland had been destroyed by Glyndwr's forces. This may have been a reference to the 1401 attack or to a further raid in 1402, prior to the battle of Pilleth, rather than to an attack in the course of Glyndwr's retreat from Woodbury Hill near Worcester *via* Leominster in 1405, e*n route* for Brecon.

A further consequence of the plague epidemics may have been to transform Presteigne from an English into a Welsh settlement. On the basis of the surnames of the taxpayers contributing to the Fifteenth of 1293, M.A. Faraday suggests that Presteigne was the most English of all the settlements in the area, with a Welsh element of less than 10%, compared with Stapleton's 28%, Norton's 53% and Knighton's 66%. Yet, during the late fourteenth and the fifteenth centuries the locality seems to have become much more Welsh in character. Presteigne became known by its Welsh name, Llanandras—the 'llan' or 'holy place' of St Andrew—and several neighbouring settlements were given Welsh variants of their previously English names; thus Litton became Llyton and Discot, Discoed. In Presteigne itself the establishment of a chantry dedicated to St David in the parish church and the naming of an important thoroughfare as St David's Street also suggests growing Welsh influence. Significantly, in 1402, after going over to Glyndwr, Edmund Mortimer appealed to 'the Welshmen of Presteigne' to give their allegiance to his newfound ally, while in 1538 Leland referred to the town as 'but a Walsche village about Edward IV's tyme'. This transformation of an English settlement into one largely Welsh in character may well have come about as a result of the depopulation of the locality; the fertile lands of the Lugg valley and the greater opportunities offered by trade attracting migrants from the now marginal uplands of mid-Wales.

The Fifteenth Century Recovery
By the mid-fifteenth century Presteigne's economy had recovered and during the second half of the century the town seems to have enjoyed renewed prosperity, judging from the ambitious and extensive remodelling of the parish church. The revival stemmed initially from the expansion of the Flanders wool trade, for the upper Lugg valley had a

reputation for the quality of its wool. It was coupled with the regranting of the market charter in 1482 through the influence of Richard Martin, a native of Presteigne, who became bishop of St David's. Towards the end of the century the town seems to have been developing a small but flourishing cloth manufacturing industry of its own. A contributory factor assisting the recovery may have been Presteigne's apparent immunity, at least until the closing decades of the century, from the serious plague epidemics which affected the kingdom every decade or so and which may have stemmed from its relative isolation. Using the number of probates as an index of mortality, M.A. Faraday suggests that only in one year between 1442 and 1500, that of 1488-89, was the town's mortality rate amongst the highest in the diocese.

Presteigne and the Wars of the Roses
The direct Mortimer connection with the town came to an end when the fifth Earl of March died of the plague in 1425. His lands passed via his sister, Ann Mortimer, to her husband, the Earl of Cambridge and then to his son Richard, Duke of York. On the defeat of the Yorkists in 1459 the former Mortimer estates passed into the hands of Henry VI. After his victory at Mortimer's Cross in 1461, Richard of York's son, Edward, Earl of March ascended the throne as Edward IV and in 1477 he bestowed the former Mortimer estates on his son Edward, Prince of Wales, the future Edward V.

After the battle of Bosworth in 1485, these estates passed into the hands of Henry Tudor as Henry VII, and he, in 1493, granted the lordship of Maelienydd and the other former Mortimer lands in the locality to his son, Prince Arthur. Included in the grant was 'the town and lordship of Presteinde', but the manor of Presteigne was not specifically mentioned in the grant, which raises the possibility that the lordship of Huntington continued to have some interest in this until the attainder and execution of the Duke of Buckingham in 1521. It is possible its omission was a clerical error, though in other respects the terminology of the grant is highly specific, referring, for example, to 'the manor, castle, and town and lordship of Reidour (Rhayader)'. Lord Rennell suggests that the manor passed to the crown by forfeit at some time in the reign of Henry VII.

For administrative purposes all the lands granted in 1493 were grouped into the lordship of Cantref Maelienydd. However, Roy Adams suggests that Presteigne was not initially included in the lordship, only coming under its jurisdiction during the sixteenth century. Even so, Presteigne clearly took a pride in its royal associations, for Symonds in 1645 noted a window in the parish church bearing the quartered arms of England and France, with Prince Arthur's name beneath.

Presteigne Parish and Wigmore Abbey
Since no records are known to have survived relating to the church prior to 1236, nothing is known of 'the household of priests': and questions as to the number of priests serving there, the sources of its revenue are matters of conjecture. Similarly, it is not clear whether or not it was subject to some other jurisdiction in addition to the diocesan authorities prior to its being granted to St Guthlac's Priory in 1145 by Thomas de Fraxino, or if this grant was revoked following the fall of the Port family in 1172 or the Braose acquisition of Presteigne in 1203.

However, within a few years of their acquiring Presteigne, the Mortimers ensured that the parish church became subject to the authority of Wigmore Abbey. In 1236 William de Fraxino, holding Presteigne from the Mortimers, granted the advowson to the abbot of Wigmore, who in return for the tithes and other revenues of the church provided a priest, possibly a canon of the abbey, to serve in the parish. In a further charter of 1244, confirmed in 1249, Thomas de Fraxino made further grants to the abbey, including extensive and valuable rights of pasturage and of justice.

The land in Presteigne granted to Wigmore Abbey lay outside the jurisdiction of the manor and seems to have been farmed directly by the abbey as a grange rather than leased out to lay tenants, certainly into the fifteenth century and possibly later. A deed of 1438 relating to a sale of land in the east field of Presteigne identified the plot as being 'under Le Grange', while the sale of Presteigne manor house by John Bradshaw III to John Read of London in 1619 included a parcel of land 'where the grange barn lately stood'.

This arrangement, by which the abbey appropriated the entire income of the parish church, persisted until the later fourteenth century. In 1386 a John Scot is mentioned rather ambiguously as vicar of Presteigne, though the first specific appointment to the post came in 1391, when the abbot instituted Richard Baker as vicar. Under this new arrangement the abbey retained the great tithes, those on grain, hay and timber, while the vicar received as a stipend the lesser tithes, those on wool, pigs, milk and labour, together with the glebeland and fees for baptism, marriage and burial. Though this was more equitable, it still meant that the bulk of the revenue of the parish church remained with the abbey. As Lord Rennell

*Part of the remains of Wigmore Abbey incorporated
into the present house on the site*

shows, in 1291 the church was worth £17 6s. 8d. in tax, yet in 1405 the incumbent, John Cascoppe, had an annual income of between £5 and £6 33s. It is not surprising, therefore, to find that on most occasions when a clerical tax, the subsidy, was levied, Presteigne was exempt either on the grounds of poverty or because the living was worth less than twelve marks (£8). There is also evidence that the new arrangement was not always adhered to, for diocesan records show on some occasions the appointment of only a chaplain or stipendiary rather than a vicar to serve the parish.

The incumbent may have been assisted occasionally in his duties by the priests of the four chantries which had been established in Presteigne in the fifteenth century or possibly rather earlier, for the duties of such chantry priests were not onerous, normally the saying of obits or the celebration of mass on the occasion of their patron's death and on other specified occasions. Presteigne had four such chantries, dedicated to St David, St Mary of Grace, St Mary of Piety and the Holy Trinity. They enjoyed annual revenues totalling £18 4s. 10d. in 1548, (St David's, £2 13s.; St Mary of Grace, £7 4s. 8d.; St Mary of Piety, £4 10s. 8d.; the Holy Trinity, £3 16s. 6d). These were substantial sums, consisting in the main of rents on houses and land, most of it in the vicinity. Such priests lay outside the jurisdiction of the abbey and the diocese, being appointed by and responsible to the trustees of the chantries, who also administered the endowments.

The Presteigne incumbent also served the chapels which may have existed in the extensive parish, though the abbey seems to have ignored parochial boundaries in their allocation of responsibility for the chapelries within their jurisdiction. Thus in 1536 as now, St Michael's, Discoed was a dependent chapelry of Presteigne, yet as P.E.H. Hair shows, in the fourteenth and fifteenth centuries it was a chapelry of Norton. Similarly Lingen was listed as a chapel of Presteigne in 1536, whereas in 1400 it was a dependent chapelry of Aymestrey. He also cites a fifteenth century reference to chapels in Upper and Lower Kinsham as dependencies of Byton, though showing that by the sixteenth century the Lower Kinsham chapelry was dependent on Presteigne. He also notes a single reference in 1474 to a chapel at Nash, though this seems to have been no more than an oratory or private chapel. An oratory may also have existed at Stapleton Castle, though there is no evidence to support this assumption.

The Fabric of the Parish Church

Dr and Mrs Taylor see the original stone church as a pre-Conquest aisleless structure, forty feet long and nineteen feet wide, occupying what is now the eastern half of the northern aisle. Externally the western limit of the original church is marked by a slight change in the alignment and by a marked change in the type of stone used, about half-way along the present wall. They suggest that the Anglo-Saxon church had been almost completely destroyed in the course of a Welsh raid in the mid-eleventh century and was rebuilt shortly after the Conquest to its original dimensions, only the lower ragstone courses of the original Anglo-Saxon church remaining to be incorporated in the new structure. The upper brownstone courses and the blocked windows on the eastern part of the exterior northern wall date from this early Norman church. Within the church, the blocked window and part of the chancel arch of the early Norman structure are clearly visible.

At some time in the later twelfth century the earlier church was extended to its present length and a tower was built rather away from the body of the church. Two elements from this church survive in the present structure in addition to the extended wall of the north aisle; part of the doorway arch in the internal west wall and two round pillars at the western end of the north aisle, presumably moved to their present positions during the next rebuilding.

During the first half of the fourteenth century, probably c.1320-40, the church was greatly enlarged; the present nave was built, a south aisle was added, connecting the tower to the main body of the church and a new, larger chancel built. The carving, which W.H. Howse suggests is a 'Majesty', but which others consider to be of St Andrew blessing the

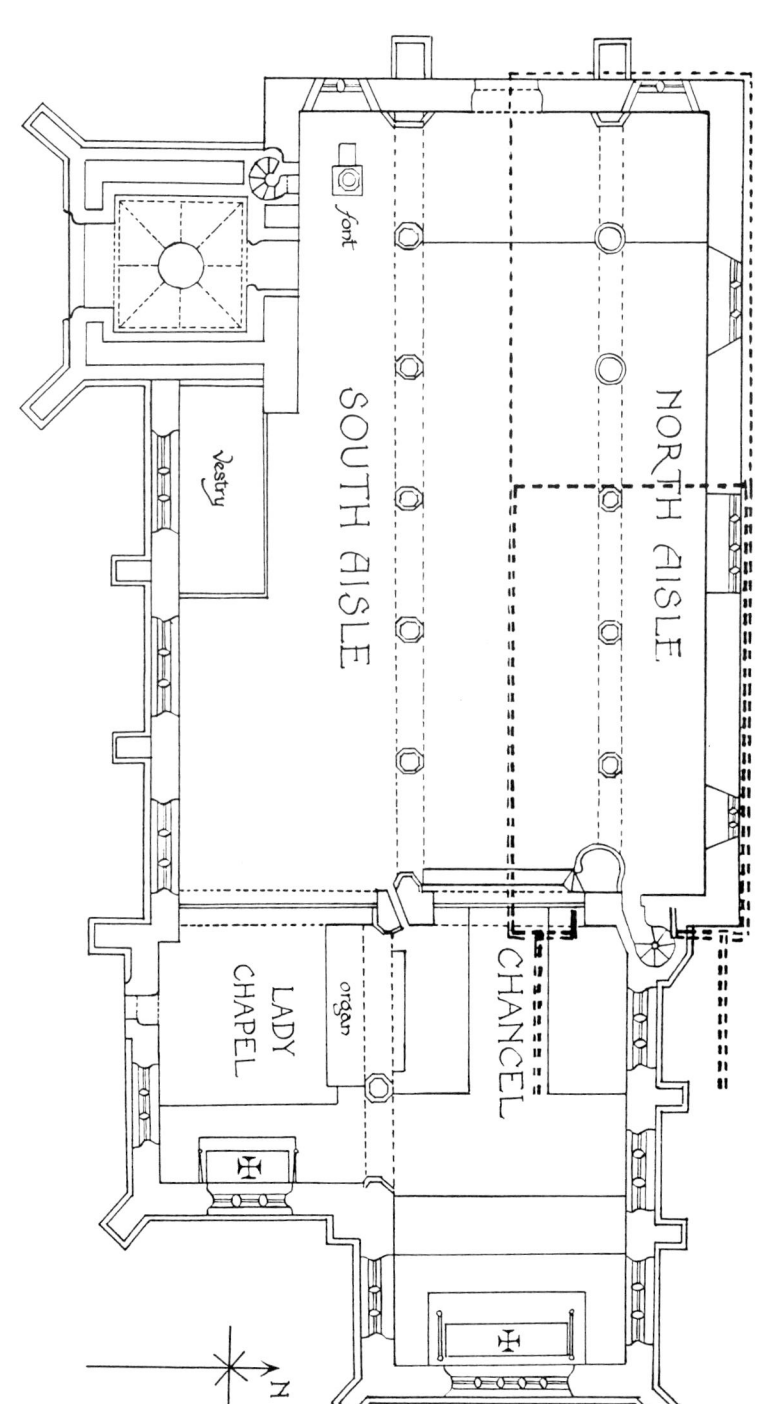

*Fig. 5: The Parish Church of St Andrew
---- represents the walls of the earlier church*

town, may be of earlier date, but was probably placed above the west door at this time.

The last major phase in the construction of the church was carried out c.1460-1520. The chancel was extended to its present size, the south aisle was extended to incorporate most of the tower into the main body of the church and the Lady Chapel was built. It has been suggested that the extension of the south aisle was carried out to accommodate altars for three of the chantries, that of St David having an altar in the north aisle adjacent to St David's Street, though one if not both of the chantries dedicated to St Mary may have had altars in the Lady Chapel.

However, it must not be assumed that the medieval fabric was entirely constructed in four such discrete phases, for it doubtless evolved in a more piecemeal fashion as succeeding generations fashioned and adapted the building in response to their own needs.

CHAPTER III

Tudor Presteigne

Writing in 1585 Camden described Presteigne as 'so greate a Mercate Town and Fair withall that at this day it dammereth and dimmeth the light in some sort of Radnor' which suggests that during the century or so after the re-granting of its market charter, the town had developed into rather more than a market town serving purely local needs.

Its growing significance stemmed in part from its location at the junction of two contrasting physical regions and at the intersection of two routes of some regional importance, that between Leominster and Aberystwyth via Cascob and Rhayader and that between Hereford and Montgomery via Knighton. From Presteigne there also radiated a number of locally important roads, to New Radnor via Evenjobb, to Kington via Nash and Rushock, to Painscastle via Walton and Gladestry, and to Llangunllo via Whitton and Pilleth.

Presteigne's growing prosperity also owed much to the steady extension of royal authority in the Marches which curbed the almost endemic lawlessness and disorder, though the pace at which this occurred must not be exaggerated. The Council of Wales and the Marches established by Edward IV in 1472 and revived by Henry VII was essentially the personal council of Prince Edward and then Prince Arthur and possessed little continuous or effective authority. Even after the Council was institutionalised after the death of Prince Arthur in 1502 it functioned only sporadically and with limited effectiveness, for Wales did not at first feature prominently in the Tudor scale of priorities. Thus the Marches remained plagued by brigands and outlaws, many of whom took refuge in the wilds of Radnor Forest, and bribery, intimidation and the suborning of juries remained all too common.

This relaxed approach to Wales and its problems came to an end in the 1530s when the break with Rome brought the threat of an invasion by the Catholic powers. In this situation Thomas Cromwell, Henry VIII's chief minister, began to assert royal authority in Wales and the Marches in a much more vigorous manner, revitalising the Council of Wales by appointing Rowland Lee, bishop of Coventry and Lichfield, as Lord President in 1534. He administered the law with a ruthless efficiency and in the course of his duties visited Presteigne regularly. In a letter to Cromwell in 1535, he describes Presteigne unflatteringly when writing of a visit he intended to make to the town: '... I entend after Easter to lye one month at Presteyne, even among the thickest of the theves to doo my master such service as the strongest of them shall be affrayed to doo as much as to fore, God willing.'

Traditionally, it was when Lee was presiding at a sitting of the Court of the Council at Presteigne in 1535 that he began his campaign to eliminate the use of the patronymic 'ap' from Welsh surnames.

Such a strict regime provided a foundation for the union of England and Wales by the Acts of Union of 1536 and 1542 which swept away the marcher lordships, incorporating some into existing Welsh and English counties, the remainder being formed into the new counties of Brecknock, Radnor, Montgomery, Denbigh and Monmouth. The Acts fostered the growth of towns such as Presteigne by sweeping away the penal laws which had hindered Welsh involvement in trade and industry. By the imposition of English land law on Wales the Acts helped the growth of larger landholdings, while the introduction of the English system of local government provided opportunities for social and political advancement on the part of the Welsh gentry. The decision in 1542 to share the role of county town between New Radnor and Presteigne certainly assisted the rise to prominence of the latter.

However, the sixteenth century was not one of unbroken growth and prosperity for the town. M.A. Faraday's analysis of the probates granted in the Hereford diocese suggest that in six of the twenty years between 1500 and 1542 for which records exist, Presteigne was one of the parishes suffering the highest mortality rates in the diocese. In three of the six years, 1501-02, 1525-26, and 1537-38, Presteigne may have suffered plague epidemics, for in those years there was certainly plague in Ludlow and Shrewsbury. It is probably no coincidence that Ludlow featured with Presteigne in five of those six years; 1501-02, 1502-03, 1525-26, 1529-30 and 1537-38; and Leominster in three; 1502-03, 1529-30 and 1537-38. All three towns were cloth-making towns, as was Shrewsbury, and infection could have spread through personal contacts and through the wool and cloth frequently transported between them. The reappearance of plague in the Presteigne locality after a respite of half a century or so may therefore have been a consequence of the rise of the cloth trade which brought the town into contact with potential centres of infection after its period of relative isolation in the fifteenth century.

Given the high mortality rates suggested by M.A. Faraday, the inclusion of Presteigne in the list of decayed towns in the 1544 Act may not have been due, as W.H. Howse suggests, to an over-rapid expansion and the jerry-building which this produced, but to a sharp fall in population in the previous decade or so, which left many houses derelict and decaying. This view is supported by a rent roll of the town in 1544, which Lord Rennell believed to be complete, showing a total of sixty landholders in the town, compared to the seventy or so of 1304. Against this backcloth, the bill presented to the Commons in February 1552, the year when Presteigne endured its last outbreak of the mysterious 'sweating sickness', to reserve the role of county town to New Radnor exclusively, may have been motivated by more than local rivalry. Fortunately for Presteigne, the bill failed after the first reading.

The Rise of the Cloth Industry

By the opening of the sixteenth century cloth production in the area seems to have grown beyond that needed to meet a purely local demand. Thus by 1514 it was worthwhile for Hugh Dee, a yeoman of the crown, to secure a grant from the crown of the ulnage, a type of excise duty, on woollen cloth made in Presteigne.

During the first half of the century the depreciation of the English coinage made English cloth cheap as against European currencies, thus increasing continental demand. In response to this, output rose, not only in the traditional cloth towns where craft gilds exercised tight control on output in terms of both quantity and quality, prices, the number of workers employed and apprentices in each business, together with wage levels, but also in 'greenfield' sites such as Presteigne where merchants could evade such restrictions to some degree.

Presteigne enjoyed two advantages for an ambitious merchant: its easy access to the high quality wool of the upper Lugg valley, which could produce cloth markedly superior to the usual Welsh friezes and flannels; and its proximity to the capital and expertise of Ludlow. The Bradshaws, who moved to Presteigne in the 1540s, were a prominent Ludlow merchant family, and John Beddoes, the eminent Presteigne cloth merchant, came of Ludlow stock and always maintained close links with the town. The earliest evidence of Beddoes' presence in the locality comes in a deed of May 1535 when, described as 'weaver', he bought some land 'lying between the way leading to Bultibroke and the stream called lugo [Lugg]'. Not until the 1550s is he described as 'esquire' or 'gentleman'.

The town's relatively late emergence as a cloth-making centre and its apparent freedom from guild restrictions also gave it a degree of flexibility which the older centres lacked. Thus in the second half of the sixteenth century, when the traditional broadcloth was losing ground to the lighter 'new draperies', Ludlow's cloth industry, based on the manufacture of a broad white cloth, went into a sharp decline, whereas Presteigne's cloth trade continued to flourish, which suggests that it was able to adjust production to suit changes in demand.

The evidence for large scale cloth production in Presteigne is relatively slight. To a large degree the hypothesis is based on the wealth and status of those involved in the industry, such as the Merediths and John Beddoes. The local power base of the Meredith family was established by Rhys ap Meredith in the opening decades of the sixteenth century through his involvement in the cloth trade. In addition, towards the end of the century his grandson Richard Meredith (d.1598) owned two fulling mills and a dyehouse in Frog (Ford) Street, close to the Lugg. Another townsman of substance involved in the cloth industry was John Gittowe who, in his will of 1535, left to his son Richard 'all my weaving loomys with all geers and other appurtenances'. The remainder of his estate included more than £34 in cash and unspecified amounts of land, both freehold and leasehold. He was clearly a man of some social standing for he nominated as his overseers John Baker, a future MP and sheriff of Radnorshire and John Bradshaw, though it is not clear if this was John Bradshaw the elder or his son.

John Beddoes' wealth has also been attributed to his involvement in the cloth industry. In his will in 1576 he left land in twenty parishes in Radnorshire, Herefordshire and Shropshire, nearly £400 in mortgages, £200 in personal estate and 100 marks for his funeral expenses, all in addition to the generous endowment of his school. On the basis of his bequests of ten shillings towards the paving of Hereford Street and of a house and other property on that street, W.H. Howse believed his residence to have been there. Local tradition places his weaving shed and fulling mill on the low ground near the Lugg below West Wall, a site certainly large enough to have accommodated substantial premises. He

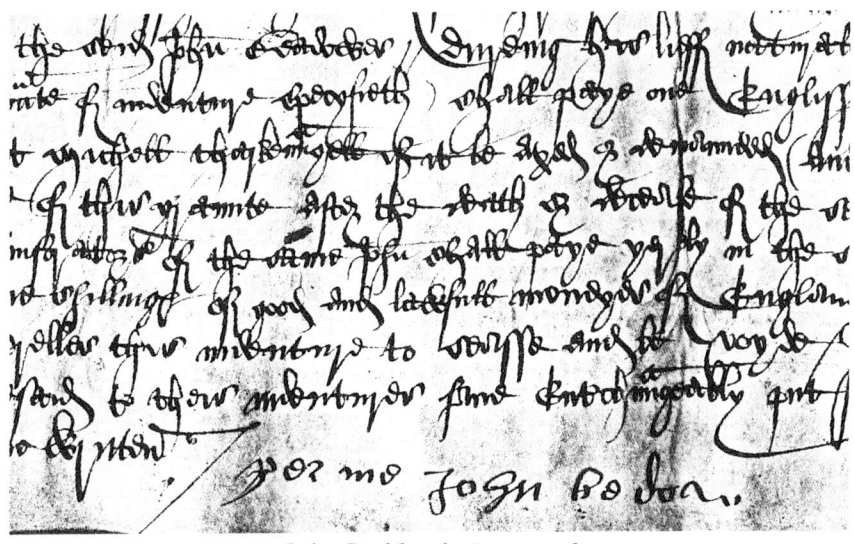

John Beddoes' signature?
This lease of 2 June 1556 between David Apowell and John Beddoes
is endorsed on the back 'In John Beddow's Writing'.
If this is so then the signature is that of John Beddoes

may well have also had an interest in the weaving sheds on Back Lane. However his will makes no mention of stocks of wool or cloth, or of premises and equipment connected with the cloth industry. This suggests that he had left the industry some time before his death and part of his fortune may well have been derived from dealings in land. He was frequently involved in land transactions in the locality in the 1550s and 1560s, often in conjunction with John Seymour, the purchaser of the Presteigne, New Radnor and Old Radnor chantry lands. In 1562 Seymour appointed John Beddoes, whom he called 'my well beloved in Christ' as his agent for land sales in the area. Beddoes' will mentions several plots of land obtained because mortgages had not been redeemed and suggests that he was advancing money on the security of land and livestock at a rate of more than 10% per annum, for the 'rent' of two shillings in the pound (a rate of 10%) that he suggests in his will should be charged on outstanding mortgages in the two years following his death is clearly regarded as a generous concession.

The bequests made in 1559 by William Morris, a Presteigne mercer with commercial links with London and possibly Bristol also shed some light on the scale of the local cloth industry, for they included land, livestock, four houses, a lease of Lingen tithes and more than £200 in cash.

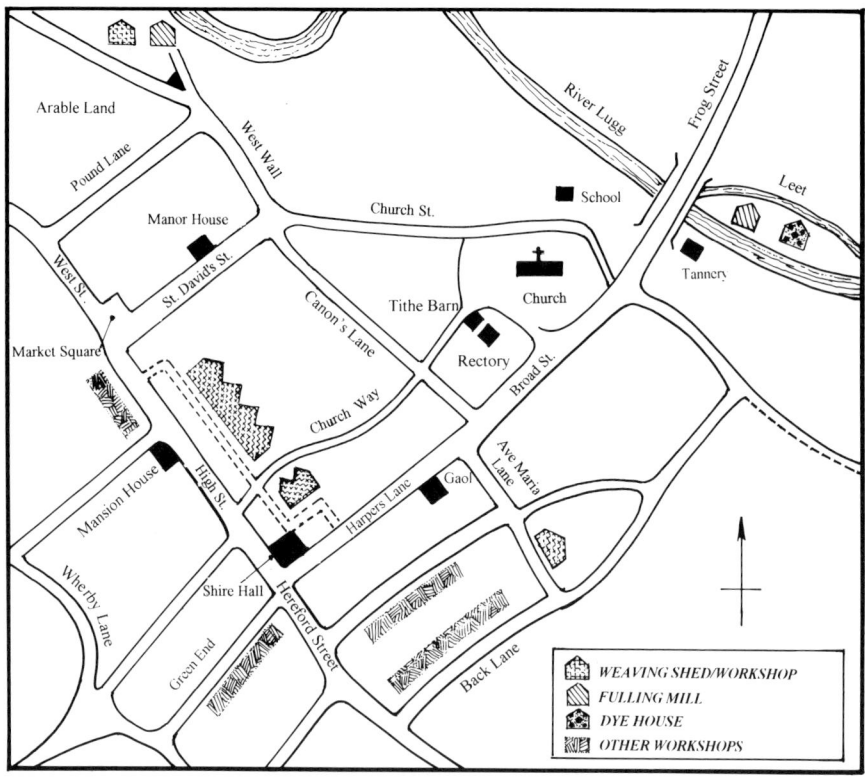

Fig. 6: The Urban Landscape of Presteigne in the late sixteenth and early seventeenth centuries

The presence of 'Mark the Fleming' and 'Gyles the Fleming' in the Presteigne subsidy roll of 1550 also supports the concept of a relatively large-scale cloth industry, for their presence may indicate that skilled craftsmen were being brought over from Flanders to train the local labour force.

However, testamentary evidence also suggests that at least part of the local cloth industry was on a small scale. In his will of 1544 John ap Powell left to Jenkyn Heb, 'ii peyre of looms and a peyre of geers' and to his wife 'geyre, the which is over the looms', but the scale of his other bequests give the impression that he was no more than a prosperous artisan. That not everyone engaged in the industry was making a good living is clearly shown in the will of Thomas a Morgan, a weaver and fuller, of 1551. After bequests of 4d. to Hereford Cathedral and to 'the poor men's box', the remainder of his estate was to go to paying his debts of more than £9 and 'to keep my children.'

*The courtyards on the northern side of the High Street
as they appear today*

The industry was located in four main areas of the town, the best known being that near West Wall, which traditionally contained John Beddoes' weaving shed, but which may have also have housed smaller businesses located in cottages and workshops in West Wall, Church Street and the lower part of Pound Lane, for weavers were certainly working in these streets a century or so later. The second industrial area was at the lower end of Broad Street and along Frog Street, possibly on both banks of the Lugg, for there is testamentary evidence of at least two fulling mills and a dye house in the locality, which also contained a tannery in the sixteenth century. The third area was towards the lower end of Back Lane and Harper's Street, the latter named after the prominent Harper family of the fifteenth century, one of whom was auditor for the Earl of March for the manors of Radnor and 'Melenith'. One weaving shed at the lower end of Back Lane, which W.H. Howse thought may have belonged to Beddoes, survived into the 1920s according to Colonel Drage. Again, the area might also have housed smaller workshops and weaving sheds. According to Jonathan Williams another area associated with the cloth industry was the northern side of High Street, workshops and weaving sheds probably being located in the cluster of courtyards at the rear, linked together by narrow alleys, and continuing behind the upper section of the west side of Broad Street.

However, the industry was not confined to the town itself for there were fulling mills at Little Brampton, Nash, Discoed and, in 1571, at the 'Overhethe' on Broadheath. The remains of what may have been weirs elsewhere on the Hindwell Brook between Wegnall Mill and Combe and on the Lugg between the town and Broadheath suggest that there may have been fulling mills or dye houses in these localities. These outlying townships were certainly more populous in the sixteenth and seventeenth centuries and there is some evidence to suggest that the cloth industry survived in these outlying areas some time after it had declined in the town itself as a result of recurring plague epidemics, the last happening in 1636-37.

Though care must be taken not to exaggerate the scale of Presteigne's cloth industry, since the population of the town never exceeded the 1,000 possibly reached in the late sixteenth century, it clearly made a substantial contribution to the prosperity of the town.

Presteigne the County Town
With the national boundary running across the centre of Lugg Bridge, Presteigne is the most easterly town in Wales and it may have been its peripheral position which led initially to the role of county town being

shared by Rhayader and New Radnor. However, on his first visit to Rhayader in 1540 to preside at Great Sessions, the judge was attacked and killed by the Plant Mat, a band of brigands. Thus in 1541 Presteigne replaced Rhayader as the venue of Great Sessions and became joint county town with New Radnor in 1542. This shared status suggests that Presteigne had not conclusively overtaken New Radnor in importance and may reflect the wish of the Council of Wales to placate the influential Lewis family of Harpton Court while enhancing Bradshaw authority in Radnorshire. Towards the end of the sixteenth century Presteigne had clearly outgrown New Radnor in terms of population and wealth, while the influence of the Lewis family declined in the early seventeenth century as a result of the connection with Sir Gelly Meyrick, implicated in the rebellion of the Earl of Essex in 1601. Following this Presteigne began to play the dominant role in the administration of the county. However, not until after 1660 did Presteigne claim county town status for itself alone. This was unjustified, since the county court, presided over by the sheriff, with a jurisdiction over civil cases involving less than 40 shillings and at which the county MP was elected, continued to hold its monthly sittings alternately at Presteigne and New Radnor until the opening decades of the nineteenth century.

Whilst the Lent and Mid-summer sittings of Great Sessions, broadly speaking the equivalent of the English assizes, were usually held at Presteigne by the end of the sixteenth century, the town became the normal venue for Quarter Sessions. Here the JPs of the county not only tried lesser crimes, but also oversaw the administration of the county, supervising the administration of poor relief, the maintenance of roads and enforcing legislation over a wide range of topics such as weights and measures, wages, employment, brewing and baking bread. Both courts met at the Shire Hall which, from at least the later seventeenth century, stood at the junction of High Street and Broad Street.

At some time in the late sixteenth or early seventeenth century the county gaol, which had previously been in a gate tower of New Radnor Castle, was relocated in Presteigne. The first documentary evidence that the gaol had been moved to Presteigne comes in a Star Chamber case of 1609 in which John and Charles Vaughan, described as 'county gaolers at Presteigne' were sued for wrongful imprisonment. The gaol was in Broad Street, on the lower half of the site now occupied by the Shire Hall, with executions being carried out in Broad Street outside the gaol, though later the place of execution was moved to Gallows Lane, leading off the Discoed road, on the outskirts of the town.

In Wales and the Marches the system of local government as established by the Acts of Union was closely supervised by the Council of Wales and the Marches from its headquarters at Ludlow. The Lord President of the Council served as Lord Lieutenant for each of the Welsh counties and the Council played a leading role in the appointment of deputy lieutenants, sheriffs, JPs and other posts in the Welsh counties and took a close interest in parliamentary elections. Given Presteigne's proximity to Ludlow and the close personal and commercial links between the two towns, it is likely that the Council welcomed Presteigne's replacement of Rhayader as joint county town since it offered a means of enhancing its influence in Radnorshire.

The extent of conciliar influence in Presteigne and the opportunities for advancement it offered its clients can be seen in the public careers of Presteigne office-holders of the sixteenth century. John Baker, who lived in High Street, probably at the Mansion House, was the first sheriff of Radnorshire in 1540-41 and the first MP for the county between 1541 and 1544. His father had fought for Henry VII at Bosworth and as a reward had been appointed forester of Radnor, a position to which John Baker succeeded in 1524. Baker was appointed Clerk of the Peace for the lordship of Radnor in 1530 and became a trusted associate of Lee in the curbing of disorder in the locality. Through his marriage to Katherine Williams, the widowed daughter of John Bradshaw the elder, he ultimately became Lee's kinsman, for Bradshaw married Lee's niece Alice Fowler in 1538. No doubt it was through his connection with Lee that he was able to secure the profitable grant of Beguildy tithes in the later 1530s.

The 'Ludlow connection' can also be seen in the public career of John Knill, MP for Radnorshire in the parliaments of 1545 and November 1554. A lawyer by training, he had served as steward of Ludlow in 1541 and as recorder in 1542. He served as a JP in Radnorshire from 1543 until his death in 1561 and in 1547 was *custos rotulorum* or Keeper of the Rolls, responsible for keeping the county records. He owned a substantial estate in the Presteigne locality and was a kinsman by marriage of the Lewis family of Harpton and the Vaughans of Hergest. Given his Ludlow connections on the one hand and his local standing on the other, he was well placed to implement conciliar policies in the county and to extend its influence with Radnorshire's leading families.

However, it is the Bradshaw family which best illustrates the mutual self-interest which characterised the relationship between the Council and the dominant families of east Radnorshire in general and of Presteigne in

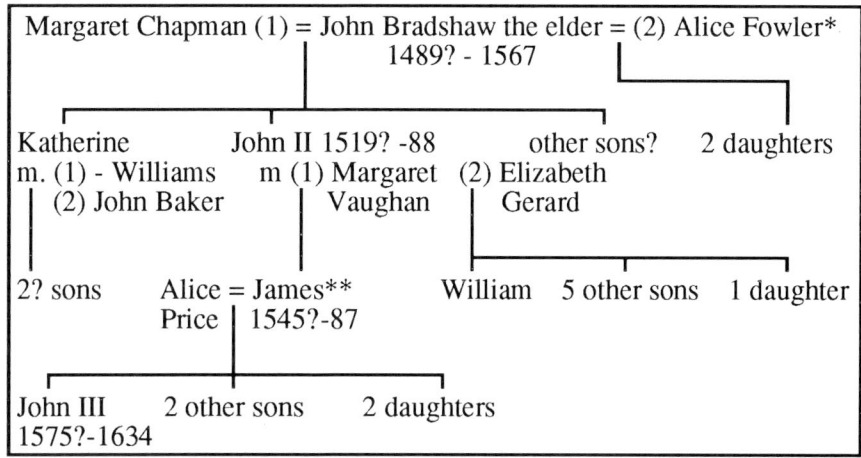

Fig. 7: The Bradshaw family of Presteigne, a tentative pedigree

*E.J.L. Cole sees Alice Fowler as the first wife of John Bradshaw the younger, rather than the second wife of John Bradshaw the elder as is shown here.

** James Bradshaw played no role in the public life of Radnorshire, either because of ill-health, or because he was absent from the county for long periods, administering the family estates in Pembrokeshire.

(Sources:
Lewis Dwnn (ed. S.R. Meyrick): Heraldic Visitations and Part of the Marches, 1846
P.S. Edwards:'John Baker IV' and Alan Harding: 'John Bradshaw I' and 'John Bradshaw II' in The House of Commons, 1509-1558, Vol. I, 1982
E.J.L. Cole: 'Brief Notes on the Early High Sheriffs of Radnorshire' TRS, Vols. XXXVI (1966) to XLII (1972))

particular. John Bradshaw the elder, 1489?-1567, was a member of a Ludlow merchant family who had served as bailiff of Ludlow on three occasions and as MP for the town in 1545. Assisted by the patronage of Lee and the goodwill of Cromwell, he began to acquire former church lands in Radnorshire, Pembrokeshire, Herefordshire and Shropshire in the later 1530s, including short leases on Dogmael Abbey and Caldy Manor in Pembrokeshire in 1537 and on Wigmore Abbey lands in 1538, converting the latter to a 21 years' lease in 1540. Though Cromwell was executed in 1542 and Lee died in 1543, Bradshaw's links with the Council remained close, possibly through the appointment of his close associate Adam Mytton to the Council in 1543. In 1544 he acquired Dogmael Abbey and Caldy Manor in fee simple together with a grant of extensive lands in the Presteigne locality, which formerly had belonged to Wigmore Abbey (E.J.L. Cole describes these lands as 'the lordship and manor of Presteigne') for a payment of £512 to the crown. In 1552 he obtained a grant of the rectory and advowson of Presteigne, thus consolidating his position as the dominant proprietor in the locality.

The Bradshaw connection with the Presteigne area possibly pre-dates the building up of this estate by some decades, for a James Bradshaw featured as a witness in a Presteigne deed of 1506, and John Bradshaw's first wife, Margaret Chapman, may have been of the Chapman family of Discoed, who owned substantial lands in the Presteigne area. She may also have been related to the Thomas Chapman who, in 1565, was granted the tithes and advowson of Shobdon parish. John Bradshaw moved to Presteigne in the middle 1540s, probably in 1546 when he gave up his pew in St Lawrence's Church, Ludlow, taking up residence at the Manor House in St David's Street. But even before this he had begun to play an influential role in Radnorshire, serving as sheriff in 1542-43. For the remainder of the sixteenth century he, his son John Bradshaw the younger (1519?-88) and his great-grandson John Bradshaw III (1574-1634) exercised considerable political influence in the county, establishing marriage alliances with prominent local families such as the Prices of Monaughty and Pilleth, the Cornewalls of Stapleton and the Vaughans. Between 1540 and 1600 six of the eighteen MPs for Radnorshire were Bradshaws, their kinsmen or their close associates, and for forty of the sixty years the post of sheriff was in similar hands. Given their connections and influence, the Bradshaws may have been responsible for the choice of Presteigne to replace Rhayader in 1542 and for the failure in 1552 of the attempt to make New Radnor the sole county town.

The Bradshaw family was thus an important channel through which the Council of Wales was able to exert its influence within Radnorshire. When seeking in vain to justify the appointment of John Bradshaw III as deputy lieutenant in 1598, the Lord President of the Council, the Earl of Pembroke, wrote: ' ... his father [sic] 50 years since was used by my father in that kind of service, Sir Henry Sidney continued him and so did I until his death. His grandson, whom I recommend is heir to his fortune, his years are not many, but sufficient.'

However, the cost of the patronage needed to maintain the Bradshaw's pre-eminence and influence in the county in the last decade or so of the sixteenth century, in face of the growing influence of the Earl of Essex in the person of Sir Gelly Meyrick, and the failure of John Bradshaw I's successors to extend the family's estates or increase the revenues derived from them sufficiently in face of inflationary pressures, meant that in the opening decades of the seventeenth century John Bradshaw III found himself in increasing financial difficulties.

The status of joint county town offered families such as the Bradshaws the chance to enhance their standing and influence, and the influx of JPs, lawyers, clerks, plaintiffs, defendants and witnesses, together with their friends and supporters, when Great Sessions or Quarter Sessions were sitting, would clearly benefit the town materially. The same could be said of parliamentary elections, though a contested election, rare in those days, could lead to disorder. The ruthless exercise of family influence and local power led to serious trouble in the town during the contested elections of 1572, 1597 and 1621. On such occasions the day and time of the poll were manipulated and 40 shilling freeholders created or disenfranchised to suit the interests of the candidate favoured by the sheriff, while freeholders were intimidated by shows of force on the part of armed supporters of the rival candidates. Thus in 1572 the atmosphere was so tense in the town that the probably outnumbered supporters of Roger Vaughan of Clyro were placed in the church to protect them from the adherents of his rival Thomas Lewis of Harpton. Even so, there was serious disorder and weapons were drawn, and it was only with the connivance of the sheriff that Roger Vaughan was elected. In 1597 James Price of Monaughty was returned, with the sheriff manipulating the date of the election in order to ensure that the poll was held at Presteigne rather than at New Radnor, to the disadvantage of Roger Vaughan, Price's opponent. In 1621 the sheriff again manipulated the poll in favour of James Price at the expense of William Vaughan of Clyro while Price's supporters paraded through the town 'in warlike manner, armed with swords, daggers and other unlawful weapons' threatening and taunting the outnumbered supporters of Vaughan.

Presteigne and the Reformation
Though the Lollard movement had attracted support in the immediate area, with William Swynderby charged before the bishop of Hereford in 1391 with having 'celebrated' frequently at Chapel Farm in Deerfold Forest and at Newton, both no more than a few miles from Lingen, there is no evidence to suggest that it made any impact in Presteigne itself. However, as Lord Rennell indicates, the dispute of 1458 between Wigmore Abbey and the parish as to who should find the sacristan or deacon for the parish church suggests some local resentment at the appropriation of the bulk of parish revenues by the abbey. The decision of the abbot in 1511 to grant the next presentation to the living of Presteigne to William Clayton and Thomas Blackbourne may well have been an attempt to appease this local opinion. In 1515, on the death of Clement ap Gruffydd, who had held the living since 1480, Clayton exercised that right, presenting William Herryson as vicar. He remained in office until at least 1536, though he seems not to have been particularly effective. In 1521 it was alleged that he was frequently absent from his duties and the task of overseeing the repair of the neglected parish property was entrusted to John Baker, John Dyer and Richard Davyes, 'chaplain', possibly one of the chantry priests.

The first local impact of Henry VIII's attack on the Church came with the surrender of Wigmore Abbey to the king's commissioners in 1538, whereby the abbey with its estates and other assets passed to the crown. Among these were the rectory of Presteigne valued at £18 16s. 8d. and the abbey lands in the parish, the latter passing into John Bradshaw's hands in 1544. The history of the rectory over the next decade or so is far from clear. Lord Rennell maintains that at one time it was held by William Rodd, while Jonathan Williams states that it was also held for a time by Walter Devereux, Lord Ferrars, Henry VIII's chief justice of south Wales. In October 1552 the rectory was granted by the crown to William Thomas, clerk to the Privy Council and an associate, if not a kinsman, of John Bradshaw, to whom it was transferred in November 1552 in reward for an annuity of £17 6s. 8d., 'a debt of 400 marks granted to the king' and the remaining years of Bradshaw's lease of Wigmore Abbey. This proved to be more of a bargain than Bradshaw could have anticipated, for Thomas was executed in May 1554 for plotting the death of Queen Mary I.

Of the incumbents of Presteigne between 1536 and 1548 nothing is known with any certainty. Walter a Rode, a clergyman named in Presteigne wills of 1539 and 1546 as an executor, may have been vicar at this time, for he is not known to have been attached to any of Presteigne's chantries. His surname would support this assumption, given Lord Rennell's assertion that the rectory was in William Rodd's hand at this time, though other sources suggest that an Edward Davies was the incumbent between 1540 and 1548. Bradshaw's grant of the the rectory did not allow him to present an incumbent until 1555 when Adam Mories, the incumbent since 1548, was deprived of the living on 'the aucthoritate parliamentorum', which suggests that Mories held protestant views and refused to accept Mary I's restoration of catholicism.

The Bradshaws seem to have used their position as patron to build up their local power base by presenting kinsmen or members of prominent local families to the living: Peter Weaver was the incumbent 1555-59, John Rodd 1559-81 and Roger Bradshaw, of a cadet branch of the family, held the living 1590-1611. The Bradshaw family evidently retained the rectorial tithes since all the above three incumbents were designated vicar.

The transfer of the rectory into lay hands probably had little impact upon the religious life of the people of Presteigne, but the same cannot be said for the dissolution of the chantries in 1549, for this struck at the institutional fabric which sustained deep devotional piety and naive superstition, the two strands of pre-Reformation lay religion. One would expect that the destruction of the chantry altars, the confiscation of plate and vestments and the sale of the endowments, with those of New and Old Radnor, to John Seymour of London for £1,600 would have provoked much local resentment, for sixteenth century Presteigne, like most of Wales and rural England, was deeply conservative in religion.

In 1548 Presteigne had three chantry priests; John Morgan, Philip Kyngley and Henry Wellington. The latter, a former canon of Wigmore Abbey, pensioned off at its dissolution, seems to have made a deep impression on the parish, for he figured as executor or overseer in a number of Presteigne wills of the 1540s. The duties of chantry priests were rarely onerous and sometimes, as at Old Radnor, they also served as parochial schoolmasters. W.H. Howse thought that this may have been the case at Presteigne.

Initially some hoped that the religious changes of the 1530s were temporary and reversible and Lord Rennell suggests that this may have been behind the appointment in 1539 of William Rodd as steward for life of Wigmore Abbey and his retention of the Nash and Little Brampton tithes. Traditional ideas on purgatory and good works were still current in the Presteigne of the 1540s. Thus in his will of 1544 Moryce ap Lellowe, after bequeathing his property to his wife, son and grandson, declared: 'I will that they or he which shall have the premises shall keep two obits yearly, the one obit one month after the feast of St Michael the Archangel, the other obit one month after the feast of the Annunciation of our Lady the Virgin, in the parish church of Presteyne for the soul of Marster John Shurley and all Christian souls.'

Against this background, if the appointment of Adam Mories was an attempt to foster the spread of protestantism in the locality, it stood little chance of success. Certainly all the Radnorshire MPs, with the exception of Charles Vaughan of Hergest, supported Mary I's restoration of Catholicism with varying degrees of enthusiasm and from a variety of motives ranging from religious conservatism to political opportunism. Local attitudes to the Elizabethan church settlement were also somewhat ambiguous, for in the 1560s the magistrates of the county, including John Bradshaw and John Beddoes, were described as being no more than 'neuter' in matters of religion. Indeed W.H. Howse regarded Beddoes' foundation of his school in 1565, with its close connection with the ringing of morning and evening bells, as an affirmation of his religious conservatism, a view supported by the purchase of former chantry lands by Beddoes and his associates in the 1550s and 1560s.

John Beddoes and his School
The school established by John Beddoes has its origins in a deed of uses of 20 April 1565 and a deed of enfeoffment signed three years later on 20 August 1568, whereby revenues of about £30 per year derived from properties in and around Presteigne were to be used 'To find, keep and maintain one meet and able learned man in the Latin tongue to be nominated and appointed ... to keep one Free Grammar School within the said town of Presteigne for ever, and therein to teach and bring up the youth that shall come and repair to the same School in virtue, discipline and learning.'

The deed of enfeoffment also stipulated that the rent from a meadow 'lying and being at St Mary Mill' should be used 'to maintain and keep one able person to ring the bell hanging in the steeple of the parish church of Presteigne every morning for ever between the feasts of All Saints and the Purification of Our Lady for the space of one hour, which shall be called (the) Day Bell, and also nightly for ever ring and peal with the same bell at every eight of the clock at afternoon as well in the summer time as in the winter time by the space of one half hour which shall be called Curfew.'

Should the ringing of the bell be discontinued for 'one whole year altogether' without reasonable cause, or if the school did not function for 'the space of three half-years together' without due cause, the endowment of the school was to revert to Beddoes' heirs.

Within decades of its introduction the day bell was rung throughout the year, by the nineteenth century at 6a.m. in the winter and at 5a.m. in the summer. Just before the First World War the day bell was discontinued and the ringing of the curfew was reduced to five minutes' duration at 8.15p.m. It ceased to be rung during the Second World War, but began again in 1945 and has continued ever since, apart from brief intervals when difficulties have arisen over the payment of the ringer. Thus today Presteigne is one of the few places in the country where the curfew is still rung on a regular nightly basis.

In past years when wage levels were low, the rent from Bell Meadow, the land given by Beddoes, was usually more than enough to pay the ringer. Thus in 1877 the bell ringer was paid £4 per year, while the rental amounted to ten guineas. However the Charity Commissioners wrote the wage of £4 per annum into the Scheme of 1878 and it thus proved impossible thereafter to increase the payment to the bell ringer from the endowment. In 1952 the payment to the ringer was increased to £12 per annum, the additional funds being provided by the Welsh Church Fund. Currently the ringers receive £320 per annum; £4 from the endowment, £16 from the Welsh Church Fund and the remainder generously donated by Mr Mike Oldfield.

W.H. Howse suggests that John Beddoes was Presteigne born and bred', the son of a John and Johane Beddoes who were witnesses to the will of Moryce ap Lellowe in 1544. However it is now clear that he was the son of a Ludlow merchant, Lewis Bedoe, and thus the John Beddoes of the 1544 will is likely to have been the founder of the school. If this is so, then Johane must have been his first wife, for the parish register of 1561 records the burial of 'Ales, the wife of John Beddoes', presumably his second wife. John Beddoes clearly maintained his Ludlow connections for his will reveals that his sister and his nieces married into prominent families in the merchant oligarchy which dominated the town—the Hucks, the Blashfields, the Hanleys, the Farrs and the Rascolls.

Beddoes' endowment of the school was very generous and certainly amounted to more than the $71^{1}/_{2}$ acres of today, for in addition to four pieces of land amounting to 71 acres, the deed of enfeoffment lists eleven other plots whose acreages are not given, several houses and a water mill.

In all the endowment was estimated to yield an annual income of £30. With the exception of three plots at Rodd, the properties making up the endowment lay in Presteigne and its immediate vicinity. Over the years some of the endowment has been sold, but clearly part was lost in the seventeenth and eighteenth centuries, through neglect and carelessness on the part of the trustees.

The original eleven trustees charged with putting Beddoes' wishes into effect were local men of some eminence. Thomas Wigmore was sheriff of Radnorshire 1579-80 and 1594-95 and MP for Leominster 1584-84 and 1586-87. His mother had married as her second husband Sir John Croft, sometime comptroller of the household of Elizabeth I. Wigmore was a personal friend of Beddoes who bequeathed him his signet ring. John Weaver, a lawyer and a substantial landowner whose principal estate lay in Stapleton, was sheriff in 1584-85 and the husband of Beddoes' niece, Anne Hanley. He was held in high esteem by Beddoes who named him as his principal executor of his will since Weaver 'knowest most of my dealing ... in whom my special trust do lie.' Peter Lloyd of Boultibrooke had been sheriff in 1544-45 and died in 1566 stipulating in his will that his heir should pay to the 'free grammar school to be kept at Presteigne' a yearly rent of 20s. John Blayney of Lower Kinsham was a kinsman of John Dee, Wigmore and the Merediths and through the marriages of his daughters was also connected with the Prices of Pilleth and the Greenlys of Titley Court. Nicholas Meredith, who left a rent of 20s. yearly to 'the schole mayster of the free grammar schole of Presteigne for the time beinge' came of an important Presteigne family with a large estate and interests in the cloth industry. Of Roger Bradshaw nothing is known with any certainty. W.H. Howse suggests that he may have been the father of Roger Bradshaw who was vicar of Presteigne 1590-1611, alternatively he may have been the Roger Bradshaw mentioned in 1621 as having served in the office of the clerk to the Council of Wales for 58 years. John ap Owen of Little Brampton and Nash was a former Clerk of the Peace for Radnorshire and a close associate of John Beddoes and a witness of his will by which he and his family received substantial bequests. The remaining four original trustees seem to have been less eminent: John Jenyns was a Presteigne mercer who had married John Beddoes' niece, Alice Hanley; Roger Vicares was another Presteigne mercer; Philip Gough or Goz was a mercer with some Ludlow connections who also owned land in the Presteigne area; of John Jenkin little is known beyond that he lived at the Dolley at Ackhill.

There was an inherent risk in appointing local grandees as trustees for men of such status were frequently absent from the locality, moreover their public duties were such that their responsibilities as trustees would tend to occupy a relatively low position in their scale of priorities. The provision in the deed of uses that new trustees should only be appointed when just three trustees remained also proved to be a weakness for three was a dangerously low number—should one of the surviving three die before new trustees had been appointed, it was necessary to have recourse to cumbersome legal processes before new trustees could be nominated.

The original school building was located in St David's Street which then included what is now Church Street, the 'schoole and schoolehouse' seem to have been on part of the site now occupied by Garrison House and that of the neighbouring house to the north. Both were destroyed in the fire of 1681 and by 1827 the school was located to the south and west of Garrison House.

The Manor and Borough of Presteigne

As indicated above, the conventional view that Presteigne became a component of Cantref Maelienydd in the mid-fifteenth century needs some modification. Initially royal control seems to have been limited to the town itself, since the manor may not have come into royal hands until either the reign of Henry VII or until the attainder and execution of the Duke of Buckingham in 1521, while the lands belonging to Wigmore Abbey did not pass to the crown until its dissolution in 1538. The significance of the town compared to the rest of the manor can be judged from their relative revenues from fees, fines and customary dues, which in 1544 amounted to no more than 10s. in respect of the town and £1 5s. $4^{1}/_{2}$d. from the rest of the manor.

Once within the lordship of Cantref Maelienydd, Presteigne was administered on behalf of the steward by a bailiff who presided over the courts and supervised the administration of the manor and borough, passing on the revenue to the exchequer. In practice however, the situation was more complex, for in 1544 John Bradshaw I had acquired the former Wigmore Abbey lands from the crown and with their manorial rights these remained in Bradshaw hands until 1625. It would thus seem that there were two manors of Presteigne, the crown manor and borough, and the former Wigmore lands which formed the Bradshaw manor of Presteigne.

In theory the bailiff received the market and fair tolls and fees on behalf of the crown, but in practice some of these had been granted away by the crown. The ulnage had been granted to Hugh Dee and the market

The Manor House

tolls were granted first in 1516 to Hugh Wylly, a groom of the chamber, then in 1519 to Wylly and William West, a page of the chamber, subsequently in 1547 to Sir Thomas Seymour, brother of the future Duke of Somerset, and in 1552 to William Thomas, clerk of the Privy Council. Almost a century later, in 1649, the toll on cattle on fair days was in the hands of Sir Edmond Sawyer, with the bailiff claiming the remainder.

    The town of Presteigne was always considered to be a borough, though since there is no evidence of a charter of incorporation, its borough status seems to have been by prescription. The area to the south of the present Station Road was known for centuries as the Burgage, which suggests a continuing local consciousness of the town's borough status. The borough consisted of four wards, Hereford Street, Broad Street, High Street and St David's Street, and Discoed, all administered by the bailiff, usually a man of at least local eminence. Thus in the 1550s and 1560s the post was held amongst others by Lewis Lloyd, lord of the manor of Boultibrooke; Richard Walsham, an ancestor of the Walshams of Knill;

and Nicholas Meredith. The bailiff was assisted by two constables and the petty constables appointed for each ward.

The bailiff presided at the manorial courts, the court leet, which met twice a year for the election of the manor's officials, and the court baron which met every three weeks and dealt with the management of manorial lands, recording the alienation of land, the surrender and renewal of copyhold leases, the settling of petty disputes and the payment of rents, heriots and other dues. (The heriot was a fine, originally the best beast, later commuted to a cash sum, paid by the heir to enter into his inheritance.) The bailiff also kept the manor accounts, forwarding them and the proceeds, fixed at £11 12s. 11d., to the crown or to the lessee of the manor. He also received the market and fair tolls on grain and the fees for market stalls, totalling £10 10s. and was charged with keeping the manor's roads in repair, having to spend at least £3 per year on this. The manorial courts continued to meet into the second half of the nineteenth century, thus in 1853 at a court leet held at the Radnorshire Arms, presided over by the steward, William Stephens, William Went was appointed bailiff. The lordship of the manor and borough of Presteigne has never been alienated and remains in crown hands.

It would seem likely that as joint county town, Presteigne would have shared in the franchise for the Radnor Boroughs, but since no details of the extent of sixteenth century franchise survives, no firm conclusion can be reached. In the election of 1690 one candidate, Sir Rowland Gwynne, claimed that originally the burgesses of Painscastle, Presteigne and Norton had shared in the franchise with New Radnor, Knucklas, Knighton, Rhayader and Cefnllys, where the right to vote was held by burgesses or freemen elected by the borough court, rather than all male property owners. His opponent, Robert Harley produced as a witness 'Mr John Miles Aged Eighty Two', who declared that he had heard that Painscastle had been disenfranchised for refusing to contribute to the MP's expenses. It seems possible that Presteigne may have been disenfranchised on similar grounds, probably in the late 1580s or 1590s when its prosperity had been threatened by plague. Such a step would have provoked little resentment, for in the sixteenth century parliamentary representation was usually regarded as a burdensome obligation rather than a privilege. However, another Harley witness, John Williams, a Presteigne freeholder, though only 64, was prepared to swear that the town had never shared in the Borough franchise. Not until after 1832 did Presteigne share in the election of the Radnor Boroughs MP; prior to that date the only enfranchised townsmen were those owning land worth forty shillings a year and thus qualified to vote in the election of the county MP.

The precise boundaries of the borough of Presteigne are not known. When seeking to define its boundaries after the Reform Act of 1832, no conclusive evidence could be found either in documentary form or from local tradition, and in consequence they were fixed in a rather arbitrary manner.

The Urban Landscape of the Late Sixteenth and Early Seventeenth Centuries

For most of the second half of the sixteenth century Presteigne seems to have shared in the general population growth of the time, with the urban area probably expanding along the south side of Hereford Street east of the present Station Road as far as Cromwell Cottage. Many of the houses in this area date from this period and most were built on the same pattern as those in the old plantation town, gable end on to the road and standing at the head of long narrow strips of land.

As previously indicated, along both sides of the High Street the regular pattern of burgage strips was being modified by infilling. On the eastern section of the north side this consisted of a long narrow alley running parallel to the street at the rear of the burgage plots and linking a number of courtyards. These and the alley were lined with workshops, many of which were connected with the cloth industry. Similar infilling seems also to have occurred to the rear of the west side of Broad Street where the burgage courtyards and workshops may have been linked by Church Way, though the first reference to this lane occurs in a mid-eighteenth century deed. At the junction of High Street and Broad Street stood the Shire Hall. Ince's painting of Broad Street, *c*.1830, shows the site occupied by a building in the style of the late seventeenth or early eighteenth century. Its predecessor was probably a timber-framed building, with the court room on the first floor and the open arcade below used as a market hall. To the south of the junction of Canon's Lane and Church Way and to the rear of the then rectory stood the tithe barn where the rector stored the tithes of grain and hay he had collected from the landholders of the parish. On the south side of High Street the infilling also took the form of a series of courtyards, though this seems to have been as much residential as industrial in character.

The expansion of the town in this period may also have seen building in the old ecclesiastical sector, along Church Street, and towards Frog Street, thus bringing Fold Farm within the limits of the town. On Frog

*J.M. Ince's engraving of Broad Street c.1830
The large building to the left of centre is the old Shire Hall,
sometimes known as the Town Hall*

Street the corn mill and tannery were already well established by the mid-sixteenth century and the new development was largely industrial rather than residential and connected with the cloth industry. The period probably also witnessed the continued development of the industrial area off Hereford Street along Harper's Lane and Back Lane. The northern part of Back Lane may have been occupied by pigsties, cowsheds, barns and stables, as it was in the eighteenth and early nineteenth centuries. To the west, there was some expansion of the town along West Street, now Scottleton Street.

Any estimate of Presteigne's population at this time must be regarded as highly speculative. Lord Rennell implies a population of 350 or so for the town in 1544 with perhaps a further 1,000 in the remainder of the parish. Reverend J.T. Evans, on the basis of 500 'houseling people', that is, aged 14 or more, suggests a population of 750 in 1546. This would seem to underestimate the number of children, moreover it is not clear whether this figure refers to the town or to the parish as a whole. Accepting Lord Rennell's figure of 350, it needs to be stressed that this represents an artificially low base after the heavy mortality of the later 1520s and the mid-1530s, and demand for labour on the part of the booming cloth trade would lead to inward migration, pushing up the population relatively quickly. The continued expansion of the cloth industry in the second half of the century, together with a period of rather more than thirty years without exceptionally heavy mortality would probably lead to sustained population growth, possibly giving the town a population of 1,000 by the mid 1580s.

CHAPTER IV

Plague, War and Fire

The seventeenth century was a time of controversy and conflict nationally as the political and religious structures developed in the sixteenth century came under strain. Inevitably such stresses would have some impact in Presteigne as the leading families of the locality were drawn into declaring themselves on the great issues of the day. However the history of the town in the seventeenth century is not only to be seen in the context of the broad issues of church and state, for it had to contend with its own local uncertainties: its prosperity threatened by plague and the fire of 1681, the decline of the Bradshaw family creating a power vacuum within the town, while the local control of the rectory remained in doubt into the second half of the century. Inevitably these local issues rapidly became entangled with the broader controversies.

The Plague Epidemics

The epidemic of bubonic plague that first reached Britain in the mid-fourteenth century returned from time to time in the next three centuries to various localities and it is clear from the parish register that Presteigne suffered plague epidemics in 1593, 1610 and 1636-37 for these years are listed as *anni pestiferi et lethales*. Indeed, Presteigne acquired an unwelcome reputation as a plague town in the early seventeenth century. The markedly large number of burials in 1586-87 and 1597 suggest that the town may have also been ravaged by plague in those years. Plague was certainly present in Ludlow and Leominster then and possibly also in Wigmore and Leintwardine in 1597. However the harvests of 1586 and the early 1590s were very poor and thus the high mortality of 1586-87 and 1597 in Presteigne may have stemmed from malnutrition and the reduced resistance to disease which this produced. Even at the best of times the poorer sections of the community lived at bare subsistence levels and in times of dearth the elderly and infants were particularly vulnerable.

However, plague was certainly responsible for the very heavy mortality of 1593, for of the 383 burials recorded, 343 were of plague victims, identified as such by the parish clerk, who wrote 'p' before the names of the plague victims. The figure may well understate the severity of the epidemic, for the first acknowledged plague victim was not buried until 10 May, though the number of burials in the previous few months had been higher than average.[1] Again some plague deaths may have gone unreported in order to evade the tight restrictions placed on the victim's family. The epidemic peaked in the summer and early autumn, with plague victims accounting for 114 out of 115 burials in July, 148 out of 149 in August, and 49 out of 50 in September. The largest number of burials in one day, twelve, occurred on 21 July with ten being the largest number in August. Any estimate of the mortality rate is highly speculative for we have no firm knowledge of the town's population in 1593, nor of how many of the plague victims lived in the town itself rather than elsewhere in the parish. Assuming that 80% of the victims lived in the town, since plague was essentially an urban disease, and that the population of the town was no more than 1,000, a 'best guess' estimated mortality rate would be in the 25-30% range.

Of the 1610 epidemic and its impact little is known. The parish register records 165 burials in the year, 117 in the period May to September, a seasonal pattern consistent with a plague epidemic. The average annual total of burials 1607-09 was forty-one, which suggests that plague accounted for between 115 and 125 deaths in the locality in 1610. Since the number of burials rose sharply in the closing months of 1609, it is possible that the epidemic may have begun then rather than in the early summer of 1610.

Of the plague epidemics affecting Presteigne, that of 1636-37 is the best documented, though even here there are gaps and ambiguities. On the evidence of the parish register, the epidemic began in June 1636 and lasted until August 1637, with plague victims accounting for 132 out of

---

1. The figures given for 1597 and 1636-37 differ from those quoted by W.H. Howse since they are calculated on the basis of a calendar year beginning 1 January, whereas his figures are based on the old style calendar year which began on 25 March.

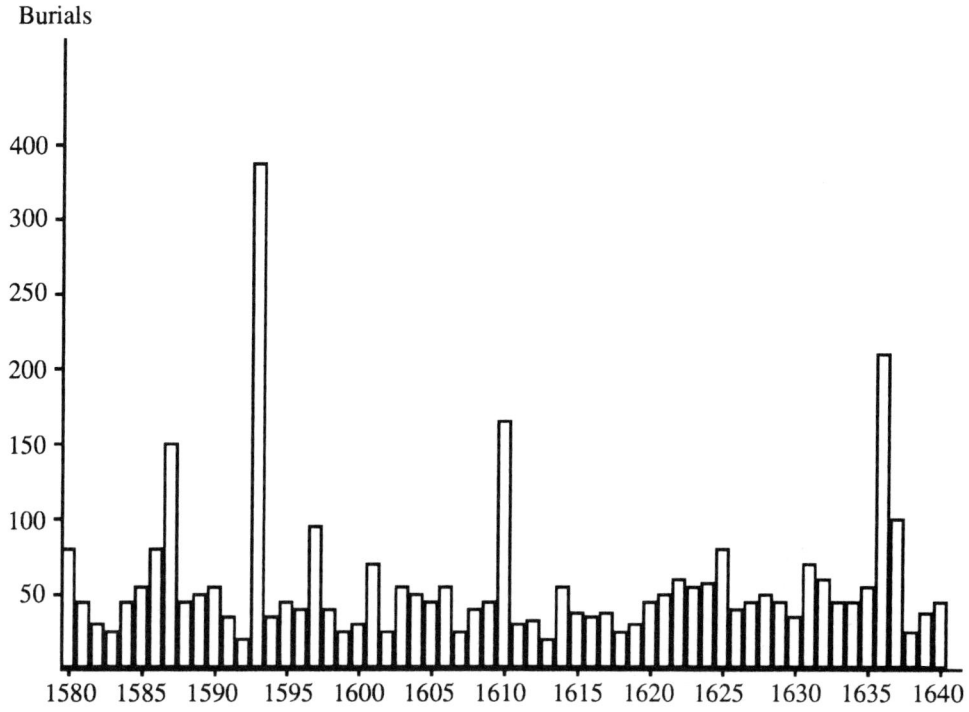

Fig. 8: Annual Total Burials in Presteigne, 1580-1640
(Source: Presteigne Parish Register)

the 208 burials in 1636 and 71 of the 101 burials in 1637. The seasonal pattern of mortality is typical of a plague epidemic with the peak occurring in August-November 1636 when 44 of the 46 burials were of plague victims. However there are grounds for believing that the parish register data seriously underestimates the extent of the plague in 1636, for the number of non-plague burials in that year is abnormally large, almost double the average of the 1630s. The register may also understate the duration of the epidemic, for although the practice of indicating the burial of plague victims only began in June, there had been an abnormally large number of burials in the previous three months, and also in the closing months of 1635. In November 1638, the retiring sheriff, Brian Crowther, writing to the Privy Council, claimed that plague had persisted in Presteigne until April of that year.

Though Wigmore, Leintwardine, Ludlow and Ross experienced plague in 1636-37, with Ross experiencing a larger number of deaths, the

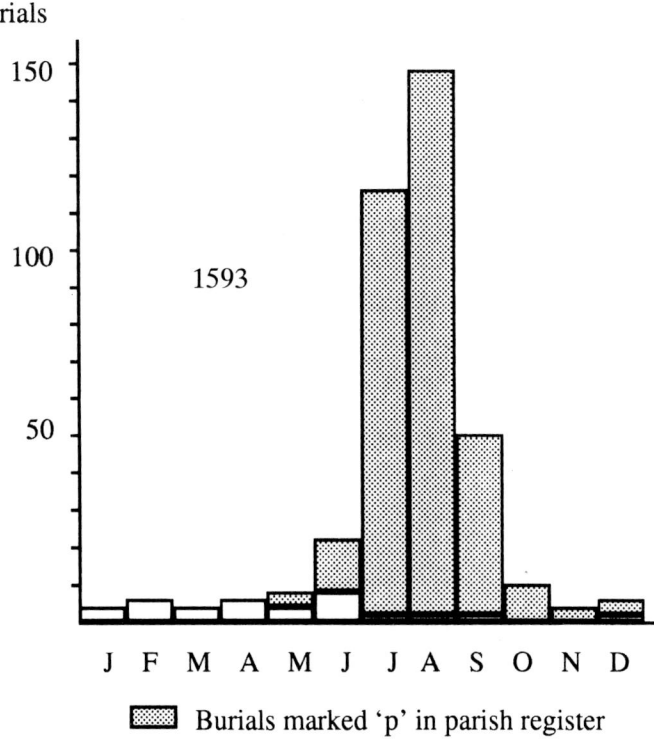

*Fig. 9: Burials in Presteigne
(Source: Presteigne Parish Register)*

Presteigne epidemic seems to have made the greatest impact on public awareness over a surprisingly large area, probably because of the protracted nature of the epidemic. J.F.D. Shrewsbury demonstrates that it was the Presteigne epidemic which led the corporation of Bishop's Castle to exclude strangers from their town and describes how, at Worcester in June 1637, an Upton on Severn man was bound over 'for saying he could find it in his mind to go to Presteigne to fetch the plague and bring it to his wife and children at Upton on Severn.'

Though death at an early age was not uncommon at this time, three epidemics in three successive generations must have had a profound impact upon the people of the town, for with the epidemiology of the plague not understood, there were no effective remedies and traditional remedies such as lozenges of dried toad or charms and amulets containing sapphire, amber, or a bead of mercury in a hazel-nut shell were of little

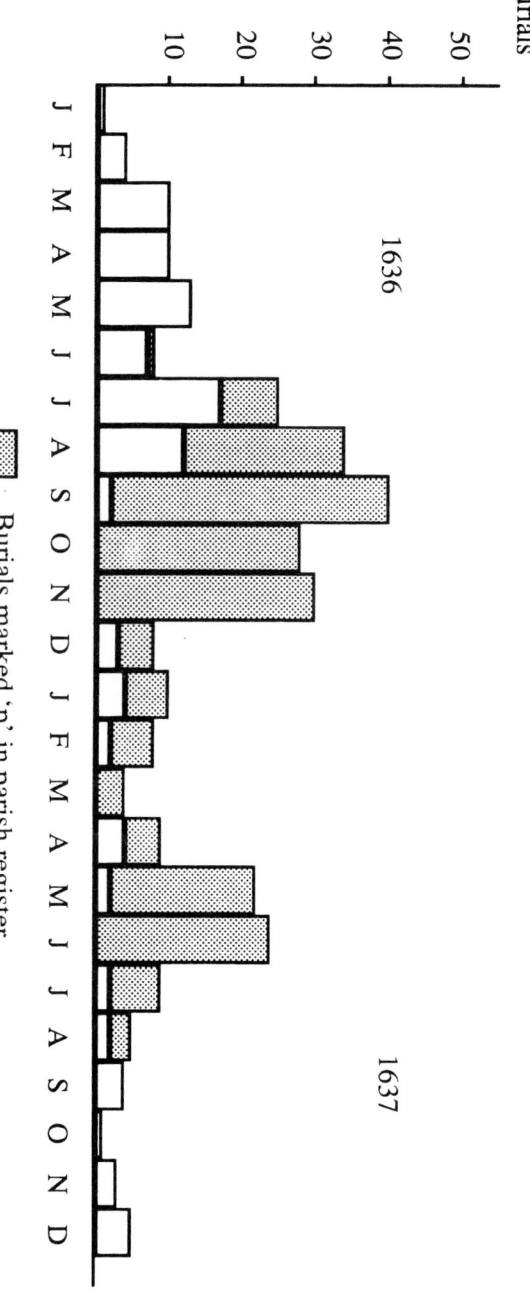

*Fig. 10: Burials in Presteigne, 1636-7
(Source: Presteigne Parish Register)*

use. Again, if plague struck a household it tended to lead to multiple deaths; nor was it the poorer families alone that suffered, for the wealthy Monnington family buried a son and three daughters in the summer and autumn of 1636. If the phrase 'the son/daughter of' indicates the burial of a minor, the 1636-37 epidemic seems to have affected the younger age groups in the town disproportionately.

It is only with the 1636-37 epidemic that we have evidence of the steps taken to contain the plague and relieve the suffering. With the town's economy shattered and the people of the surrounding countryside unwilling to bring food supplies into the town, there was a risk of real hardship or the spread of infection as inhabitants left the town in search of food. To prevent such occurrences the bailiff and constables sought to restrict the movement of the townspeople while the county authorities levied a weekly rate on the surrounding townships to relieve the suffering. In 1636 the magistrates of the neighbouring Herefordshire Wigmore hundred ordered the weekly collection of £3 8s. 3d. from its fifteen townships, this sum to be paid to John Price of Combe. The Radnorshire magistrates, meeting at New Radnor, took similar steps, levying £400 for this purpose by October 1637. Supplies for the town were left at clearly defined points, half a mile or so away: at Market Lane, off the Leominster road; at Chicken Lane, at the intersection of the lane from the Brink to Stapleton and Letchmoor Lane, and at 'the Broken Cross', whose precise location is unknown, though references in property deeds indicate that it was in the Broadheath area, which suggests that it may have been an alternative name for Market Lane.

Such measures were only partially effective, for it proved impossible to keep the inhabitants within the town and food supplies were clearly inadequate. In the spring of 1638 the justices reported that 'By reason of the plague the better sort of the inhabitants of Presteigne departed thence and have not returned' and another witness reported to the Privy Council that, while in Radnorshire in 1636-37, he had seen 'divers of Presteigne begging relief thereabouts, the chief constable and bailiff being unable to keep them in.' Understandably this provoked some resentment in the vicinity of the town and Paul Slack describes how Sir Robert Harley advocated halting the supply of bread to the town if the people continued to 'wander abroad ... in troops', while another landowner refused to contribute to the weekly rate for this reason.

In the face of such a severe and prolonged epidemic some social and economic dislocation was inevitable. The market was closed in the early summer of 1636 and did not open until the spring or early summer of 1638 at the earliest. The market had probably also been closed during the epidemics of 1593 and 1610, but it is doubtful if such closures had any profound and long term impact upon the town's economy for, given the poor roads of the period, only those living at the limit of the town's hinterland would find it easy to find an alternative market for their produce at Kington or Knighton, towns which seem to have escaped the plague.

Kington and Knighton's apparent immunity from severe plague epidemics is puzzling. Possibly, since neither town was a seat of county government, they were less likely to be in frequent contact with potential centres of infection, while if their cloth industries were more closely geared to local markets than Presteigne's this would again reduce the risk of outside infection. However, such factors would not appear to offer a complete explanation.

The impact upon the local cloth industry was probably more profound, for its reputation as a plague centre would have an adverse effect on the demand for its cloth and it may have been difficult to maintain a skilled labour force after three epidemics in successive generations. The 1636-37 epidemic seems to have led to the closure of most if not all the large scale cloth businesses in the town, including that which had once belonged to John Beddoes. However the industry seems to have continued on a small scale both in the town and the surrounding area into the eighteenth century.

The epidemics do not seem to have had any marked long term impact upon population levels in the locality, judging by annual totals of burials recorded, for though in the years following an outbreak the number of burials tended to fall sharply, they rose again in the following decade, thus suggesting that the population loss from plague was rapidly made good by in-migration. Thus, if plague years are excluded, the average annual burials in the 1580s were 48, only to fall to 39 in the 1590s, rising to 47 in the period 1600-09. In the next decade the average annual number of burials fell to 36, rising to 53 in the 1620s and falling to 47 in the 1630s. The population loss may well have been made good as a result of migration from the Welsh uplands, thus maintaining a strong Welsh influence in the locality. Thus in 1620 18% of the land holders in the townships of Presteigne, Discoed and Maes Treylow included the Welsh patronymic 'ap' in their surnames.

At first sight, given Presteigne's reputation as a plague centre, such rapid re-population would seem unlikely. However, the decades of the plague epidemics were periods of dearth—there were several successive poor harvests and wool prices fell sharply in the opening decades of the seventeenth century as a result of increasing imports of Spanish wool. Migration to the town from the Welsh uplands was thus driven by sheer necessity, moreover the element of risk, once an epidemic had run its course, may well have appeared acceptable to a population inured to early and sudden death.

The Eclipse of the Bradshaw Family
Though the plague epidemics came at a time when the Bradshaw influence was declining sharply, there seems to have been little significant causal connection, though the family's income may well have been reduced by the impact of the plague upon the local economy. The threat posed by the Essex faction had forced the Bradshaws into an aggressive display of their local influence and of the twenty sheriffs between 1584 and 1603, eighteen were in the Bradshaw camp, as were at least half of the local members of the commission of the peace for Radnorshire. The use of patronage on this scale seems to have been beyond the family's means and in the opening decades of the seventeenth century John Bradshaw III (1574-1634) was compelled to gradually dispose of the family estate.

In 1605 the tithes of Presteigne and Broadheath were leased, possibly to a relative by marriage, Humphrey Cornewall of Stapleton, for it was he who presented John Scull to the living in 1611, while in 1609 the tithes of Leintwardine, Adforton and Walford were sold. In 1611 Presteigne tithes were sold to a Robert Williams and in 1612 the Pembrokeshire estates of Dogmael Priory and Caldy Manor were disposed of. In 1613 John Bradshaw conveyed extensive property in Presteigne to his uncle William Bradshaw, the head of the Pembrokeshire branch of the family, for £400. This transaction was probably not an outright sale but rather a mortgage, for it was a very low sum in view of the assets involved; twelve messuages, eight cottages, three mills, twelve tofts (small cottages usually with rights of common), twenty gardens, 500 acres of arable land, 50 acres of meadow, 330 acres of woodland, 100 acres of pasture and 500 acres of heath.

In spite of these transactions John Bradshaw seems to have remained in financial difficulties, for in 1615 he appeared before the Star Chamber, along with his kinsman James Price of Monaughty and the sheriff, accused of embezzling part of the subsidy which they had been collecting in the county. In 1616 he was once more before the Star Chamber, this time accused of attempting to bribe the sheriff not to arrest him for debt. In 1619 he sold the manor house and its estate, which presumably included the properties listed above, to John Read of London for £1,200. Finally, in 1625 he conveyed the manorial rights of Presteigne, granted by the crown to his great-grandfather, to Sir Robert Harley of Brampton Bryan.

His last years were spent living quietly in his new home, the Cross House, now the Radnorshire Arms. He had been excluded from the bench since 1616 and although he was appointed a deputy lieutenant in 1625, the Bradshaw influence had clearly waned, hence the bitterly contested election of 1621. In the 1620s political dominance in the locality passed into the hands of the Price family of Pilleth who, with their client Richard Jones of Trewern, monopolised both the county and borough seats until the civil war.

Though Charles Price took care to maintain his political power base, the deputy stewardship of the crown boroughs in Radnorshire, he was principally concerned with his military and parliamentary career and this may have created a power vacuum in Presteigne. John Read, sheriff of Radnorshire 1622, may have had political ambitions, but he died in 1624 leaving an heir little more than a year old. For a time in the late 1620s the Jones family, represented by Griffith Jones, clerk to the peace in 1621, his brother Evan, and his nephew Richard, seemed to be assuming a local ascendancy. Possibly a junior branch of the Jones family of Trewern, they had built up substantial estates in the Presteigne area, including the Boultibrooke estate and the manor house. Griffith Jones, who had acquired the lordship of the Presteigne manor from Sir Robert Harley in 1626, was sheriff in 1628, but was murdered during his year of office. Thereafter the family seems to have concerned itself with its estates and with establishing itself more firmly in the social hierarchy of the borderland. In the absence of a single dominant family, leadership in Presteigne seems to have passed to a loose coalition of lesser gentry such as the Merediths, Taylors, Blayneys and Rickards. However the interests of these families did not always coincide and they did not always possess the power nor the resources necessary to defend the interests of the town.

Regaining the Rectory
After the sale to Robert Williams in 1611 the rectory and advowson changed hands frequently in the following few years. Williams sold them to William Wigmore who in turn disposed of them in 1614 to a syndicate headed by Sir Thomas Wolseley, and in 1619 they were sold to Sir Robert Harley of Brampton Bryan for £1,020. In 1627 Harley sold them to a puritan group, the feoffees (trustees) for the impropriations, who

planned to use the income from the Presteigne rectorial tithes, along with the tithes they had acquired or impropriated from other livings, to support puritan lecturers in the London church of St Antholin's. The price of £1,400 gave Harley a handsome profit, though this may not have been the motive for the sale for Harley, a devout puritan, strongly sympathised with the aims of the feoffees, two of whom, Richard Sibbes and William Gouge, were his close associates.

It may have been the realisation that local control of the living was under threat which led to the revitalisation of an old parochial institution, the Twelve Men. Lord Rennell regards the Twelve Men as having been formed to safeguard local interests in the days when the living was controlled by Wigmore Abbey, but which had lapsed at some time in the first half of the sixteenth century. There is no mention of the institution in the parish registers, which date from 1561, until 1603 when an entry in the register states: ' ... for as much as some of the XII men of the parishe of Presteyne are dead and departed out of this transitorie liefe, and, that the number is to be supplied by ancient custom of the gravest and substantiallest men of the parishe It is ordered and decreed that the persons undernamed shalbe and remayne of the number of the XII men ...'

The names listed include those of some of the most prominent men in the locality: Peter Lloyd of Boultibrooke, the bailiff of Presteigne; Thomas Weaver of Stapleton, a great nephew of John Beddoes; John Walsham, soon to be lord of the manor of Knill; Nicholas Taylor, a lawyer and a substantial landowner; and Francis Owen of Nash and Little Brampton, another lawyer and a minor functionary of the Council of Wales and the Marches. Men of such standing, some with a legal training, could be expected to champion local interests, should these be threatened by an absentee lay impropriator. Significantly, once the rectory had passed out of immediate local control, care was taken to keep the Twelve up to full strength, thus in 1621, 1623, 1627, 1630 and 1631, the parish register records the appointment of new members. The institution would thus appear to have been more than an interesting medieval survival, though there is no evidence to indicate any success which it may have had against the absentee owners of the rectory.

In 1632, in the course of the crown's campaign against puritanism, as a result of an action brought by the Attorney General, the feoffees were declared to have acted illegally and were ordered to forfeit Presteigne rectory, along with their other assets, to the crown. In January 1639 Charles I granted the rectorial tithes to Thomas Turner, bishop of London, and John Juxon, but in April this grant was rescinded and by letters patent, Reverend John Scull, vicar of Presteigne, and his successors were constituted as rectors, the advowson of the living remaining with the crown.

Of Scull, who obtained the rectory at a cost of £300 and with the assistance of Lord Willoughby, whom he served as chaplain, little is known. He may have been distantly related to the Crofts of Croft Castle and also to the Meredith family, for the will of Morgan Meredith, a former sheriff of Montgomeryshire, drawn up in 1594, mentions bequests to his son-in-law William Scull and his children, who included a John Scull. Presented to the living in 1611 by the Cornewall family, he does not seem to have been an effective or popular incumbent. In addition to the living of Presteigne, Scull also held the living of Llanbadarn Fawr and the prebend of Llangunllo, and in a survey of the clergy of the Hereford diocese, probably drawn up for Sir Robert Harley, *c.*1640, was described as 'of very ill life.' In the contested election of 1621 he had been prepared to use his influence to the full to secure the return of James Price of Monaughty, while the letters patent of 1639 granting him the rectory recognised that he had been frequently absent from the parish and stipulated that in future the rector should 'continuously make ... residence at Presteigne.' Since the entries in the parish register between 1611 and 1632 are in the handwriting of his curate, Reverend Hugh Bevan, it would seem that Scull had been largely non-resident for the first twenty years of his incumbency. In 1639, shortly before his appointment as rector, the parishioners had petitioned the crown requesting the appointment of a Richard Bretton and portraying the parish as 'having for many years been destitute of a preaching minister.' Not until opinions had been polarised by the bitterness of the Civil War does Scull seem to have won the general support and sympathy of his parishioners.

The survey drawn up for Sir Robert Harley, though by no means impartial, suggests that neighbouring parishes fared little better than Presteigne. Titley, Byton Kinsham and Lingen were all served by curates paid £10 a year who could do no more than read the service, while Knill was served by a rector who was described as 'neither of good life nor learning.' Only the conscientious Reverend Edwards, vicar of Kington, emerged with some credit since the survey noted that he preached 'for the most part once a Sabbath.' Even so, since he also served the churches of Huntington, Brilley, Michaelchurch and 'Llandeveylocke', he had to spread himself rather thinly.

Pilleth Court (c.1940), the home of the leading Radnorshire Royalist, Charles Price

Presteigne and Charles I

Presteigne, like the rest of Radnorshire, has a reputation for unswerving loyalty to the royalist cause. Thus in 1627 Francis Rickards of Presteigne, clerk to the peace and later collector of ship money in south Wales, could proudly claim in a letter to the Privy Council: 'Radnor is one of the least and poorest counties within the Kingdom, but most willing to yield all service and supplies.'

In part this stemmed from the county's relative isolation which created an inward looking conservatism which viewed with suspicion any ideas which threatened the *status quo* in church and state. The Presteigne area also had personal links with Charles I for in 1617 Northwood, 240 acres of woodland and waste lying between Presteigne and Evenjobb, had been leased to Sir Thomas Trevor for the use of the then Prince Charles, an enthusiastic huntsman.

This loyalty to the crown and the pride in the county's royal connections was demonstrated in 1633 when the tenants of the lordship of Cantref Maelienydd, including those of Presteigne, together with the tenants of other royal manors in the county contributed £741 12s. to repurchase the lordship and the other manors which Charles had sold in 1631, the tenants requesting: 'that the same lord king should reassume the same lordships, of late alienated, for a royal estate, and that they themselves might continue as tenants of the king of England as they formerly had been ...'

Self-interest probably also played some part in the tenants' action, for in 1632 the original purchasers had disposed of the property to Sir William and Sir George Whitmore, who promptly sought to exploit their rights to the full. No doubt the tenants preferred royal control as it had been exercised by the Earl of Pembroke, steward between 1616 and 1630, and his deputy in the 1620s, Charles Price of Pilleth, who seem to have exploited their positions for electoral advantage rather than for financial gain. It is rather more than coincidence that Charles Price represented the Radnor Boroughs in the parliaments of the 1620s, for as the steward's deputy he had considerable influence in the admission of burgesses within the boroughs and thus determined who had the vote.

Charles' response to the petition of 1633 was to confirm the privileges and liberties of the tenants, promising that never again would he alienate the lordships. Typically however, he almost went back on his word for in 1639, when Sir Robert Harley sought a lease of the lordships, it was only after a fierce debate in the Privy Council and another petition from the tenants that Harley's proposal was rejected.

Throughout the 1620s and for most of the 1630s Radnorshire met, without protest, the crown's financial demands, in spite of poor harvests, low wool prices and the burden of relieving Presteigne during the plague epidemic. Thus, when the collection of ship money, revived in 1634, was extended to inland areas, Radnorshire met its quota of £490 10s. in full. This sum was markedly lower than the quotas of its neighbours—Montgomery's at £833 6s., Brecknock's at £933, and Herefordshire's at £4,000—reflecting the county's smaller population and relative poverty.

However, in 1637, Evan Davies, the sheriff of Radnorshire, reported that he had been unable to collect £12 8s.10d. of the £28 ship money due from Presteigne and his successor, Brian Crowther, failed to recover this sum, despite several requests to Lewis Meredith, the bailiff of Presteigne. Ship money had originally been a means of providing ships to protect the coast from piracy, but after its revival by Charles I it soon became virtually a non-parliamentary annual property tax. Within Radnorshire as a whole there are signs that traditional loyalty to the crown was wearing thin and in 1639 there was a shortfall of more than 30%, though this may have been, to some extent, a local response to widespread and heavy defaults elsewhere in Wales and the Marches.

However, and despite the conservative loyalty, it may also have been a reaction to royal policy which stressed the authority of the bishops, the importance of ceremony and the pre-eminence of the sacraments. The 1639 petition from the parishioners of Presteigne complaining of the lack of 'a preaching minister, able and qualified to dispense the mysteries of salvation' is reminiscent of the aggressive protestantism of the Elizabethan age and is mirrored by the protestant stance adopted by Charles Price in the Long Parliament of 1640-42. Only in June 1642, when parliament sought to wrest control of the army from the king, did Price declare for the crown; later returning to Radnorshire to execute the commission of array, thus securing the county train band (militia) for the royalist cause. Price's reaction to the crisis of 1640-42, though more coherent, probably mirrored the attitude of Presteigne and of Radnorshire as a whole, a committed though imprecise loyalty to the traditional institutions of church and state, rallying to the crown in the final crisis.

Presteigne and the Civil War
Presteigne was the scene of one of the earliest skirmishes in the Civil War in Wales, when it was raided on the night of 27 October 1642 by a detachment of parliamentarian troops drawn from a force commanded by the Earl of Stamford, stationed at Hereford, to block a possible royalist advance from Wales. Stamford's position was very exposed and royalist forces were preparing to advance on Hereford from Raglan and Presteigne. Acting on information from William Jones, a parliamentary sympathiser, that royalist leaders were to meet at Presteigne to co-ordinate their attack, Stamford decided to raid the town to capture local royalist leaders and to disrupt their plans. A party of sixty men—forty troopers and twenty mounted musketeers—left Hereford at 3p.m. and arrived at Presteigne seven hours later.

By then the meeting had broken up, but a few Royalists were still at the home of Francis Rickards in Broad Street. After a brief struggle in which three royalist soldiers were killed, six of their leaders were captured and imprisoned. Charles Price was sent to Gloucester and Rickards to Coventry. In a petition for his release Rickards paints a picture of injured innocence: 'On 27 October last the captain of a troop of horse under the control of the Earl of Stamford seized Captain Charles Price, Knight of the County. Petitioner went in a friendly way to visit Price and was then, without cause, taken by the Captain of the troop, ... carreyd to Coventry where he remained ever since in chains.' Rickards was freed in February 1643 and Price a month or so later.

In the meantime the Royalists had placed the informer, William Jones, in the county gaol and plans were made to attack Brampton Bryan Castle, the home of Sir Robert Harley and the local parliamentarian stronghold. The attack was scheduled for February 1643 with a force drawn from the

Radnorshire train bands, stiffened by troops from Herefordshire, but the plan was abandoned when the train bands, assembled at Presteigne, refused to fight outside the county.

In April 1643 Presteigne was again raided by parliamentarian forces when two troops of cavalry occupied the town briefly, freed Jones from the gaol and plundered local Royalists. Jones took shelter at Brampton Bryan, from where he launched a raid on the Nantmel home of Hugh Lloyd, the sheriff whom Jones blamed for his imprisonment. Though Presteigne remained a royalist stronghold, it played no part in the attack on Brampton Bryan of July 1643, foiled by Lady Brilliana, nor in the successful attack of the spring of 1644.

1645 began with a tragedy for the royalist cause in Radnorshire with the death of Charles Price at Presteigne, stabbed by Colonel Robert Sandys, possibly in a duel, on 17 January. W.H. Howse assumes that Sandys was a Parliamentarian, but the *Weekly Accompt* of 29 January implies that he was a catholic Royalist, for it attributes the dispute which led to Price's death to Price 'showing some discontent that Papists were received with greatest favour and Protestants shut out of office and they put in.' Given Price's aggressive protestantism, this explanation has the ring of truth about it. If not a catholic, Sandys, a kinsman of Samuel Sandys, the former royalist governor of Worcester, was certainly a member of the pro-catholic faction surrounding the queen, for in May 1645 he went to Paris to seek her assistance in securing a pardon from the king for Price's death.

With both sides plundering friend and foe alike, the Clubmen and their policy of 'armed neutrality' gained some support along the eastern fringes of Radnorshire, though the county in the main remained loyal to the crown. Thus after his defeat at Naseby, it was to south Wales and the borderland that Charles I came to rally his supporters and to regroup, and in the late summer and early autumn of 1645 he and his troops passed through Radnorshire twice.

The first visit was in early August when, *en route* for Oxford from south Wales via Brecon and Ludlow, he passed through the county with a force of 3,000 men. Entering Radnorshire on 6 August, the royalist force passed through Painscastle, Newchurch and New Radnor. The king and some of his courtiers stayed the night of 6-7 August 'at a yeoman's, the court dispersed'. Tradition has it that that this was at Bush Farm, Evenjobb, which Charles renamed Beggar's Bush to commemorate the plain fare on which he had dined. The troops pushed on ahead of the royal party, passing through Presteigne, Wigmore and Ludlow, the *Weekly Accompt* of 29 August carrying a report from Wigmore that

'3,000 horse and dragoons came over by Prestene.' Whether the king took the same route is unknown and contemporary sources are silent on the point. Webb suggests that he may have travelled the longer Knighton route to throw off possible pursuers.

Charles I returned to the area in mid-September, *en route* for Chester from Hereford, via Newtown, though the authorities disagree on the details of his stay in Presteigne. Originally he had planned to make for Worcester, but with parliamentarian forces blocking the way he changed his route, travelling from Stoke Edith to Presteigne via Leominster or Weobley and possibly Pembridge, a journey of more than thirty miles which began at 6a.m. on 18 September and ended at midnight. However the sources disagree as to the length of his stay in the town and as to his host. The *Iter Carolinum* states that Charles stayed at the house of a 'Master Andrewes' for the night and resumed his journey on 19 September, reaching Newtown safely. As Symonds describes in his diary: 'This day we marched from Presteyne, and except in the first three myles, we saw never a house or a church over the mountaynes.' However, an entry in the parish register, written in 1793 by the rector, Reverend William Whalley, asserts that Charles spent two nights, 19-20 September in Presteigne as the guest of Nicholas Taylor at Lower Heath, two miles to the east of the town.

Most authorities cast doubt on this local tradition, preferring the *Iter* account which is confirmed by Symonds, though 'Master Andrewes' remains unidentified. W.H. Howse rejects the tradition on the grounds that Nicholas Taylor was only 19 in 1645 and that the earliest date known for his residence at Broadheath is 1651, though J. Southwood has since shown that Taylor's father was described as being 'of Lower Heath' in 1619. Even if Nicholas Taylor was in residence at Broadheath in 1645, it is difficult to reconcile this tradition with that attached to King's Turning, a turning to the left near Wegnall Farm leading to Broadheath. Tradition has it that riding eastward from Presteigne on this visit, as though making for Kington, New Radnor, or Leominster, Charles turned left here towards Broadheath, in order to confuse possible pursuers, fording the Lugg and joining up with his troops, who had left Presteigne on the Stapleton road, making for Stonewall Hill on the way to Knighton and Newtown.

Closely connected with this royal visit to Presteigne was the pillaging of Willey Court by the pursuing parliamentary troops. With the men of the household working in the fields, the house was unprotected and some of the female servants were molested by the soldiers. When the owner,

Lower Heath House

Colonel William Legge, discovered what had happened, he and his men, some of whom were armed with pitchforks, caught up with the troops at Knighton where one soldier was killed and others wounded.

To assert some degree of control over the largely royalist borderland, Colonel Birch, after occupying Hereford in December 1645, established garrisons at Presteigne and Montgomery. Coming only a few months after the town had quartered the troops accompanying Charles on his two journeys through Radnorshire in 1645, the garrison must have placed a great strain on its resources. This may well have been the garrison of which the town complained in its petition of 1669, when it was stated that the town had been compelled to maintain a parliamentary garrison on free quarter for twelve months.

Nor was the hardship confined to the town itself, for nearby communities such as Whitton and Norton were compelled to give free quarter to detachments drawn from the garrison from time to time, in addition to providing supplies for it. In 1646 Whitton farmers provided three oxen and a heifer for the Presteigne garrison, while in February 1646 Norton had to provide twenty bushels of oats, two loads of hay, a hundredweight of bread, sixty pounds of cheese and forty pounds of beef and bacon, and a further twenty-six bushels of oats a few weeks later. In January Norton had had to provide six teams of horses to carry timber from Stapleton to Presteigne for the use of the garrison and on two occasions in February teams of horses to transport 'turf' (possibly peat) to the garrison, presumably for use as fuel.

The garrison had been withdrawn by 1648, for when south Wales rose for the king in the summer of 1648, the few parliamentarian troops in Presteigne were rounded up and placed in the county gaol, and when the authorities wished to arrest the presbyterians Edward Harley and Thomas Blayney later in the year, a troop of Colonel Horton's cavalry was dispatched to the town. The execution of Charles I probably increased hostility in the town to the new regime, for in 1650, in response to a petition from troops in Presteigne, the Council of State instructed the judge at the sitting of Great Sessions in the town not to let them 'be oppressed by lying and mischievous witnesses'.

In 1651 five young men from leading families of the locality, Nicholas Meredith, William Taylor (a cousin of Nicholas Taylor), John Bull, Thomas Gomey and Andrew Higgins set off to fight for Prince Charles at the battle of Worcester. Their story is best told in the words of John Lloyd of Presteigne in his deposition as reported to the Committee of Accounts in London in March 1652. The five men met 'with Major General Montgomery at Bewdley, [and] told him that they had sent him some wine ... There being then an order to march, on an alarm, Meredith and the others accompanied the Major with his brigade of 2,000 horse to Worcester and rode with the Duke of Buckingham in his troop. When Lord General Cromwell came against Worcester, they joined the Duke of Buckingham and advanced into the field, but perceiving their party retreating, the whole troop retreated likewise, and were all scattered.'

The young men remained defiant and refused at first to accept the charges laid against them. They received local support, for when their lands were confiscated and advertised for lease at the Cross in Presteigne and in New Radnor, none but the existing tenants were prepared to take them, while the tenants would only do so at the existing rents and leases, which presumably would provide indemnification in the future. In the event Nicholas Meredith sought to evade confiscation of his lands by claiming that they were for the most part a jointure for his mother, and as late as December 1654 his case had not been decided.

A tradition persisted in the locality until at least the end of the nineteenth century that Prince Charles had sought shelter in the Presteigne area after the battle of Worcester, though since his itinerary is so well documented, it has no factual basis. The enduring royalist sympathies of

*Knill Court, the seat of Walsham family.
It was destroyed by a fire in 1942*

the area can be seen in the celebration of the restoration of the monarchy on Oak-apple Day, 29 May, which persisted into the 1940s.

Royalist sympathies did not, however, preclude co-operation with the new regime, for the roads had to be maintained, the poor relieved, wrongdoers punished, and family interests and the social hierarchy maintained. Thus William Monnington served as bailiff of Presteigne for most of the 1650s and, as Ruth Bidgood shows, Reverend Philip Lewis, the future rector of Presteigne who was later to describe the parliamentarians as a 'black sacrilege', was prepared in 1654 to use the puritan under-sheriff, John Dauntsey, to evict a Lewis Morgan from property which he considered belonged to his wife.

The willingness of John Walsham of Knill and Nicholas Taylor of Lower Heath to serve as JPs throughout the 1650s might be construed in the same light. Walsham served as sheriff in 1654 and, it is alleged, assisted Vavasour Powell in his plans to resist by force Cromwell's seizure of power. Nicholas Taylor was more deeply implicated with the new regime, serving as sheriff in 1651 and as a member and on most county committees for assessment throughout the Interregnum, though he changed loyalties in 1659-60 and helped to prepare the way for the Restoration. His kinsman, Peter Taylor of Evenjobb, also took a prominent role in the new regime at county level.

Other local figures who had been active on the parliamentarian side during the war, Sir Robert Harley, his sons Edward and Robert, and their kinsman and client Thomas Blayney, were also prominent in local administration in the years following the defeat of the king. As T. Bassett shows, the Harleys and their east Radnorshire clients dominated the early Radnorshire county committees. Robert Harley was also MP for Radnor Boroughs 1647-48 and his older brother Edward was one of the MPs for Herefordshire in the same period, while Blayney, as G.E. McParlin demonstrates, played a prominent role in the parliamentary government of Herefordshire, serving as collector of revenues under the Earl of Stamford, treasurer of the Gloucester committee 1643-45 and as a member of the Herefordshire county committee and sometimes treasurer between 1646 and 1649. However, all were presbyterians and, apart from Nicholas Taylor, took no part in affairs after the seizure of power by the Independents in December 1648 and the execution of Charles I in January 1649.

Walsham was no doubt influenced by his wife's puritan connections, for she was the sister of Jenkin Jones, the prominent Breconshire Baptist, but the case of Nicholas Taylor is more puzzling, for he had few sympathies with the new religious regime, though under the 1653 ordinance he, as church warden, solemnised a marriage in the parish. Possibly it was no more than an accommodation with a regime with which he had no real sympathy, but whose existence he had to accept to further family interests. For its part, the new regime, anxious to secure any degree of cooperation, was prepared to accept the most lukewarm allegiance.

Presteigne and the Puritans
If the townspeople were prepared prepared to temporise in varying degrees with the new regime in the political sphere, this does not appear to have been the case in matters of religion. Even so, few were prepared to go to the lengths of Nicholas Taylor, whose children Nicholas (1654), Charles (1657), Elizabeth (1658) and John (1660), were christened privately by visiting ordained clergymen since, as he explained in 1672, 'in those bad times there was no lawful minister settled in our Parish.' Another strand in the local attitude to the new religious order was the obvious local resentment that the rectorial tithes were once more under threat. However, one must not write off the puritan cause in the town completely, for there are some hints at some puritan presence. The puritan overtones of the 1639 petition and the presbyterian beliefs of Thomas Blayney have been noted above. Again, Vavasour Powell, the Puritan who dominated mid Wales in the early 1650s had married a Mrs Quarrell 'of Presteigne', who might be expected to be sympathetic to his

religious views. Finally, Sir Robert Harley, who held the manor briefly in the mid-1620s and was building up his estate locally, is known to have favoured his puritan co-religionaries in his choice of tenants elsewhere and may have followed the same course in Presteigne. Certainly one of his tenants at Willey, Richard Strangward, citing the plague epidemic at Presteigne as due cause, preferred in May 1637 to have his daughter baptised at puritan Brampton Bryan, rather than in a nearer parish such as Norton, Lingen or Byton.

In April 1643 parliament had restored the rectorial tithes to the feoffees, but this had no real impact since the town was still under royalist control. However in March 1647, the victory of St Antholin's seemed complete when the verdict of 1632 was declared null and void and the rectorial tithes restored to the feoffees. In practice this decision may well have been ignored in Presteigne, for Reverend Philip Lewis, writing after the Restoration, maintained that the tithes had been seized by parliament, leaving the incumbent, Reverend John Scull, in great financial difficulty. Even so W.H. Howse demonstrates that Scull remained rector until at least a few months before his death in August 1652 and seemingly in receipt of the rectorial tithes until March 1652 when the Commission for the Propagation of the Gospel in Wales instituted an itinerant preacher, Richard Lucas, as vicar of Presteigne. Shortly afterwards parliament ordered that the profits of the rectory be paid into the hands of Colonel John Jones for the time being.

In the summer of 1652 the parishioners petitioned parliament, asking that St Antholin's claim be set aside, but this request was rejected and the rights of St Antholin's reaffirmed. Thereafter, until at least 1657, £100 *per annum* from the tithes were paid to St Antholin's, with the balance, apart from a grant of £39 to Mrs Scull, going to Richard Lucas. In February 1655, though Lucas was still officiating in the parish, a Thomas Cole was appointed to the rectory. This confusing situation, by no means unique, arose from the fact that at this time clerical appointments in Wales were being made by at least three bodies. A local *modus vivendi* was soon arrived at whereby Cole officiated as rector in Presteigne with Lucas in charge at St Michael's, Discoed, with a stipend of £20. Cole's appointment seems to have lasted only a year and Lucas was once more officiating as vicar with the parishioners attempting, without success, in 1657 to buy out St Antholin's claim on the parish, in order 'that the union of the Rectory and the Vicaridge ... may continue.'

Richard Lucas remained as vicar until at least 1660, though he never seems to have won over his parishioners. A former London tailor and a committed Puritan, whose spelling and grammar suggests that he had received little formal education, he may have lacked the social status expected of an incumbent. However the real objection to him may have been that he was not an ordained clergyman. Thus it was argued in 1652-53 that the portion of the rectorial tithes not paid to St Antholin's should not be paid to Lucas but to an assistant to officiate 'in regard of the inability of the said Mr Lucas.' Nicholas Taylor's refusal to have his children baptised by Lucas has been noted above and it may also be significant that on two occasions, June 1654 and June 1655, laymen officiated at marriage services, on the latter occasion Nicholas Taylor solemnising the marriage of two servants of a fellow church-warden.

Ostensibly Lucas lost the living in June 1660 with the presentation of Phillip Lewis to the vicarage, which encouraged St Antholin's to reassert its claim to the rectorial tithes. However, it was to no avail for on 30 November 1660 Lewis was presented to the rectory of Presteigne. It seems that Lucas did not go quietly and Thomas Richards suggests that he clung on until 1662 before he was effectively ejected. His resistance may explain why Lewis was not formally inducted until 1664.

In general, one gains the impression that the regimes of the Interregnum lacked the means, if not the will, to adopt an aggressive religious stance in their dealings with the parish. Scull retained the living until at least March 1652, possibly under the protection of Nicholas Taylor, and thereafter he, and later his widow, were treated more generously than Lewis implied in 1671. Reverend John Jones continued in his post as master of the grammar school, which appears to have functioned throughout the period despite its close links with the established church. Nor was there apparently any determined attempt to puritanise the parish until 1652. Neither is there any reference to Vavasour Powell being active in the parish, for his local activities seem to have been centred primarily in New Radnor. The situation in Presteigne may not have been so confrontational in the religious sphere as Lewis and Taylor imply.

The Fire of Presteigne, 1681

Thanks to M.A. Faraday's analyses of the hearth tax returns for Herefordshire and Radnorshire for 1670-71 it is possible to gain an impression of how Presteigne stood in relation to its neighbours in terms of size and prosperity in the mid-seventeenth century. With 128 houses, compared to Knighton's 100 and New Radnor's 66, one could see how Presteigne was increasingly able to reserve to itself the status of Radnorshire's county town. However, it was much smaller than its Herefordshire neighbours,

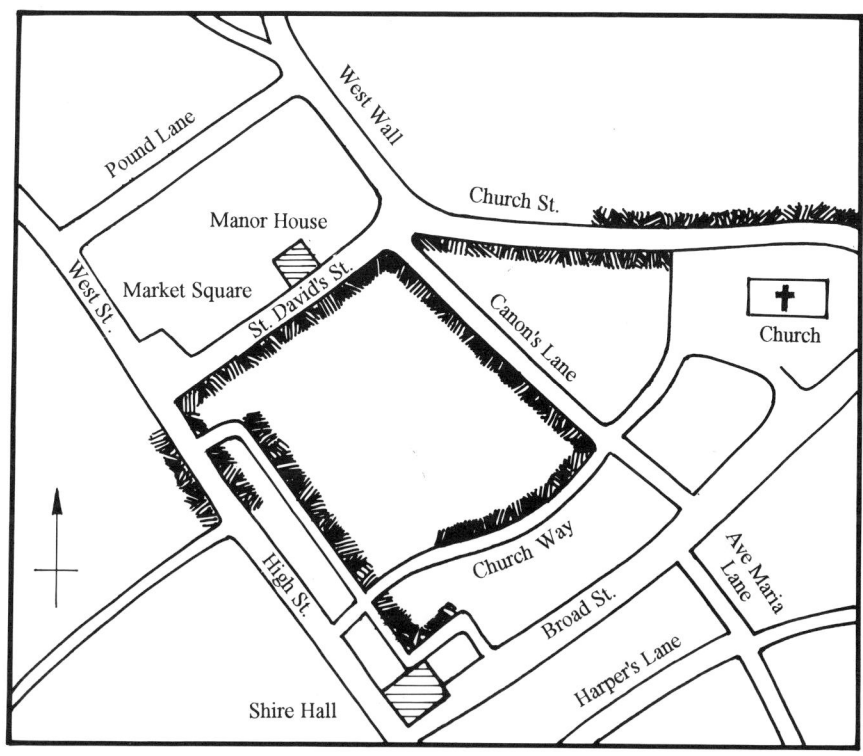

Fig. 11: Possible areas affected by the fire of 1681

Kington with 258 houses and Leominster's 420. The number of houses in the town, together with the constables' lists of householders in 1660, suggests a population of 750 or so, which implies that the ravages of plague and the resulting decline in the cloth trade may have brought about a sharp fall in the town's population since the 1580s. Even so, if the average number of hearths per house can be taken as an indicator of relative wealth, Presteigne, with an average of 2.7 hearths per house, was the most prosperous town in the county and compared favourably with Leominster's 1.98. However the Presteigne figure is distorted by the high proportion of large houses, some 23% of the stock having four or more hearths. Again it can be argued that the quality of housing in a locality indicates the accumulation of wealth in past decades rather than current income generation. However, whatever level of prosperity Presteigne enjoyed in 1670, the fire of 12 September 1681 was a severe blow.

Fire was always a real hazard in towns of the period, for most houses were timber-framed, with walls of wattle and daub and thatched roofs, and once a fire had taken hold it could spread rapidly. It is more than coincidental that most town fires occurred in early autumn when the building fabric was tinder dry after a hot summer and when, with households moving indoors at the start of autumn, more domestic fires were needed for cooking and warmth.

The fire of 1681 was certainly extensive, for it caused damage estimated at £6,150 and Luttrell's *Brief Relation of State Affairs* could describe Presteigne as being 'almost burned to the ground'. One list drawn up in 1681 gives the names of sixty-three owners or occupiers of houses destroyed in the fire while other lists name forty-eight people in distress as a result of the fire and in receipt of food and twenty-nine apparently in receipt of money, the latter lists including nine names not included in the first. The first list also states that the school and school house, which were opposite the church, were also destroyed. Assuming that none of the houses were in multiple occupancy, it would appear that a maximum of seventy-four and a minimum of fifty-one buildings were destroyed, but making some allowance for non-resident owners and for some owner-occupiers having sufficient means not to require relief, it would seem likely that the number of buildings destroyed was between fifty-five and sixty-five. The documents also suggest that there was one fatality, for 'the Blind woman' initially in receipt of relief is noted as having died later.

A comparison of the 1681 lists with the constables' lists of householders in 1660 and a 1675 list of heriots suggests that the fire was confined to the High Street and St David's Street, which then included Church Street. Thus fifteen of the owners or occupiers of houses destroyed are shown in the 1660/1675 lists as resident in High Street and six as resident in St David's Street. Significantly, none of those named in the 1681 documents are shown as householders in any other street in the town in the lists of 1660 and 1675.

In 1660 these two streets contained seventy-six houses, fifty-two in High Street and twenty-four in St David's Street. However a number of houses in both streets still contain substantial elements which pre-date the fire. Thus in High Street it would seem likely that the fire was confined to the western half of the street, on the south side as far as the former Castle Inn, which was badly damaged in the fire, and on the north side no further than the marked change in the building line. In St David's Street the fire seems to have affected the eastern side where all the houses are clearly post-seventeenth century. On the west side, St David's House and the Manor House for the most part pre-date the fire, though their later facades may suggest that they suffered some damage. On Church Street the houses on the south side are clearly eighteenth century, as are those on the north side, opposite the churchyard and adjacent to the site of the former school house and school.

However, it is unlikely that the areas indicated could have accommodated the sixty or so houses destroyed and thus other possible localities need to be identified. One possibility is that the fire may have destroyed more houses in High Street and St David's Street than has been suggested. Ince's engraving of Broad Street in 1832 shows the old Shire Hall, which stood on the site now occupied by the post office, at the junction of High Street and Broad Street, as a brick structure in early eighteenth century style, and W.H. Howse suggests that this may have replaced an earlier building, destroyed in the fire, though this hypothesis is not supported by any evidence. Another possibility is that the fire may have destroyed houses and alleyways behind the north side of High Street, which may have stretched back further than the vestiges which remain today, together with houses on Church Way and Canon's Lane. Ogilby's *Britannia* of 1675 shows a solid block of building behind this side of High Street, though the plan of the town is too small to show any detail.

If the fire was limited to this area and still destroyed half the town's housing stock it would seem that Hereford Street and Broad Street were thinly populated at this time. However, the 1660 constables' lists show twenty-nine householders in Hereford Street and forty-seven in Broad Street, a total of 152 in all, as opposed to the 128 houses of the 1670 hearth tax returns. To some extent this discrepancy can be explained in terms of multiple occupation and tax evasion, but we must bear in mind that not all houses were liable to pay the hearth tax; householders in receipt of poor relief and those not eligible to pay poor rates were exempt. It also seems likely that some houses may not have possessed even one hearth: in 1690 Elenor Eckley claimed that she was living 'in a poor cot without any shelter of walls and almost exposed to all weather.'

The fire undoubtedly caused a major dislocation of the town's economy, for it destroyed a substantial proportion of its commercial and manufacturing premises. If the original Shire Hall was destroyed it would not only have deprived the town of its only covered market accommodation, but also placed its status as county town under threat, for there were no other premises in the town of sufficient size and status to house the sittings of Quarter Sessions and Great Sessions. It may have been more than coincidental that by the 1690s Quarter Sessions were sometimes held at Knighton rather than at Presteigne.

Farming Patterns and Land Holding

Following his purchase of Presteigne tithes in 1619, Sir Robert Harley instituted a survey of the parish, excluding Rodd and Lower Kinsham, whose tithes were not included in the transaction, in order to assess the tithe liabilities of the landholders. The survey, summarised in Figures 12 and 13, provides a valuable insight into patterns of farming, land utilisation and landholding in the locality in the opening decades of the seventeenth century.

The arable acreage in 1620 was almost 55% of that recorded in the mid-nineteenth century, and probably underestimates the true position, for in 1620 two of the largest farms in Stapleton were under grass. This seems a surprisingly high proportion in view of the later specialisation in barley production for the local malting industry and emphasises the local self-sufficiency so characteristic of the early seventeenth century rural economy.

In each township oats was the predominant crop and in the area as a whole occupied more than 63% of the arable acreage. In the upland townships, notably Maes Treylow, Rowley and Gommey, and Dolley and Ackhill, the dominance of oats is so overwhelming as to suggest that monoculture was the rule. Even in more favoured townships oats clearly dominated the crop rotation to such an extent as to suggest that oatmeal was a staple food for most inhabitants. In all but two townships rye was the second crop, and occupied more than 23% of the arable acreage in the area as a whole. Only in Presteigne and Little Brampton did barley occupy second place and in the area as a whole barley accounted for 13.5% of the total arable acreage. It would seem that rye bread was a staple for much of the parish, though the nutritionally superior bread made from barley or a mixture of barley and rye may have been in use in the lowland areas. With only five acres of wheat grown in the locality, wheaten bread was clearly a luxury, enjoyed only by the few.

In all there were 154 landholders, twelve holding only meadow and forty-two holding only arable land. The average holding of arable and meadow was 21.5 acres, though this may be an an under-estimate, for it assumes that none of the landholders held land in Kinsham or Rodd, townships not included in the survey. Moreover, the 'day's math', by which holdings of meadowland were measured, the area mown by one man in a day's work, was rather more than the acre assumed in this analysis.

The large proportion of very small holdings, many of them entirely arable, suggests that much of the arable farming was subsistence in

Township	Nos. of landholders	Barley (acres)	Rye (acres)	Oats (acres)	Meadow ('days' math')	Other Crops (acres)
Presteigne	55	108	76.5	164.5	151	4 (peas)
Litton	19	4	25.5	71.5	44	-
Maes Treylow	13	5.5	6	45	18.5	-
Discoed	11	18	24.5	68	28	-
Rowley, Gommey	8	0.5	9.5	64	21	-
Dolley, Ackhill	11	7.5	36.5	136	34.5	-
Stocking	6	-	7	13.5	40	-
Little Brampton	7	31.5	18	83	53	-
Nash	6	24.5	36	58.5	39	-
Willey	21	10	59.5	143	79.5	5 (wheat)
Stapleton	15	10.5	52	121	100	-
Heath	15	8	18	90.5	104.5	6 (peas)
Combe	5	13	47.5	57	33	
Totals		**241**	**416.5**	**1,115.5**	**746**	**15**

Fig. 12: Land Utilisation in Presteigne, 1620

nature, with grain production for the market being the preserve of the larger landholders. The many small holdings also suggest that a system of open field farming still existed in the early seventeenth century. Surviving deeds show that open fields were present, in vestigial form at least, in the second half of the sixteenth century. Thus Beddoes' deed of enfeoffment mentions 'Claterbrookefield', which was located between Broadaxe and Corton, and also Netherwest field and Inneston field, while deeds in the Brampton Bryan estate papers refer to a West field on the south bank of the Lugg towards St Mary's Mill; 'Astefield' or East field, which seems to have been to the south of Whitewall Farm; Nether field which was 'near a certain cross called Herstoncross' on Broadheath; and finally Nether Inneston field, which seems to have been to the east of Presteigne and which may be the fuller name of the Nether field mentioned above. Other deeds of the period refer to a Nolton field, apparently lying between Clatterbrook and Broadheath. Frequently such deeds identify 'lands' or closes in terms of the owners of the lands or open strips adjoining on all four sides. Some of the enclosures were old enough to have been given specific names, such as Bryne Glyce, and they varied

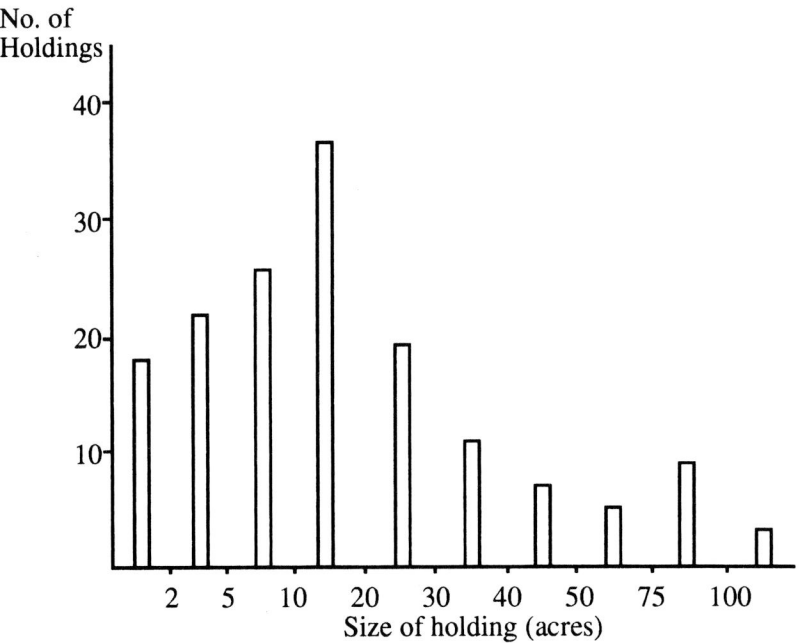

*Fig 13: The Pattern of Landholding in Presteigne, 1620
(Source: 1620 tithe survey)*

in size from an acre or so to as much as sixteen acres. Such enclosures had the effect of dividing the original larger fields which were still in multiple ownership and worked in common. Thus a lease between John Bradshaw the elder and Peter Hyde, 'sherman', refers to ten acres of lands 'in sundry fields' in Presteigne. At Broadheath it seems that a large open field had been thus divided into a number of smaller fields including 'Graselokes Furlong', 'le Medell Furlong' and 'Ryholl' by the mid-sixteenth century. Nolton field had been similarly broken up into a number of smaller fields by 1509.

Though there are few references to the pattern of arable farming in the locality for the remainder of the seventeenth century, it seems likely that the wheat and probably the barley acreage increased substantially at the expense mainly of rye; thus there are references to the 'Wheatlandes' at Combe in 1665 and at Presteigne in 1688, while in the course of a tithe dispute between Reverend Richard Lucas and Thomas Cornewall in 1658 it transpired that the latter had raised 2,000 sheaves of wheat in Stapleton that year, in addition to 1,000 sheaves of rye and 2,000 sheaves of oats.

Even with such growing specialisation it seems that some arable land was in open fields, for in 1688 Thomas Willetts was presented before the manorial court for blocking a path leading to the 'Wheat Landes' and thus obstructing the access of landholders.

Of pastoral farming in the locality during this period there is little direct evidence, though clearly meadow, pasture and rough grazing made up more than the 5,500 acres of the mid-nineteenth century and much of the latter two categories probably consisted of common grazing land, as it did at the beginning of the nineteenth century. Much of the pasture was grazed by sheep, kept for their wool which was used in the local cloth industry, rather than as stores. Though Presteigne did not have a specialised stock market until 1649, wills of the sixteenth and early seventeenth centuries suggest that cattle were kept in substantial numbers, and the relatively large acreage of meadowland (probably nearer 900 acres rather than the suggested 700) used to produce hay for fodder in 1620 would seem to bear this out. With one recognised minor drovers' road, that from Llanbister via Llangunllo and Pilleth, passing through the town *en route* for Lingen and then Leominster or Ludlow, and with two 'feeder' roads, one from Rodd and Cold Harbour and the other from Beggar's Bush and Cold Oak joining this at Presteigne, many of the locally produced beasts would join the stream of Welsh cattle making for the English lowlands and ultimately the London meat market. Oxen would also be required locally for the plough and as draught beasts, to be slaughtered at eight years for meat for local consumption, salted and finally boiled to make it palatable. Roast meat was normally only eaten by the wealthy.

During the first half of the seventeenth century there are some indications that specialised stock rearing was beginning to develop in the locality. The 1620 survey shows that in Little Brampton, Nash, Stapleton and Broadheath, meadowland amounting to thirty-seven days' math was being utilised as grazing. Some of this may have been used as water meadow, for an agreement of 1612 between Peter Child and Nicholas Taylor to divert a stream 'for the watering and bettering' of closes near Barland shows that the principle was well known locally. The establishment of a weekly 'Beaste Markett' in the town in 1649 together with livestock fairs on the Tuesday before Easter and on 3 September also points to the growing importance of livestock. The market and fairs lapsed with the restoration of the monarchy in 1660, discredited by their republican origins. But in 1669 the town successfully petitioned the crown for the restoration of the fairs and for the right to hold a livestock market on Saturdays, the normal market day, having proved that no other livestock markets or fairs were held on those days with a thirteen miles radius of the town. The livestock market was initially held in Broad Street, but though stock markets were held in Presteigne until the second half of the present century, the town never succeeded in wresting dominance from its rivals Knighton and Kington.

CHAPTER V

Stagnation and Recovery

The impression one gains of the town in the opening decades of the eighteenth century is one of a community doing no more than marking time. On the evidence of the parish register the population was static and may have declined to below the level of the third quarter of the previous century, for the number of baptisms barely exceeded the number of burials in the period 1700-20. Nor was there any obvious reason for inward migration, since in terms of commercial development the period was one of transition; one previously important sector of the local economy, the cloth industry, was in the last stages of decline, while alternative commercial opportunities had not been fully exploited. At the institutional level the administration of the school and the gaol throughout much of the century seems to have been characterised by a casual neglect. Although by the end of the eighteenth century Presteigne had reasserted its role as county town, it never again exercised the political leadership over the county it had enjoyed prior to the Civil War, and in the opening decades of the eighteenth century the great political issues of the day, the succession of the Hanoverians and the Jacobite rebellions appear to have had no local impact.

Presteigne's Loss of Political Influence
At first sight Presteigne seems to have retained its political ascendancy within Radnorshire for in the course of the century the Presteigne-Norton area provided fifteen sheriffs, a disproportionate share compared to other areas of similar size in the county. However, in terms of parliamentary representation, its loss of political influence is clear for the locality did

not provide a single MP for the county or for the Radnor Boroughs, until the closing years of the century. Nicholas Taylor, very briefly, and Edward Price of Boultibrooke may have entertained parliamentary ambitions in the second half of the seventeenth century, but in the eighteenth century no Presteigne family possessed the wealth and standing to challenge the dominant political forces within Radnorshire; the Harleys, the Lewis families of Harpton and Downton and Sir Humphrey Howorth of Maesllwch.

Edward Price, of Montgomeryshire origins, had acquired Boultibrooke and the manor of Presteigne, along with the Manor House, by marriage with the daughter and ultimate heiress of Richard Jones, and may have been an unsuccessful candidate in the election of 1677. Thereafter he seems to have enjoyed an eventful life; chronically in debt, he seems to have had Jacobite sympathies, for his loyalty to William and Mary was suspected by some. He lost his position as a JP and though chosen as sheriff in November, 1693, he was replaced during his year of office by Robert Cutler of Knighton. He seems to have redeemed himself later, for he retained his position as colonel of the Brecon and Radnorshire militia and served as sheriff in 1700. He died in 1703 as a result of a wound in the groin received in a duel with Thomas Baskerville of Bryngwyn. Jonathan Williams states that the duel arose out of a quarrel over a cock fight at the Oak Inn in Broad Street, the duel taking place in a yard at the rear of the inn, though another local tradition is that the duel took place in an upstairs room at the rear of 9 Broad Street. In spite of his financial difficulties the family retained Boultibrooke and the manor of Presteigne into the second half of the century, for his grandson, also Edward Price, served as sheriff in 1741. His daughter and heiress Anne married Bell Lloyd in 1758, bringing him Boultibrooke and the lordship of the manor of Presteigne.

The inability of Presteigne landowners to build up a power base from which to launch a political career may have stemmed in part from the town's economic decline in the late seventeenth and early eighteenth centuries. However the main obstacle was probably the overwhelming ascendancy of the Harley family, whose patronage and estates in the locality were so extensive as to preclude any other local family from enhancing its status to a point sufficient to justify a bid for political influence independently of the Harley interest or even to warrant Harley patronage. Throughout the period the major families functioned as no more than minor clients of the Harley family whose local seats were at Brampton Bryan and Eywood, Titley.

The Harley family had begun to build up its influence before the civil war and by the eighteenth century the sources of its authority in the area were many and various. The family were lords of many of the surrounding manors, notably Stapleton, Litton and Cascob, Evenjobb, Norton, Lower Kinsham and Rodd, Nash, Byton, Combe, and Downton. Some of these manors included areas which were part of Presteigne itself. Thus, included in the manor of Downton were Broadheath Common, Whitewall Farm, properties in High Street, St David's Street, Back Lane, and West Wall, together with land in the vicinity of Rowley, Paradise, Cold Oak, King's Turning and Letchmoor. The lordship of a manor brought with it authority and prestige, for the manorial court, presided over by the lord or his steward had jurisdiction over such matters as trespass, strays and property rights, and the right to collect an heriot, usually the best beast, before an heir could enter into his property.

Though the manor and borough of Presteigne itself remained in royal hands, for much of the eighteenth century the Harley family leased from the crown the right to collect heriots in the manor, in addition to acquiring the lordship of the other Presteigne manor in either 1775 or 1797. As stewards of Cantref Maelienydd 1647-49, 1660, 1671-73, 1691-1714 and 1768-1848, the Harley family had the ability to appoint the bailiff of the town without reference to the wishes of the townspeople. From 1712 until 1848 the family also held the advowson of the rectory and were thus able to appoint the rector.

As W.H. Howse demonstrates, the Harleys also owned substantial properties in the Presteigne locality, notably Stapleton Castle (455 acres), Nash Court (595 acres), Rodd Court (452 acres), Broadheath House (146 acres), Upper Broadheath (50 acres), Hill Farm (231 acres), Byton Farm (287 acres), and Highlands Farm (145 acres). This is by no means an exhaustive list, for they also owned Taylor's Farm, Norton; Mill House, on the site of the present Grove House, and several other town properties.

Undoubtedly the town gained from Harley patronage: Auditor Harley, the brother of the first earl of Oxford, founded a parochial library and may have been the 'gentleman of quality' who established a charity school in the town; the third and fourth earls were instrumental in securing the appointment of new trustees for the grammar school in 1744 and 1780, while the fifth earl gave the Warden to the town in 1805. On the other hand, its power and prestige in the locality was such that other families were unable to exert any real political influence save as minor clients of the Harleys while that family dominated the local political scene, and, as Roy Adams shows, exercised considerable influence in county elections. However, with the accession of the fifth earl in 1790 and the appointment of his nephew, Lord Rodney, as lord lieutenant of Radnorshire, neither of whom took any real interest in politics, local figures such as Richard Price of Norton Manor and Sir Harford Jones Brydges of Boultibrooke began to exercise significant political influence within the county.

The Grammar School
After the fire of 1681 the school was rebuilt within a few years, possibly rather to the south of the original site, with funds raised by a 'brief' or appeal circulated to every parish in the kingdom. The original master's house, 'a very small low building, scarce fit for the master to live in' was replaced, at his own expense, by Reverend James Bayley, the master of the school since 1676, though he chose to live in his own house close by, probably on the site now occupied by Garrison House in Church Street.

Bayley was rector of Byton and also held the living of Kinsham, in addition to his post as schoolmaster until the early 1720s. It was during his tenure that the fortunes of the school reached a low ebb, though the claim of Rev. Samuel Sandford, rector of Presteigne, made in a letter to the Society for Promoting of Christian Knowledge in 1713 that 'the Free School here has been without a master or scholars for more than 20 years' clearly exaggerated the situation. Sandford had at one time hoped to divert Beddoes' endowment to support the foundation of a charity school in the town and cannot be regarded as a disinterested observer. In a case brought before the Hereford Consistory Court in 1717 Sandford and other trustees sought to dislodge Bayley and appoint a more suitable person as master. Though it is not always easy to distinguish the truth in the welter of claims and counter-claims made at the hearing, the picture painted of the school is a dismal one, with the number of pupils declining to single figures, the trustees divided and the master shut out of the school in 1713 and 1715.

Though Reverend Bayley, according to some witnesses, had begun to neglect his duties some years earlier, the real problem had begun when he was appointed to a living at Burford in 1695. Within a year or so Bayley had moved to Burford, though retaining his appointments in the Presteigne locality, and it was alleged he 'did not come to the school for two or three days together' on occasions. Numbers at the school fell sharply from the previous forty or so as pupils were removed to other schools, notably one kept at Knill by an Isaac Griffiths. Matters improved for a time as a result of the conscientious efforts of Reverend Eusebius

Beeston, employed by Bayley to officiate as curate at Byton and Kinsham and to serve as master at the school. Initially Beeston was paid £20 per annum for all three posts, the remainder of the school income, along with the stipends attached to the Byton and Kinsham livings going to Bayley, though within a few years Beeston was receiving 'the whole profit of the school', amounting to £29.

After Beeston's death in 1711 the situation once again deteriorated sharply as Bayley, although living once more in Presteigne, entrusted the Byton and Kinsham livings and the school to a succession of curates, some of whom served for no more than a year, and sometimes neglected the school. Soon the number of pupils had fallen to six or seven and this led Sandford and some of the trustees to bring the case to dismiss Bayley and replace him by the most effective of his former curates, Reverend Hugh Jones. Bayley, for his part, claimed that he had always acted with the consent of at least some of the trustees, disputed his alleged inefficiency, and claimed that the fall in numbers stemmed from Sandford setting up his own unlicensed 'Latin school' and encouraging parents to remove their children from the free school. He also alleged that Sandford had withheld the income from the school's endowment for two years, during which time he had spent at least £20 out of his own pocket repairing the building. The verdict of the court is not recorded, but it seems likely that the trustees were 'forct to own ye Master's title' and that Bayley's licence to teach was not rescinded.

This was by no means the end of the school's problems for the trustees were content to leave the administration of the endowment in the hands of Bayley's successor, Reverend Humphrey Griffiths, clearly no businessman, for by 1740 many of the tenants were greatly in arrears. Moreover, by this time only two of the trustees were living, insufficient to appoint new trustees and the Earl of Oxford was compelled to bring an action in the court of Chancery to secure an order to appoint new trustees, alleging that those surviving, John Greenly and John Meredith, denied all knowledge of Beddoes' deed of enfeoffment.

Recourse had to be made to Chancery once more in 1780 to secure a full complement of trustees, but even then the school was administered with great laxity. Griffiths died in 1779 and the school apparently ceased to function until 1781 when Reverend John Grubb was appointed as master. In addition he also served as vicar of Wigmore and was an active JP in Herefordshire and the quality of his leadership can be judged from the fact that when he died in 1821 it emerged that the school's endowment had passed into the estate of the last surviving trustee, Sir John

Boyd, who lived in Kent and who had subsequently died in 1815. Once more Chancery had to intervene to appoint new trustees and to recover the endowment from Boyd's heirs.

A Change in Direction
Though large scale cloth production had come to an end within a decade or so of the last plague epidemic, scattered documentary evidence suggests that the area was still producing cloth to satisfy at least part of the local demand into the early decades of the eighteenth century. Fulling mills were in operation at Combe, Discoed, Nash and Little Brampton in the second half of the seventeenth century and possibly at Frog Street on the Stapleton side of Lugg bridge as late as 1706. Clothworkers and dyers are mentioned in property deeds of the period, particularly at Combe and Broadheath, while the parish register records the burials of eight weavers between 1708 and 1710, though thereafter such references are few, the last being recorded in 1729. With the possible exception of Discoed, cloth production in the area had become entirely a cottage industry, carried on in the homes of the weavers such as those in Pound Lane, West Wall and Church Street.

Two types of commercial activity developed out of the decaying cloth industry. Sheep rearing continued to be an important element in the local farming pattern, given the upland nature of much of the parish. With no local industry to supply, wool stapling businesses developed, buying and sorting by type and quality the local wool to resell to the cloth industry elsewhere. In the early decades of the century, the town contained at least two such businesses, one of which, that of Richard Meredith, 1687-1760, was of a substantial nature. However, confidence in the town's future seems to have been fragile, for as J. Southwood notes, at some time after 1727 Richard Meredith moved to Kington, and by the middle of the century his two sons, Richard, 1712-79, and Bridgewater, both had flourishing woolstapling businesses there.

The demise of the cloth industry left the premises which had housed it available for other uses. The sheds and workshops of the earlier seventeenth were relatively easy to adapt, but the same could not be said of the fulling mills. With two well-established flour mills at the Wegnalls and off Mill Lane, there would seem little justification to convert fulling mills to this use, though this appears to have happened to such mills at Combe and Broadheath for a time. Many such mills were allowed to decay, but the Lugg Bridge mill was converted, unusually for the area, into a paper mill.

The mill, which seems to have used rags as its raw material, was certainly in operation by 1727, when the parish register records the baptism of a son of Edward Vaughan, 'paper maker at Frog Street'. The mill was still functioning in the second half of the century, for at his burial in 1761 Vaughan was still described as a paper maker. On the sale of Grove House to Thomas Legge by Stansil Griffiths, the mill may still have been operating, for the transaction included 'Paper Mill Close'. By 1780, as W.H. Howse notes, the premises had reverted to its former use, functioning as a fulling mill during the short-lived revival of Presteigne's cloth industry in the closing decades of the century. By 1822, as A.H. Shorter demonstrates, the premises were back in use as a paper mill, licensed in the name of Benjamin Rowley. How long it continued to operate is not clear, for the business is not mentioned in trade directories of the 1830s and 1840s, though in the *Hereford Journal* of 30 December, 1846, Mr Beebee of Willey Court was offering Grove House for sale 'with outbuildings and a paper mill'.

The staple industry of the town in the eighteenth century was that of malting. Lying in the rain shadow of the Welsh uplands, with an annual rainfall of about 35 inches, the locality was well suited to barley production. The extension of barley cultivation was also helped by the ready availability of agricultural lime for use as a fertiliser, since by 1714 lime kilns were operating at Nash. By 1695 the malting industry was already an important industry in the town for Ogilby noted in his *Description of the Aberystwyth-London Road* 'It has a good market on Saturday, especially for Barley, which is here malted in great quantities.' During the course of the eighteenth century the industry grew in importance. In 1750 Kitchen noted that 'the town's chief trade is in malt' and in 1766 Brookes, in his *General Gazette* paraphrased Ogilby, commenting that 'the market is remarkable for barley, of which they make a great deal of malt.'

Several of the town's inns, notably the Duke's Arms, the Castle, the George and the Barley Mow had malthouses producing malt for their own brewing needs, but there were also at least five malting businesses operating on a commercial scale in the town by the middle of the century. One such business was located at the bottom of Harper's Lane; a second on Hereford Street, on the site now occupied by the Midland Bank; a third was in the High Street, on the site occupied later by the parochial workhouse; a fourth at Warden Court, on the junction of High Street and St David's Street, and the fifth on Primrose Lane, off Warden Road. The scale of operation of such businesses can be judged from an advertisement in the *Hereford Journal* of 1806, offering for sale the Hereford Street malting business which produced between 4,000 and 6,000 bushels of malt per season.

In the second half of the century attempts were made once again to revive the town's cloth industry. In 1755 the Brecon Agricultural Society established a small factory on West Wall, but this seems to have been a shortlived venture. The second attempt, in the closing decades of the century, fared little better. It was certainly in operation in 1795 and in 1801 secured the contract to supply uniforms for the Radnor Militia. It used outworkers for spinning and concerned itself with weaving, dyeing and finishing. The business was carried on in the old weaving sheds in Back Lane, which were certainly modernised and possibly enlarged. According to G. Drage, 'These sheds ... had long lattice-work windows at their upper storeys (they faced south) to provide the weavers with a good light.' It was probably to service this factory that the mill near Lugg Bridge, which had served as a paper mill for decades, was converted once more into a fulling mill. A third textile business was functioning on a reasonably large scale at the close of the century at Maes Treylow, Discoed, for in an advertisement in the *Hereford Journal* of 1808 described it as possessing 'a Fulling Mill, Dye-house, Carding and Spinning Machines, Weavers' Looms with Drying Racks and Workmens' Cottages'.

However, one must not lose sight of the fact that Presteigne was essentially a market town, mainly concerned with the provision of goods and services for the surrounding countryside and in processing agricultural products—timber, leather, and more specialised crops such as flax and hops in addition to barley. At this time flax was widely grown for locally produced linen goods, but at least two farmers in the Presteigne-Whitton area were growing flax on a commercial scale. In the 1780s subsidies, given to promote flax cultivation when cotton imports had been disrupted by the American war and its aftermath, were claimed on a production of about 250 stones in weight per annum, which implies a total of 7-8 acres or so devoted to this crop in the locality. The field name Flax Plock, which survived in Norton into the nineteenth century suggests small scale flax production in this parish, probably for domestic purposes, since there is no record of any claim for the bounty. Field names also testify to hop cultivation: the Hop Yard near Gallows Lane in Presteigne, Hop Field Meadow at Norton, Hop Yard Orchard at Byton, and the Old Hop Yard at Nash were all current field names in the opening decades of the nineteenth century. The area under hops was again probably small for the average acreage devoted to this crop in the parish of Presteigne between

1807 and 1820 was no more than 18 acres. Even so this was probably more than was required for local use. As with grain production, both hops and flax were seasonally labour intensive, and thus provided further employment for the town. Such increased employment opportunities were essential, for by the end of the century the old open field arable farming, largely subsistence in nature, had virtually disappeared in the Presteigne locality, though it lingered on until 1863 in the neighbouring parish of Norton. The consolidation of farms into bigger units had also led to a shedding of labour.

County Town Functions
The holding of two sittings of Quarter Sessions each year at Knighton until 1783 somewhat eroded the role of Presteigne as the county town. However, as the venue for Great Sessions, some sittings of Quarter Sessions, and the site of the county gaol, Presteigne was assured a steady stream of visitors if little direct employment, for the county employed only two full-time staff—the hall keeper and the gaoler, relying in the main on part-time officers to assist the JPs. More importantly, it encouraged lawyers and other professional men to set up practices in the town. Moreover, the sitting of such courts had a social as well as judicial significance, for most of the county families felt obliged to attend the dinners and assemblies held in the town at such times. The inns, eating houses and the tradesmen of the town profited greatly on these occasions, as they did when the officers and men of the Militia mustered in the town for drill on a field just beyond Lugg bridge, or for target practice at the Butts, just beyond the Burgage to the south-east of the town.

Great Sessions met at Presteigne twice yearly for the Lent and Summer sittings and it was on these occasions that its status as county town was shown to best advantage. It was the custom to ring the church bells on the arrival of the judge who was met on the outskirts and escorted into the town by the high sheriff, the under-sheriff, the chaplain, two trumpeters, the twelve javelinmen, and a retinue of magistrates, gentry and freeholders amounting to as many as one hundred and fifty men. After the judge had been escorted to his lodgings at the Manor House, the sheriff's dinner would take place, with up to a hundred guests.

Though parliamentary elections in Radnorshire were usually uncontested in the second half of the eighteenth century, they provided other occasions from which the town gained commercially. The successful candidate would be expected to provide a dinner for the gentry and to 'treat' his lesser supporters to meals and beer at the inns of the town. Nor was it unknown for the prisoners in the gaol to be the recipients of free meals and drink on such occasions.

Elections and sittings of the courts were held in the court room on the first floor of the Shire Hall at the junction of High Street and Broad Street, the ground floor housing a store room and an arcaded area which accommodated stalls on market and fair days and served as the butter market. In 1781 the magistrates agreed to a request of the townspeople that the town's fire engine should be kept in the store room, the county surveyor giving his opinion that the doorway could be widened without causing any damage to the structure of the building. However, within a few years, whenever the court room was in use by large numbers of people, the floor had to be supported by large timber props, a situation which did not inspire confidence, not least on the part of the judges.

The county gaol was in Broad Street, on the lower half of the site now occupied by the Shire Hall. It housed five categories of prisoner: those awaiting trial; felons awaiting execution or transportation; petty criminals serving their sentence in the gaol; debtors; and the inmates of the bridewell or house of correction. In such circumstances, the number of prisoners in the gaol reported by John Howard and James Neild on their visits of inspection between 1774 and 1807 seems surprisingly small. However, the stay of felons in the gaol was often short, for those sentenced to death were usually executed within two days of being sentenced, either outside the gaol or, later, at Gallows Lane, off the Discoed road, while those sentenced to transportation were normally sent on their way at the first opportunity on grounds of economy, if not of security. Few petty offenders were gaoled, the usual punishment for petty theft, for men and women alike, was a public whipping on the bare back 'until the back be bloody' in the offender's home town, while assault, unless upon a person of some consequence, was usually punished by a fine of a shilling. The preponderance of debtor prisoners in the gaol in the late eighteenth century reflects a tendency on the part of the Radnorshire county court and elsewhere to imprison debtors for small sums, in one case at Presteigne in 1782, for a debt of nine shillings.

The impression gained of the gaol is one of neglect. In 1777 it was simply declared to be 'out of repair', while by 1780 the situation had deteriorated to the extent that part of the wall had to be propped up. The regime was careless in the extreme: prisoners of all categories, irrespective of sex, moved freely within the gaol, while the gaoler was non-resident, leaving the gaol at night to look after itself. Administration was so lax that Robert Lowe, sentenced to seven years' transportation in 1778,

Year	Debtors	Felons
1774	4	3
1775	3	1
1779	2	2
1782	9	4
1788	5	2
1801	5	4
1803	3	2

Fig. 14: Prisoners in Radnor County Gaol, Presteigne, 1774-1803
(Source: The reports of John Howard and James Neild)

was somehow overlooked and had to petition for release in 1785, after first escaping to draw attention to his plight. The gaol was clearly insecure, for there were also escapes in 1781, 1786 (two), 1787 and in 1794. One senses an air of desperation in the decision of the bench in 1788 to take such steps as were required 'to prevent, if possible, the prisoners from escaping'.

In the closing decades of the century, possibly in response to Howard's strictures on 'this bad prison', matters improved. In 1782 a wall twenty-one feet high was built around the gaol and the interior remodelled to provide accommodation for the gaoler and separate quarters for felons, debtors and the inmates of the house of correction. In 1787 straw bedding was provided for all, and in 1789 a daily ration of 1lb. of bread was given to all inmates, and a chaplain and surgeon were appointed. In the period 1790-93 further alterations were made, which enabled the circuit judges to confirm that the gaol was 'well and sufficiently repaired and amended'. In addition, the house next to the gaol had been acquired and converted into a separate house of correction which functioned independently of the gaol. Even so, when Neild visited the gaol in 1803 the situation was still far from satisfactory: the water supply was deficient; the prisoners had only one courtyard for the use of all categories of prisoner; and the gaoler, by virtue of his post as sheriff's officer, was frequently absent. The impression of uncaring neglect is reinforced by the inventory of 1815 listing the gaol's fittings as fourteen blankets, an old dresser with two drawers, five three-legged stools, four small benches and a bucket.

Turnpikes, Tollgates and Inns
Before the eighteenth century travellers passing through Presteigne had been on horseback or on foot, with goods carried by teams of packhorses or by packmen. It was by the latter means that the pottery made at Lingen

between the sixteenth and eighteenth centuries was marketed throughout the neighbourhood. By the opening decades of the eighteenth century one carrier's cart was operating on a regular basis between Leominster and Presteigne, with a link to London via the Leominster carrier operating a weekly service to London, with the Black Horse Inn at Holborn Bridge serving as the London depot. By the middle of the century, if not earlier, this had been supplemented by stagewagons lumbering through Presteigne *en route* for Aberystwyth from Worcester and Leominster at a maximum speed of two miles per hour.

Since 1555 the maintenance of roads had been the responsibility of the parish, though bridges and their approaches were the concern of the county. Each parish annually appointed a surveyor of roads who could call upon the parishioners to provide labour, wagons and oxen to keep the parish roads in good repair. Most roads received minimum maintenance, for the surveyor usually wished to avoid the hostility of his fellow-parishoners who resented so spending their time. Maintenance tended to take the form of throwing a load of field stone in the ruts and potholes when a road had become impassable, or if this did not suffice, ploughing a stretch of road level. In such circumstances local traffic usually took the form of sledges rather than wheeled vehicles.

In the buoyant economic climate of the mid-eighteenth century better access to raw materials and markets became essential. Under the turnpike system an Act of Parliament could be obtained (normally renewable every seven years) to establish a trust to improve and re-route roads, financed by loans raised on the security of the tolls collected from road users at gates erected at intervals along the road. The toll gates were let out to the highest bidder who recouped his outlay and received a return on his capital from the tolls he collected. The trust's affairs were managed by trustees drawn from the local gentry.

Roads in the locality of Presteigne fell within the jurisdiction, sole or shared, of four trusts: the Presteigne and Mortimer's Cross Trust, established in 1754; the Kington Trust, established in 1756; the Bluemantle or Aymestrey Trust, set up in 1759; and the Radnorshire Trust, set up in 1767. The present road pattern in the area is largely a legacy of these Trusts' efforts, though our knowledge of their activities is limited, for with the exception of the Radnorshire Turnpike Trust, most of the records have been lost.

The viability of the old London-Worcester-Aberystwyth road running via Presteigne, Cascob, Dolau and Rhayader had been threatened by the turnpiking of the Kington-New Radnor-Rhayader section of the rival

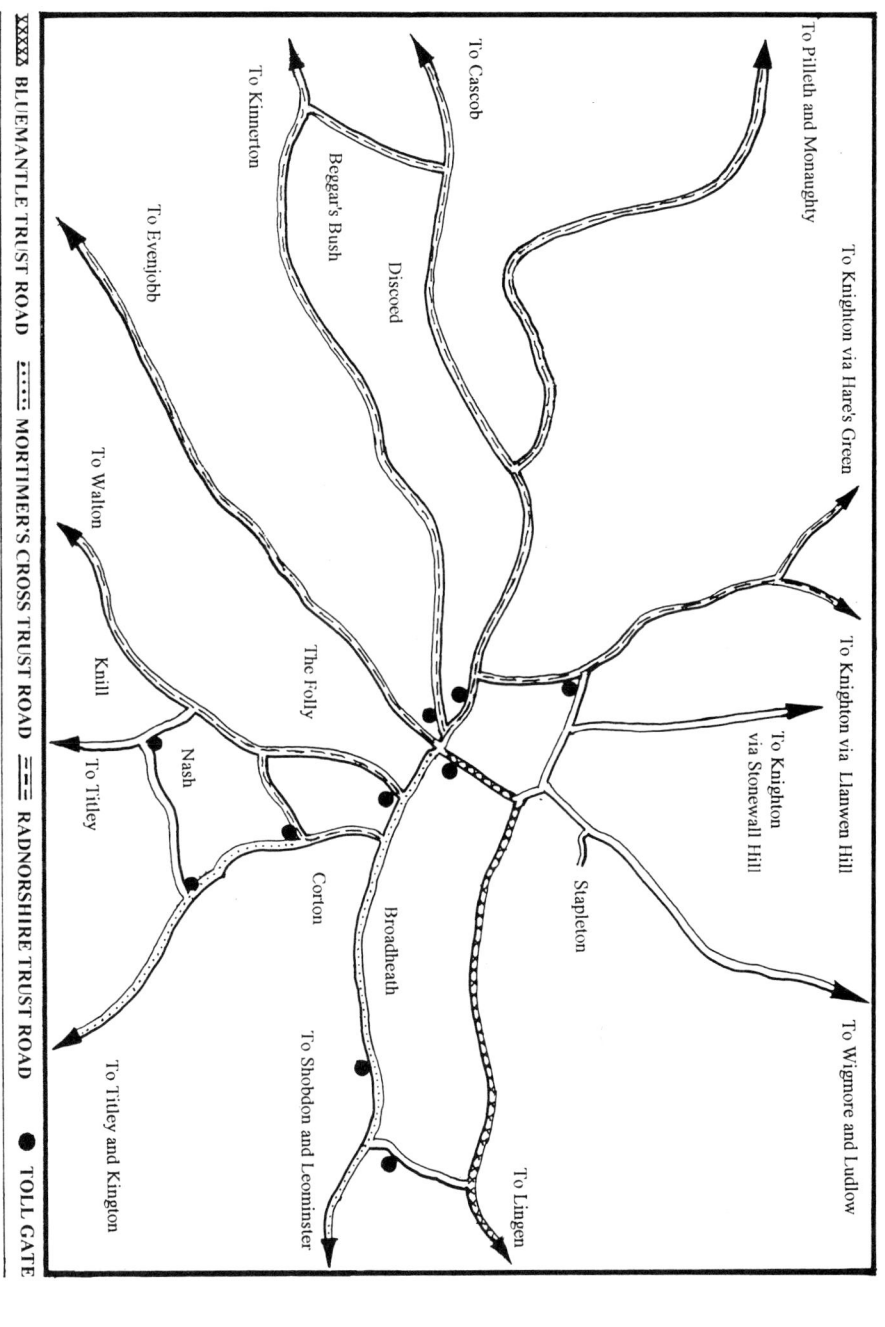

Fig. 15: Roads and Toll Gates in the Presteigne locality

London-Gloucester-Aberystwyth route, first mooted in the 1760s and completed by the early 1770s. Thus, it is not surprising to find that almost the first decision of the Radnorshire Trust was to re-route and turnpike a road to New Radnor via Warden Road, Beggar's Bush and Kinnerton to connect with the New Radnor-Rhayader road, installing its first toll gate at Beggar's Bush. In 1805 a new road to New Radnor via Discoed and Beggar's Bush was turnpiked, only to be replaced by a new road running via Discoed and Maes Treylow in 1820. Not until the late 1820s or early 1830s was the present route via Corton and Walton in operation.

The Radnorshire Trust then turned its attention to the Knighton road which originally ran via the Lugg Bridge, Stapleton and Stonewall Hill. In 1775 it was replaced by a road running via Whitton, Pilleth and Monaughty, but in 1780 the shorter Boultibrooke Bridge-Norton-Meeting House-Llanwen Hill route was turnpiked. The present Norton-Hares Green road dates from 1828.

The old Leominster road over Lugg Bridge, Letchmoor Lane, Combe Corner (where it was joined by a road from the Rodd and Corton via King's Turning) and Shobdon was turnpiked by the Mortimer's Cross and the Bluemantle trusts in the eighteenth century. The present road, which follows old estate tracks, seems to date from the 1820s. The old Kington road via Broadaxe Lane, the Folly, Nash and Titley was also replaced in the 1820s by the present road, stretches of which were controlled by the Radnorshire, Kington and Mortimer's Cross trusts. Traffic on the turnpikes was strictly regulated, the number of horses permitted to draw a vehicle being determined by the width of its wheels. Travellers on foot were exempt from charge, but all other road users were charged.

For every horse, mule, ass or beast of burden, laden or unladen and not drawing:	Weekday $1^{1}/_{2}$d., Sunday 2d.
For every horse, mule, ass or other beast of draught except oxen and other horned beasts pairs drawing any wagon used in husbandry:	4d.
For every horse drawing a coach:	Weekday 5d, Sunday 6d.
For every score of cattle:	10d.
For every score of sheep:	4d.
For every pair of oxen or horned beast drawing abreast or in pairs:	5d.

Figure 16: Radnorshire Turnpike Trust's Scale of Charges, 1811-44

Such fees were collected at the toll gates which soon surrounded each town or village. Those in the Presteigne locality are shown in Figure 15, but not all gates indicated were in operation at any one time, nor did they all belong to the one trust.

Since the majority of the Radnorshire trustees lived in the New Radnor-Presteigne-Knighton area, the roads there were rather better than in much of the rest of the county, and certainly better than the 'mere gullies worn by torrents' which they replaced. By 1794 a weekly stage-coach service was operating between Knighton and London, via Presteigne and Wigmore alternately. The journey was not for those of a weak constitution, for the coach left Knighton at noon on Friday and did not reach London until Sunday morning. Even before this date changes of horse and postchaises for hire were available at the Rose and Crown and White Hart inns on Hereford Street and the New Inn on High Street. By 1810 the same facilities were to be found at the Radnorshire Arms, the Oxford, the Duke's Arms and the Castle. By 1808, if not earlier, the Aberystwyth-Worcester coach was running via Presteigne on a regular basis. Insofar as improved roads generated additional traffic, Presteigne's recovery of the later eighteenth century owed much to the turnpike system: the capital value of land near a turnpike road appreciated significantly and, initially at least, generated more business for the town's traders, craftsmen, professional men and innkeepers. However, the extent of the turnpike roads in Radnorshire should not be exaggerated: in 1814 only 76 of the county's 485 miles of carriage roads were paved or turnpiked.

The turnpikes provoked some hostility: farmers resented paying toll on both empty and laden wagons, while tollkeepers were suspected, sometimes justifiably so, of overcharging. Thus in 1771 the tenant of the New Radnor gate was fined for putting up additional gates on a fair day. Perhaps the major grievance in the Presteigne area was that since four trusts overlapped, relatively short journeys were rendered excessively expensive by frequent tolls. Normally payment at one gate cleared the payer of further charges for a distance of seven (later ten) miles. However such a concession applied only in the case of roads operated by the same trust. Thus a journey from Presteigne to Kington involved paying three tolls; at the Corton gate to the Radnorshire Trust, at the Roddhurst gate to the Mortimer's Cross Trust, and at the Titley gate to the Kington Trust. Sometimes such resentment boiled over into violence. In 1780 John Luker of New Radnor was imprisoned for breaking down Stanner gate with a hedgebill, and in 1814 gates at Nash and Walton were destroyed by farmers who refused to pay tolls on empty wagons returning from liming.

The increased prosperity of the town in the later eighteenth and early nineteenth centuries is reflected by a steady increase in the number of inns licensed to operate in the locality. From about 1750 onwards records show thirty-two inns, beer and cider houses functioning, and the list is probably far from complete—St David's Street and Church Street are suspiciously empty of such premises and a search of property deeds relating to this area would probably yield up a few more. Not all these inns were operating at the same period, the maximum of any one year being sixteen in 1822. Present knowledge relating to Presteigne's inns, past and present, is summarised in Figure 17. Some of these beer and cider houses seem to have consisted of little more than a room in an ordinary dwelling house set aside to provide food and drink on market and fair days in order to supplement family income.

Some of these inns, notably the Castle, which may have been known as the Falcon in the seventeenth century, the Oxford Arms/Blue Boar and the Oak on Broad Street, and possibly the Barley Mow on Hereford Street date from the late seventeenth century, while the Duke's Arms, known as the Talbot before 1720, may have functioned as an inn as early as the fifteenth century. One inn was also functioning in St David's Street in the sixteenth century, for in 1562 Robert Smythe of that street appeared at Great Sessions on the charge that he 'keepithe an ale house ... and in the same maynteynyth baudry and othere mysdemeners contynualli.'

Life and Work in Eighteenth Century Presteigne
By the second half of the century a modest degree of prosperity had returned to the town and this was clearly reflected in the urban landscape, for Kitchen described the town in 1750 as 'large, well-built and populous', while a decade later Brookes could describe the town as handsome. The rebuilding and remodelling of the closing decades of the century produced the scattering of Georgian facades throughout the town, notably in St David's Street and Broad Street. However the extent of the such a remodelling should not be overstated, for in 1805 Walter Davies noted: 'The town is a motley group of good and poor houses intimately blended like a shuffled pack of cards.'

The population of the parish and of the town itself seems to have grown from 1720 onwards, largely from natural increase rather than from inward migration, for the parish register shows baptisms exceeding deaths by a significant proportion, particularly in the periods 1761-80 and

Fig. 17: The Inns and Public Houses of Presteigne

Hereford Street		
Masons's Arms	No. 14	A beer house c.1908
Barley Mow		Certainly open in 1822 and probably much earlier
Apple Tree		A beer and cider house in the 18th and 19th centuries. Closed 1912
Machine House	Br. Legion Club	Operating as a beer house in 1882
White Hart	Milford House	Functioning as an inn in 1781
Oxford Arms	Oxford House	Open in 1825
Rose and Crown	Lloyd's Bank	An inn in 1781. Closed shortly before 1835
Sun	Millfield	In the early 19th century most town functions were held here. Closed in 1906
Farmers' Arms		As the Blue Boar prior to 1867 it was very lively!
Green End		
Fountain	No. 1	Beer house open in 1838. Later known as the Stars and in 1854 as the Hope and Anchor
High Street		
White Hart	No. 2 or 53	Named as the White Horse in one deed. Precise location not clear. Open in the 1760s
Red Lion	No. 46	18th century beer house. First reference 1799
King's Head	No. 44	Early 19th century inn, possibly slightly earlier
Lion	No. 41	19th century beer house. Burned down in 1906
Castle		Certainly functioning as an inn in 1680s, when possibly known as the Falcon
New Inn	The Posting House	One reference as the Posting House Inn. Open 1784
Radnorshire Arms		The 'Cross House'. Opened as an inn in 1792
The Globe	Globe House	19th century beer house. First reference 1828

St David's St.		
The Bull		Present hotel opened 1820 on the site of the old Bull Inn. Had a reputation as the sportsman's inn
Scottleton Street		
Royal Oak		Open 1823. Known as the 'top Oak' to distinguish it from its Broad Street rival
George		Precise location unknown, probably opposite the Royal Oak. 18th and early 19th century beer house.
Queen's Head	1, Castle Dyche	18th and 19th century beer house which may have operated as an inn for a time
Bell	No. 2/3	A beer house opened in the 18th century and known originally as the Bluebell Inn
Broad Street		
Black Lion	Assembly Rooms	Later the White Hart and the New Oak Inn. Closed in 1823
Duke's Arm		16th century if not earlier. Known as the Talbot Inn until c.1720
Harp Inn	Harp House	19th century cider house
Oxford Arms	2, White House	Also known as the New Inn, Blue Boar and Bowling Green Inn. First reference 1767
Oak	Oak House	The 'old Oak', open in 17th century. Notorious for its cock pit. Scene of a duel in 1703. Closed 1912
Bridge Inn	Bridge House	Open in the later 18th century. Known as the Waterloo Inn for a time after 1815
Ford Street		
The Grove		A cider house in the 18th century
Broadheath		
Cricketers' Arms		A beer house open in 1838. Closed 1929
Cat & Fiddle		A beer house in the 1830s

1801-20, and it seems likely that the increase would have been more marked between 1781-1800 if there had not been a significant degree of outward migration from the town towards the end of that period, for this would seem to be the most likely reason for the 22 uninhabited houses in the town in 1801 out of the total housing stock of 216.

The expansion of the town over Lugg bridge into Stapleton at the turn of the century reinforces this impression of population growth. Even so, the 1801 census put the town's population at 1,057, surprisingly low in view of the rate of population growth suggested by the parish register data. Possibly there had been substantial migration from the town throughout the century or, alternatively, its population in the last quarter of the seventeenth century had been substantially less than the 750 or so suggested in the previous chapter.

Year	%
1701-20	5.2
1721-40	22.8
1741-60	20.5
1761-80	34.8
1781-1800	24.3
1801-20	72.2

Fig. 18: Excess of Baptisms over Burials in Presteigne Parish, 1701-1820
(Source: Presteigne Parish Register)

Any population growth that may have occurred in the locality took place against a background of recurrent smallpox epidemics. The first recorded burial of a smallpox victim in the parish took place in 1709, and the parish register showed that Presteigne suffered smallpox epidemics of varying intensity in 1730-31, 1758-9, 1767, 1774 and 1783-4. The abnormally larger number of burials in 1702, 1714, 1719, 1729 and 1741 suggest that the area had already suffered epidemics of some type, possibly including smallpox, though the register gives no hint of what disease was responsible for the heavy mortality of those years. However, the scale of mortality in the eighteenth century epidemics does not bear comparison with that of the plague epidemics of the Tudor and Stuart periods. Thus 23 of the 55 burials of 1731 were of smallpox victims, as were 26 of the 56 burials of 1759, 27 of the 48 burials of 1767, 6 of the 35 burials of 1774 and 14 of the 50 burials of 1783. Since the ages of the smallpox victims are not always given in the register, it is not possible to analyse the incidence of smallpox mortality across the age groups, though the available data suggests that the overwhelming majority of smallpox victims were under twenty years of age. Since exposure to smallpox conferred a degree of immunity to survivors, the frequency of the epidemics reinforces the impression of a increase in the rate of population growth as the century progressed, with a consequent growth in the numbers in the age groups most susceptible to the disease.

The expansion of the local economy does not seem to have kept pace with the growth in population, for at the turn of the century, if not earlier, poverty was widespread and living conditions for the poorer sections of the community were wretched. With a housing density of 5.5 persons per dwelling in 1801, many lived in tiny 'one up, one down' houses, some of which survived into the twentieth century in the form of workshops, sheds and stables in the alleyways and courtyards on both sides of High Street and the west side of Broad Street. Water was obtained from wells and pumps in the courtyards, since the springline is little more than twenty feet below ground level. Sanitation took the form of earth privies and open cesspits, with local farms competing eagerly for the contract to remove 'night soil' from the town to use as fertiliser on the fields. In these crowded tenements disease spread easily and it seems likely that Presteigne's two centenarians of the eighteenth century, Deborah Hacklett, who died in 1727 aged 106 and Elizabeth Lewis, who hailed from Radnor and died in 1790 aged 102, had spent their lives in rather better circumstances.

Of the wages and working conditions of non-agricultural workers in the locality little is known beyond that in the cloth factory in 1795 men received 9s. per week, women from 4s. 6d. to 5s. and outworkers from 6d. to 9d. per day. Farm workers were paid between six and seven shillings per week and female field workers 6d. per day. Working hours for farm workers were, in winter from first light until dark, in summer from 6a.m. to 6p.m., and at harvest from dawn until dusk.

At these wage levels workers would have had difficulty in maintaining their families at subsistence levels, even when grain prices were low, for at this time beef and mutton cost 3d. - 4^1/$_2$d. per lb.; pork 5d. - 6d. per lb.; bacon 10d. per lb.; butter 9^1/$_2$d. -11d. per lb.; and milk 1d. per quart; and coal 30s. per ton. In times of dearth, such as 1794-6 and 1801-2, labourers' wages fell well below the barest subsistence levels.

In his *State of the Poor* of 1797, Sir Frederick Eden gives a graphic account of the living conditions of a day labourer in Presteigne, married with five young children: 'The wages and employment of the father are extremely various at different times of the year. In the summer he receives from 1s. to 1s. 6d. per day, in winter from 10d. to 1s. a day. He is allowed his board at harvest, but not at other times ... He is sometimes prevented by wet weather from working and often cannot obtain employment, so that on the whole he thinks that the average does not exceed 6s. 6d. per week. His wife occasionally assists a neighbouring family in baking and earns about 9d. per week. The oldest children nurse the youngest ... He can give no further account of his expenses than that the family uses nearly every week about half a bushel of wheat which now costs six shillings. His house rent is thirty shillings a year. Their common breakfast is onion pottage, dinner bread and potatoes, supper the same. They very rarely can procure a bit of meat or butter.'

The situation of this family was desperate at the time of Eden's visit, but must have become impossible later on in the year when wheat rose to 14s. 6d. a bushel and in March, 1801 when it reached 18s. 3d. a bushel. No doubt at such times the family received limited assistance from the parish, as they had done in the winter of 1794-5 when they had received 5s. and three pecks of wheat. Nor was this an isolated case: Eden commented that the earnings of labourers in the Presteigne area were so low that the poor were literally starving when corn prices rose. Two people seeking help from a parish official in 1795 'were in such a state of unfeigned distress that they actually fell down in his house through hunger'. Nor had the situation improved by the opening years of the nineteenth century. In 1805 Walter Davies commented tersely on Presteigne, 'No industry, the men labour in agriculture, women and children starve', adding: 'A gentleman and lady, seeing the poverty of the inhabitants, parted money among them and this day 125 lbs. of mutton and 120 6d. loaves are distributed at the expense of the same. Some people swear they are Bonaparte and Josephine.'

In such circumstances, it is not surprising that between 1776 and 1803 poor relief expenditure in Presteigne more than quadrupled, from £98 7s. 6d. to £470 1s. 7d.

At first sight farm servants fared rather better, for in the 1790s men received between £7 and £9 per annum with board and lodging and women £3-£5 per year. Such servants were usually hired for the year at a May Fair, (that at Presteigne, on 9 May, began in 1808) when those seeking employment wore tokens of their trade on their smocks, such as a tuft of wool or a piece of whipcord. When hired, the farm servant received a shilling as 'earnest money', often frittered away in drinking and merrymaking at the pleasure fair. Once hired, their living conditions were poor, particularly on smaller farms, for if they did not live with the family they could lead very isolated lives. Often they slept above the livestock in an outhouse, while the diet, even of the farmer's family, differed little from that of Eden's farm labourer: breakfast consisted of flummery (a mixture of flour, milk, eggs and honey) and milk; dinner and supper of bread, cheese, potatoes or soup. According to Walter Davies such households were 'rarely treated with fresh meat' and 'bacon, beef or mutton, salted or dried, furnish a Sunday feast.' Farm servants could be exploited, particularly on small farms, for farmers often insisted on a very full compliance with the letter of their contract and Quarter Sessions records contain instances of farm servants imprisoned for disobedience or breach of contract in the Knighton area as late as the mid-nineteenth century.

Poverty seems to have been more widespread in the Presteigne area than in Radnorshire as a whole, possibly because common land, upon which a bare living could be scratched, was less available than in the uplands. There also seems to have been more poverty in the town than in its near neighbour Knighton, for Eden stated that the Presteigne workhouse contained 19 inmates, while 65 households were in receipt of poor relief, 60 on a regular basis, in a town of no more than 158 houses (as he estimated), whereas in Knighton, with 138 houses, the workhouse had 17 inmates, but only 12 families were in receipt of poor relief. It is unlikely that the discrepancy stemmed from generosity on the part of the Presteigne authorities, for the poor were farmed out to the lowest bidder in order to keep down poor rates. Thus a notice in the *Hereford Journal* of 6 December 1787 informed the public: 'This is to give notice that the Poor Persons belonging to the Township of Presteigne ... will be let out to the best bidder, as Workhouse Keeper for the term of one year.'

The first reference to the Presteigne workhouse in the parish register is in 1757 and by the turn of the century it was located in High Street, on the site of a former malt house. Its function was to house those of the poor who were unable, through infirmity or age, to maintain themselves, and on the evidence of the register, the inmates tended to be elderly women and young women with illegitimate children. Though no records of the workhouse survive, some impression of the regime can be gathered from Eden's account of the situation in Presteigne in 1795.

During the late 1750s the poor of the town had been farmed out for £60 *per annum* and all who needed help from the parish, usually no more than eight at any one time, were required to enter the workhouse which, according to Eden, 'stands in a fair situation but is a most wretched hovel'. It contained nine beds in 1795, each with a mattress of chaff and flock (scraps of waste wool). The diet of the inmates compared favourably with that of the labourer in Eden's case study, for the keeper claimed that he provided meat on at least three and sometimes five occasions each week, dinner on the remaining days consisting of potatoes mashed with milk. Breakfast consisted of milk or broth and bread, and suppers of bread and cheese. The keeper's annual allowance had risen to £145 per annum by 1795, and in view of the high cost of provisions at that time he had been allowed an additional £20 to maintain the workhouse and provide some outdoor relief.

Not all the townspeople relied on parochial assistance in times of need for, like Knighton and Rhayader, Presteigne had its own friendly society, later known as the 'Old Club', whose members were entitled, in return for a weekly subscription, probably 6d. or 1s., to receive a few shillings per week when too sick to work, and whose widows received a small annual pension of a few pounds. However, the regular weekly subscription would have been beyond the means of a labourer, and the eighty-one members of the society of 1795 probably consisted in the main of tradesmen and skilled artisans in regular employment. Even so, the club did not survive long into the nineteenth century, probably partly because of the testing economic environment of the day.

In part the relatively greater poverty found in the Presteigne area in the late eighteenth century stemmed from the failure of the local economy to keep pace with the growth in population; there was thus a pool of unemployed or under-employed labour which tended to depress wage levels in the locality. Walter Davies attributed the higher wages of the Radnorshire uplands to 'a few improvers [who] come from a distance' whereas in Herefordshire, with whose agricultural system the local farming pattern economy had greater affinity, 'the farmers were of the old school.' The growing importance of cash crops which had a highly seasonal demand for labour, as did the local malting industry, probably contributed to the problem.

The development of the malting industry may well have distorted the local corn market, reducing the amount of bread corn available in times of dearth and thus forcing up the price. The use of wheat as bread corn by the labourer in Eden's case study rather than a mixture of wheat and barley may not be a sign of rising living standards, but of a reduction in the supply of small quantities of barley for domestic use as a result of the demands of the local malting industry.

Given the relative proximity of the more dynamic emerging industrial areas of South Wales and the West Midlands, it would be surprising if there had not been a measure of migration from the Presteigne area in the closing decades of the century. Significantly the level of migration as measured by the proportion of uninhabited houses shown by the 1801 census was greater in the south-western and south-eastern fringes of Radnorshire than in its upland interior where subsistence agriculture still prevailed and the greater availability of common land enabled the under-employed to augment their meagre earnings.

CHAPTER VI

From the French Wars to Victoria

After a brief period of prosperity, which does not seem to have survived the ending of the Napoleonic War in 1815, the town entered another period of commercial decline which led to an increased emphasis on its twin roles as the seat of justice and the centre of local government for the county. This changing emphasis was reflected in the drive to refurbish the town's civic buildings and to maintain them in an appropriate manner.

Earning a Living
In the opening decades of the century the population of the town rose sharply, increasing by 43% between 1801 and 1831, with the housing stock increasing by nearly 50% in the same period. Parish register data suggests that the growth in population stemmed from natural increase rather than inward migration, for the excess of baptisms over burials 1801-20 almost matches the increase in population of the parish as recorded by the censuses of 1801 and 1821. The increase was the result of a marked reduction in the mortality rate rather than a significant increase in the birth rate, for although the average annual total of baptisms rose from 41 per annum between 1761-1800 to 50 in the period 1801-20, more or less in keeping with the growth in population, the annual average total of burials fell slightly between the two periods, from 31 to 30 per annum, in spite of the population increase.

W.H. Howse suggests that the growth in the town's population was, at least in part, at the expense of the surrounding rural area, arguing that those made unemployed by the changes in agriculture, moved into the town before ultimately migrating to the industrial areas of South Wales

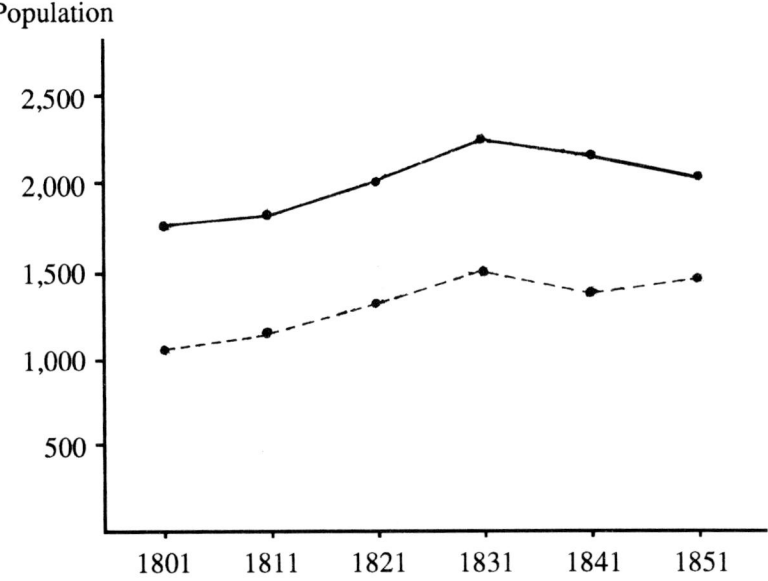

Fig. 19: The Population of Presteigne Town and Parish, 1801-51
——— *Parish Population* ------ *Town Population*
(Source: Printed census data, 1801-51)

and the west Midlands. However, an analysis of the census data does not entirely support this hypothesis, for the population of the rural parts of Presteigne parish increased by 29.7% between 1801 and 1831, in spite of the agricultural depression of the decades after 1815. On the other hand, the steady increase in the proportion of the town's unoccupied housing stock, from 2.5% in 1821 to 5.9% in 1831 and 9% in 1841 suggests that there was increasing migration from the town in the second quarter of the century. Again, a significant degree of multiple occupation in the town in the period, in spite of the growing number of unoccupied houses, suggests that there may have been a transient element in the town's population, which would lend support to Howse's hypothesis.

The marked increase in the town's population of 21.8% between 1801 and 1821, together with Carlisle's observation in 1810 to the effect that 'This is a very improving town, there being at this time ..., though after so many years of war, scarce a void house in it', suggests that the recovery of the second half of the eighteenth century persisted until the end of the war in 1815. However, some evidence, fragmentary and anecdotal, indicates that decline may have set in before that date. Neither Walter Davies

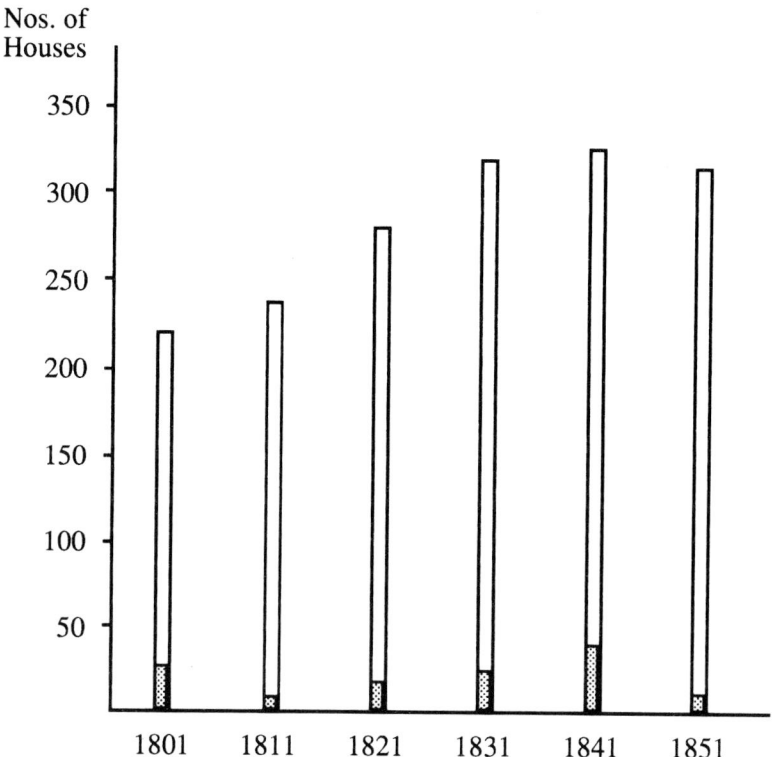

Fig. 20: Presteigne's Housing Stock, 1801-51
▓▓▓ *Unoccupied houses*
(Source: Printed census data, 1801-51)

in 1805, nor Carlisle in 1810 mentions the cloth factory which had been functioning in the town at the turn of the century; and by 1822 the fulling mill on the Stapleton side of Lugg Bridge had reverted to its previous use as a paper mill; while the press advertisement of the Discoed fulling mill in 1817 made no mention of textile machinery, which suggests that the business was in abeyance at this date, though it was functioning once more in 1841.

The opening of the Kington-New Radnor turnpike in the late eighteenth century had undermined Presteigne's role as a staging point on the London-Aberystwyth route, for it gave the Gloucester-Leominster-Aberystwyth route which ran via Kington a time advantage of an hour or so over the Worcester-Leominster-Aberystwyth route which ran via Presteigne. The latter service continued to function after 1808 on a fairly regular basis, though with periodic gaps of a few years. By 1837 there were great hopes that the new road from Presteigne to Penybont via Bleddfa would, as the shortest route to Aberystwyth from Birmingham and London, restore Presteigne's importance as a route centre, but this was not to be. The time for the journey to Aberystwyth from Presteigne had been reduced to eight hours or so by the later 1830s, but by then the time taken for the Kington-Aberystwyth journey had fallen to six and a half hours.

The decision taken in 1813 to use only Knighton market as the basis for the Radnorshire grain prices published in the *London Gazette*, rather than those of both Presteigne and Knighton, as had been the practice previously, may also have been a symptom of Presteigne's decline. On the other hand, far from indicating the town's decline as a grain market, it may have been no more than a recognition that the demands of the town's malting industry were distorting local grain prices to the point where they were becoming thoroughly unrepresentative.

Presteigne's fortunes were inextricably tied to those of the local farming industry. Ellis, writing in 1832, described the town as a sort of metropolis for five miles round, 'groceries, draperies, iron work and shop goods are bought here', going on to explain that 'the inhabitants of the town are principally professional men, tradesmen, mechanics and handicraftsmen.' This description of the town is supported by an analysis of the town's businesses listed in Pigot's *Commercial Directory* of 1830 which shows nearly one hundred businesses in the town:

4 attorneys	2 ironmongers	2 coopers
3 surgeons	3 drapers	2 corn dealers
1 veterinary surgeon	3 tailors	2 limeburners
1 bookseller/stationer	1 watchmaker	3 maltsters
	1 staymaker	2 painters/glaziers
2 chemists	2 saddlers	2 pump makers
2 land agents	2 milliners	2 skinners
1 auctioneer	2 van men	3 stone masons
1 post mistress	2 carriers	1 tanner
4 bakers	12 innkeepers	1 brazier/tinman
6 shoemakers	3 blacksmiths	1 organist,weaver
4 butchers	5 cabinetmakers/joiners	1 clog/pattenmaker
5 grocers		2 millers
1 wheelwright	1 timber merchant	

Given the small hinterland of the town, most of these activities were small-scale family businesses, with only the tannery, timber yard and the malthouses likely to have employed more than one or two workers in addition to members of the family.

A large proportion of the town's labour force was employed in agriculture, overwhelmingly the major recruiter of labour in the parish as a whole. The 1801 census suggests that more than 75% of the labour force in the locality were employed in agriculture and by 1831 the proportion had not fallen significantly. There were two major estates in the area by the nineteenth century, Norton Manor owned by Richard Price and consisting of 8,774 acres, and Sir Harford Jones Brydges' estate, centring on Boultibrooke and amounting to 4,088 acres. Most of the farms, even after consolidation, were small, few exceeding 50 acres, and most seem to have been leasehold, typically held on a 21 year lease. Most of the arable land, with the exception of that in Norton parish, was old enclosed land. What parliamentary enclosure there was in the locality was of common grazing land and came in the later war years or shortly after: 1809 in Lingen; 1810 in Stapleton (123 acres); 1812 in Pilleth (500 acres); 1813 in Cascob and Ednol (1,500 acres); and 1817 in Willey (142 acres).

During the war years the price of agricultural products had risen sharply and farming prospered, despite increasing local and national taxation and the high capital costs associated with increasing output. Farm workers shared in this prosperity, wages rising to between 8s. and 10s. per week and £10 to £12 per annum for male labourers and farm servants respectively. With incomes of landowners, farmers and farm workers rising, the town shared in the boom of the war years. With the advent of peace in 1815 the price of agricultural products collapsed and farming found itself in serious difficulties for more than two decades. The situation was exacerbated by the continuing high level of local and national taxation, the high rents negotiated during the boom years and the need to repay loans taken out at that time to finance improvements. Moreover, in the Presteigne area, the enclosures initiated in the closing years of the war were not completed until some years after the collapse of prices: Willey in 1819; Stapleton in 1824; and Lingen in 1828; and to make matters worse enclosure costs seem to have been high, £6 per acre at Stapleton.

The farmers' response was to cut costs and farm workers' wages fell back to 7s. to 8s. per week by 1824 and to 6s. to 7s. per week by the early 1830s. At this level it was generally accepted that a married labourer with children, in full time employment, could not maintain his family at a bare subsistence level without assistance from the parish, for food prices were rising rapidly; a 4lb. loaf of bread that cost 4d. in 1817, cost 9d. in 1820. In eastern Radnorshire it became customary for employed labourers to receive assistance from the poor rates on a regular basis. In some townships house rents were paid by the parish and elsewhere labourers received a weekly allowance of 1s. 6d. per week for each child after the first. Landowners' incomes also fell, for with farmers unable to pay their rents, it was expedient for estate owners to give rent abatements of about 10% rather than evict and be left with unlet farms on their hands. With incomes of all classes of rural society falling, it is not surprising that Pigot's *Commercial Directory* of 1830 commented that Presteigne was 'a place of little trade', while Ellis in 1832 reported that 'the town is said to be stationary'.

Nor did the town possess a large enough hinterland to weather the crisis easily. A useful indicator of hinterlands can be gained from a comparison of the relative size of the Presteigne, Knighton and Kington Poor Law Unions established in the mid-1830s, when groups of neighbouring parishes were combined for the purposes of poor relief in an attempt to reduce costs and hence reduce the level of poor rates. The Presteigne Union did not extend far beyond parochial boundaries and consisted of fifteen small communities in addition to the town itself and covered a population of 3,441. The Knighton Union consisted of twenty townships with a total population of 8,719, while the Kington Union served twenty-six townships with a total population of 12,022. Included in the Kington Union was the parish of Titley, which in the eighteenth century had been considered as being partly within Presteigne's sphere of influence. Not surprisingly, there was some hostility between Presteigne and its Herefordshire neighbour, a correspondent of the Poor Law Commissioners in 1836 noting that '... the rivalry of these two country towns, aggravated by political hostility, has produced a feeling more suited to the middle ages than to the temper of a civilised country in the nineteenth century.'

With the volume of its trade no more than static, the burden of local taxation remained high. Between 1813 and 1815 the town's annual expenditure on the relief of poverty averaged £437 per annum, and reached an average of £514 per annum between 1819 and 1821. Even in 1827-29 the town was spending an average of nearly £460 per annum relieving its poor. The renewal of the county's civic buildings between 1819 and 1829 meant that county expenditure and therefore the level of the county rate remained high, thus again increasing the burden on the town's businesses.

Matters were not helped by the loss of part of the town's commercial infrastructure in the decade or so after 1815. Part of its market square was incorporated into the new Bull Hotel in 1820 and when the old Shire Hall was sold in 1831, one of the conditions imposed on the purchaser was that the covered arcade which served as a market hall and which projected into Broad Street should be demolished since it represented an obstacle to traffic. In 1840 the *Hereford Journal* reported that the town's weekly market to be 'almost lost.' A meeting of the townspeople decided to move the market day from Saturday to Tuesday and to build a new market hall, but it proved impossible to raise sufficient funds. Until the opening of the Market Hall and Assembly Rooms in 1865, the butter market was held in the open air in High Street and on occasions the Duke's Arms and its yard at the rear were called into use to serve as the town's market place.

The Story of Mary Morgan

No history of the town would be complete without some account of the tragic story of Mary Morgan which has aroused such sympathy over the generations. Mary is said to have been the last woman to be publicly executed in Wales, but the real interest in her case stems from the unusual circumstances surrounding her trial and execution which have given rise to much speculation over the years.

On 23 September, 1804, Mary Morgan, the sixteen year-old undercook at Maeslwch Castle near Glasbury, the home of Walter Wilkins, MP for Radnorshire, gave birth to a baby girl in secret in her room at the castle. Almost immediately she killed the baby with a knife which she used in her work, almost severing the head from the body. The tragedy was discovered within hours, and at the inquest two days later Mary Morgan was found responsible for the death. She was taken to the county gaol at Presteigne on 6 October, where she was lodged to await trial at the Lent sitting of Great Sessions in Presteigne. Her trial opened on Tuesday, 9 April, little more than a fortnight after her seventeenth birthday, when the grand jury of twenty-five, after considering the evidence, found that the case was proved, and two days later she was found guilty by the fourteen strong petty jury chosen from members of the grand jury, and Judge Hardinge pronounced the death sentence. She was executed at noon on Saturday, 13 April 1805 at Gallows Lane.

The penal code of the day was very severe and in theory such crimes as imitating a Chelsea Pensioner or defacing Westminster Bridge were capital offences, while in practice those found guilty of sheep, cattle or horse stealing were often hanged. Nor did age or sex have any bearing; in 1787 a girl of seventeen, Susannah Minton of Kilpeck, was hanged at

Hereford for setting fire to a barn. By 1805 It was unusual, however, for the death sentence to be carried out in cases of infanticide. Neild records only one other execution for infanticide in that year in England and Wales, for the normal procedure in such cases was to commute the sentence almost immediately. The failure to do this in the case of Mary Morgan has given rise to some speculation. Walter Wilkins junior, the son of the house and possibly a gallant of Mary's, was certainly a member of the grand jury and may have been on the petty jury which found her guilty, for the jury list shows that the fourteenth member of that jury was either Walter Wilkins or Charles H. Price. Since the Wilkins family was very much part of the legal establishment in the Brecon circuit, it has been suggested that the death sentence may have been the result of an establishment cover-up. However, on the basis of Judge Hardinge's letter to the bishop of St Asaph of April 1805, this would not appear to be the case. According to this, Mary Morgan denied that Wilkins junior was the father, naming a fellow servant who had accepted paternity before the birth of the child. Again, the letter suggests that Hardinge was not on particularly good terms with the Wilkins family whom he describes as 'most profligate', for he criticises Wilkins junior severely for being a party to the concealment of the pregnancy.

Hardinge seems to have favoured harsh sentences on female defendants found guilty at Presteigne and it may have been some psychological trait in his make up which was responsible for Mary Morgan's fate. Alternatively it could have been her conduct during the trial which may have been the deciding factor, for according to Hardinge, she had decided to kill the child even before her birth, and initially at her trial she seems to have shown little sign of contrition, in Hardinge's words: '... she took it for granted (sic) that she would be acquitted, had ordered gay apparel, to attest the event of her deliverance and supposed the young gentleman (whom I well knew) [i.e. Walter Wilkins junior] would save her by a letter to me...'

Hardinge's belief that 'there was no single trace of religion to be found in her thoughts' may also have prejudiced him against her. Her initial lack of awareness of the gravity of her situation at her trial suggests that the balance of her mind had been severely disturbed by the birth of her child, a condition known as post-natal psychosis, and made worse by her long incarceration prior to the trial. However, one should avoid the late Victorian stereotype of a young woman disgraced by bearing an illegitimate child, for illegitimacy was common in early nineteenth century Radnorshire and carried no real social stigma. Of the 675 births recorded in the county in 1839, 100 were recorded as illegitimate.

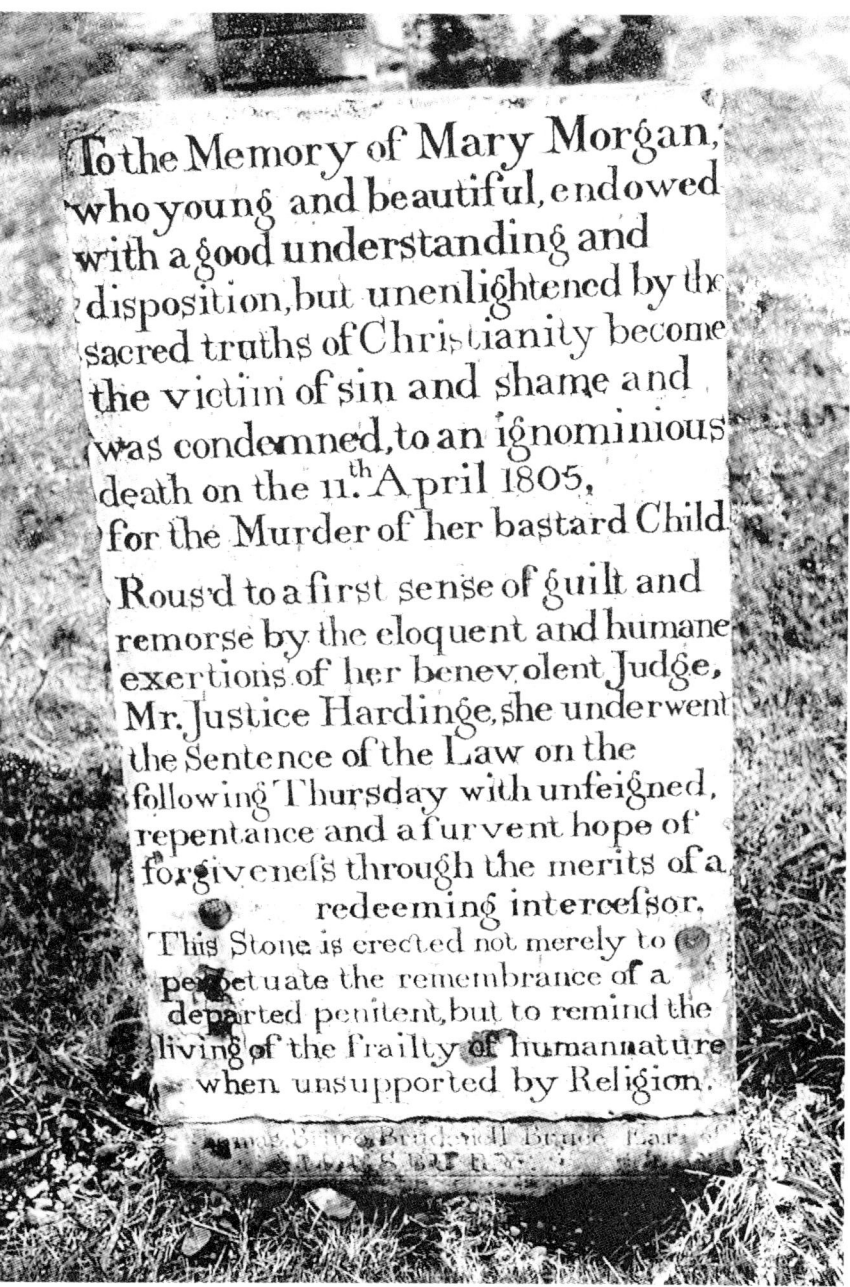

*The gravestone erected by the Earl of Ailesbury,
a friend of Judge Hardinge*

The second gravestone of Mary Morgan

Though documentary sources afford no evidence of overt local sympathy for her plight, tradition suggests that her case attracted considerable sympathy in the town. W.H. Howse, in his conversations with elderly residents uncovered many local traditions connected with Mary Morgan which had been handed down over the generations: that the householders in Scottleton Street drew their blinds out of respect for her on the morning of the execution and that if money could have saved her, she could have had 'a wagon load'; that Mary, wrapped in a winding sheet, was unconscious when lifted from the cart at Gallows Lane. In one of his notebooks W.H. Howse records the tradition that initially the authorities were unable to find a farmer willing to provide a cart to carry Mary Morgan to Gallows Lane, nor a waggoner to drive it. The strong local tradition of an attempt to obtain a reprieve also suggests that the Mary Morgan case had excited local sympathy. Mrs Parris has demonstrated that there is no evidence in the official records to support the claim that a pardon or reprieve was granted or even sought, nevertheless the tradition persists that Sir Samuel Romilly, or her young defence counsel Richard Beavan, or an unknown gentleman rode to London, obtained a reprieve or pardon, but arrived back in Presteigne too late to halt the execution as his horse went lame.

There is no evidence to suggest that the final part of the sentence, that the body should be 'dissected and anatomised' was carried out and her corpse was buried in unconsecrated ground, for that part of the churchyard containing her grave was then part of the old rectory garden. A stone bearing a sanctimonious epitaph was erected by a friend of Hardinge's, the Earl of Ailesbury, who had an inordinate enthusiasm for erecting monuments, in answer to the storm of criticism which Mary Morgan's harsh sentence had provoked. The second stone, bearing the text 'He that is without sin among you let him first cast a stone at her' is something of a mystery for it is uncertain when, or by whom, it was erected. It was in place in 1818 when Horton published his 'Elegy', but if the tradition that Hardinge visited the grave on each future visit to the town is true, it is unlikely to have been placed there prior to Hardinge's death in Presteigne in 1816, for judges were men of considerable influence whom it would have been unwise to offend. On the other hand, there seems to have been little love lost between Hardinge and the townspeople: in 1814, when Sarah Chandler, under sentence of death, escaped from the gaol with the connivance, if not active assistance of some in the town, Hardinge, beside himself with rage, expressed the belief that half the townspeople deserved to be gaoled. As to the identity of the donor of the stone, it has been suggested that it may have been the townspeople or Mary Morgan's parents, while others have suggested that her young defence counsel, Richard Beavan may have been responsible for its erection.

Any local hostility seems to have been directed against Hardinge rather than at the Wilkins family, which suggests that if there had been any speculation concerning the involvement of Walter Wilkins, it was rapidly seen to have been unfounded. Walter Wilkins senior was returned unopposed as MP for the county in 1806, 1807, 1812, 1818, 1820 and 1826, though not popular with some of the well-established families in the county such as the Lewises of Harpton. On each occasion he visited Presteigne for the formal declaration of his election he received a rapturous welcome, being chaired around the town, as was Walter Wilkins junior in 1826 when he was representing his father. On the death of his father in 1828 there was a determined effort to persuade Walter Wilkins junior to take his place, but he declined on grounds of ill health. Again, though Sir Harford Jones Brydges was the most vocal supporter of Wilkins in the county, this did not prevent his wife and children heading the list of subscribers to Horton's 'Elegy' in 1818, which suggests that the Mary Morgan case was not a sensitive issue for the Whigs or for the Wilkins family. One wonders if the ill-tempered and bitterly fought election of 1835, in which Walter Wilkins III, the son of Walter Wilkins junior, narrowly defeated the Tory Sir John Benn Walsh, revived the speculation concerning the family's involvement in the case and thus preserved it.

The Renewal of the Town's Civic Buildings
Though the Shire Hall and county gaol were the responsibility of the county rather than of the town, the unsatisfactory state of both buildings must have given rise to some unease on the part of the townspeople since the loss of the courts and the gaol would have involved the loss of status and business at a time when Presteigne's fortunes seemed on the wane. Fortunately the Radnorshire Bench, chaired by Sir Harford Jones Brydges, decided to replace both buildings and between 1819 and 1829 spent more than £10,000 on the construction of a new gaol and Shire Hall in the town.

Given that the county's annual revenue was in the region of £1,850, expenditure on this scale was not undertaken lightly and the decision of the Bench owed much to the pressure brought to bear by the judges of Great Sessions. In 1818 the Shire Hall and the gaol were presented by the grand jury as being unsatisfactory. The Bench decided to give priority to the building of a new gaol at a cost of no more than £3,300, resolving that it '... should be erected in as plain a manner as possible and with every economy consistent with it being a substantial building, hoping at some time to erect a new Court House for which ... all expense of ornament, which the County can afford, should be reserved.'

The judges of Great Sessions were not happy with the county's order of priorities, arguing that, out of respect for them, a new Shire Hall should have taken precedence.

RADNORSHIRE.

NOTICE

IS HEREBY GIVEN,

That the General Quarter Sessions of the peace for the County of RADNOR, are further adjourned to, and will be holden at

The Shire Hall, in Presteigne,

On TUESDAY, the 8th day of DECEMBER next, at Eleven o'Clock in the Forenoon,

For the purpose of considering the Expediency of applying to Parliament in the ensuing Session, for an Act for Building a new

SHIRE HALL,

With Court of Justice and other necessary Buildings attached thereto, and a new

Gaol and House of Correction, for the said County;

And also of considering the powers and provisions necessary to be inserted in the Act, for carrying such undertakings into execution, and for raising and defraying the expences thereof.

By order of the Court,

November 7th, 1818.

DAVIES,
Clerk of the Peace.

This notice of 1818 shows the concern of the Bench at the condition of the old Shire Hall and County Gaol

Probably the main factor influencing the decision of the bench was the highly insecure nature of the gaol, for escapes were becoming embarrassingly frequent, occurring in 1814, 1815, 1818, 1819 and 1820. Though the escape of John Williams in 1820, double-chained and without his trousers, no doubt excited much comment, it had been the escape of Sarah Chandler in 1814 which had brought the gaol and its administration into some disrepute.

Of an upper Teme valley family, several of whom had previously been transported, Sarah was the wife of Thomas Chandler, a tenant farmer of the Dolley, Ackhill. Accused of forgery in that she had attempted to alter two £1 pound notes of the Kington Bank into £5 notes, at her initial trial in 1813 she had been released on bail of £100. At the Lent sitting of Great Sessions in 1814 she was tried before Judge Hardinge and sentenced to death, in spite of a petition sent to the Prince Regent and signed by the sheriff, James Davies, the clerk of the peace who was also the banker she had sought to defraud, and twenty-seven other local dignitaries. Probably because of the petition, the Home Secretary, Lord Sidmouth, granted a fourteen day stay of execution for Hardinge to reconsider the case, but the latter was adamant. On the eve of her execution, during a violent thunderstorm, her husband, brother and friends scaled the gaol wall, forced an entry into her cell and freed her. Hardinge was furious, secured the dismissal of the gaoler whom he suspected of colluding in the escape and offered a reward of fifty guineas for her recapture. The reward notice described Sarah Chandler as 'Rather tall, of a Lusty Habit and a florid complexion and is well known in the neighbourhood of Presteigne and Knighton. It is reported that she was seen very lately dressed in man's apparel in the Northern Part of the County.' She later moved to Birmingham where she made a living selling milk. She was recaptured in 1816, a Wilson Payn receiving the reward. By the time she had been returned to the gaol Hardinge had died and in 1817, after several petitions for mercy, including one from the sheriff and bailiff of Birmingham, the death sentence was commuted to transportation for life. She sailed for New South Wales in 1818 on the 'Friendship', to be joined in 1826 by her son who was transported for life for horse stealing.

Designs for the new gaol were submitted by Edward Haycock, a Shrewsbury architect and builder; Sir Charles Smirke, who designed some of the galleries of the British Museum, Hereford Shire Hall and the library at Boultibrooke; and by Benjamin Wishlade, the county surveyor. The plans submitted by Haycock and Smirke were considered too ambitious and too expensive and Wishlade's plans, estimated to cost £3,248,

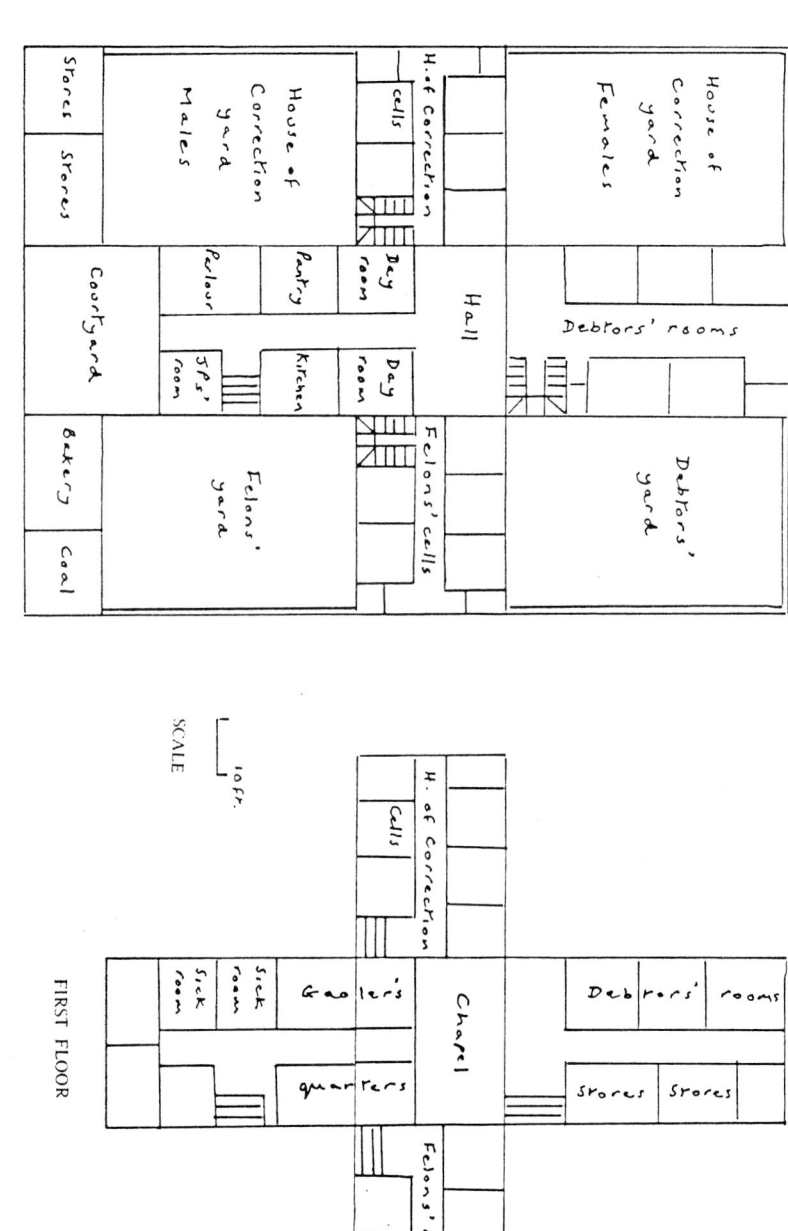

Fig. 21: The plan of the New Radnor Gaol, Presteigne, 1821
(Source: Radnor Quarter Sessions records)

just below the limit set by the bench, were accepted, and Wishlade was also awarded the contract to build the gaol.

The project was financed by borrowing £2,000 on the security of the county rate, Walter Wilkins advancing £1,500, and he duly obliged with a further loan of £500 when it proved impossible to borrow this from any other source. A number of sites were considered for the new gaol; Went's Meadow near Boultibrooke bridge, the Hop Ground near Gallows Lane and an orchard at the rear of the Apple Tree Inn, but the choice finally fell on a piece of land between Broadaxe Lane and Clatterbrook Bridge, which was purchased from Edward Rogers of Stanage for £120. Work started on the new gaol in July 1819, the foundation stone being laid by Richard Price, MP for Radnor Boroughs, and in August 1821 the work was completed.

Under constant pressure from the judges of Great Sessions concerning the inadequacy of the Shire Hall and the judge's lodgings, in 1825 the bench decided to proceed with the construction of a new Shire Hall on the site of the old gaol and house of correction in Broad Street, with only the shell of new judges's lodgings included in the initial phase since it was considered that the county's finances would not permit the completion of the latter until a later date. Plans were drawn up by Edward Haycock and by May 1826 three tenders had been submitted for the building contract: Haycock's for £4,800; Wishlade's for £4,770, and that of a local building firm, Cole, Luggar and Young, for £5,931. The contract was awarded to Haycock and, under the impression that Wilkins would advance the necessary funds, the Clerk to the Peace, James Davies, was authorised to borrow £4,500 from him. Wilkins refused to lend the money, and since Davies was only able to borrow £1,000 from other local sources, a further £3,000 was borrowed from the Exchequer Loans Office, the county presumably deciding to find the other £500 from its own resources.

In the meantime Haycock was ahead of schedule in constructing the new building, in spite of modifications to the original plan such as the addition of colonnades at the front. The bench was highly satisfied with the quality of his work and decided to press ahead with the completion of the lodgings, a further £1,500 being raised from the Exchequer Loans Office, though not without some difficulty. By October 1829 the work had been completed to the satisfaction of the supervising committee of magistrates who reported that: '... the execution of both contracts reflect very great credit on the ability and skill of Messrs. Haycock as architects and on their integrity as individuals.' The new premises were used for the first time on 25 August 1829 for a sitting of Great Session, though

Quarter Sessions did not meet in their new setting until Easter 1830. All that remained to be done was to dispose of the old premises and these were sold to Thomas Coates of Leominster in 1831, the hall for £93 and the record room at the rear for £128.

The new Shire Hall had barely been completed when doubts were cast on its future, for in the autumn of 1829 it was proposed that on the reorganisation of the Welsh judicial system, Radnorshire should be placed within the jurisdiction of Hereford Assizes. Such a proposal created a storm in the county, the grand jury objecting to the expense and inconvenience which such a scheme would create, adding that '... ample and convenient accommodation for holding the assize and also for the accommodation of His Majesty's Judges has been recently created at Presteigne ... at the great and heavy expense of the county.' The proposal was also heavily criticised in the local press and was soon withdrawn, to be resurrected thereafter every decade or so. However, Assizes continued to be held at Presteigne until the dismantling of the assize system by the Courts Act of 1970 and the setting up of the new Crown Court at Welshpool in 1971. The last Assizes to be held in the town were held in October 1970, Mr Justice Mars-Jones presiding.

At first the authorities guarded their new premises jealously and were most reluctant to allow their use by other public bodies. The guardians of the Presteigne Poor Law Union were denied the use of a room in 1837 and later that year, when it was decided to establish a library in the town, permission to locate it in the Shire Hall was only granted on condition that the room in which it was located should not be used as a public reading room. However, it seemed unreasonable to leave the lodgings unused for all but two or three weeks in the year and in 1834 these were let to James Barnes, a local JP, for a rent of 10s. per week, presumably on condition that he would vacate the premises when Assizes were sitting.

Politics and Society
Life in Presteigne in the first half of the nineteenth century was not always as tranquil as Ince's picture of Broad Street in 1830 might suggest. Apart from the boisterous high days and holidays and public occasions such as general elections and the sittings of the courts, the town could appear quiet. Even as late as the mid 1820s cattle and pigs roamed the streets with impunity, much to the annoyance of the turnpike authorities. However, the decades following 1815 saw social tensions increasing and with the labourers of the town pauperised and no effective police force, there was always a possibility that unrest might spill over into

public disturbances such as those which occurred in Rhayader in 1818-19 and 1826 and more generally in the rural counties of southern England in the 'last labourers' revolt' of 1830-31.

The town authorities therefore tended to react strongly to any perceived threat to the existing social order. Thus the formation in 1801 of the Presteigne Society for the Prosecution of Felons and the attempt to set up a Society for the Protection of Game in 1816 with draconian powers of search, reflect the fears of the propertied classes of a social upheaval. In 1831 the authorities were still clearly nervous, for a labourer found guilty of sending a threatening letter demanding money from Edward Lee James, a prominent Presteigne lawyer and property owner, was sentenced to fourteen years transportation. Echoes of such social tensions can be seen in the *Hereford Journal* of 10 December 1845 when a local correspondent, commenting on the attempted suicide of a domestic servant in Presteigne, remarked: 'A few months imprisonment in the House of Correction and a good flogging once or more are well merited for hurting the feelings of a good and indulgent mistress.' A few months earlier the Poor Law Commission in London had reacted with alarm when it was discovered that unemployed, able-bodied labourers were not being given the poor relief to which they were entitled, but were compelled to work for the Radnorshire Turnpike Trust, breaking stone at a wage rate of 8d. per ton, half of this being paid in kind.

Though the loose coalition of property owners, professional men and prosperous tradesmen which controlled the town under the patronage of the Jones Brydges family of Boultibrooke was broadly Whig in sympathy, it did not always present a united front. Deep personal rivalries meant that political feeling could run high in the town as factions sought to manoeuvre their nominees into public appointments and appealed to public opinion in the town for support. Such divisions in the establishment were exploited with glee by the more mischievous elements as the townspeople took sides with some enthusiasm.

Until the Green Prices inherited the Norton Manor estate in 1861, the Jones Brydges family dominated Presteigne socially and politically. The first baronet, Sir Harford Jones, who assumed the additional surname of Brydges by royal licence in 1826, was a descendant of the Jones family of Trewern, prominent in Radnorshire in the sixteenth and seventeenth centuries. Born at Harford House in 1764, he had entered the services of the East India Company in 1783, adding substantially to the family fortune and gaining a baronetcy in 1806 for his services in keeping Persia within the British sphere of influence in the face of heavy pressure from

Boultibrooke House c.1930, the seat of the Jones Brydges family

Harpton Court c.1910, the seat of the Lewis family

France and Russia. He returned to Persia as British envoy in 1807, after taking a lease on Boultibrooke, and on his return to Britain in 1811, having failed to secure the governorship of Bombay, he resigned from the Company and purchased the Boultibrooke estate and the lordship of the manor of Presteigne from the Harleys in 1812.

He renovated and enlarged Boultibrooke House and on taking up residence began to play a prominent role in the public life of the county. In 1816 he served as sheriff and between 1818 and 1822 he was chairman of the Bench, steering through the building of the new county gaol. He was a committed Whig and his political beliefs and his personal antipathy towards Thomas Frankland Lewis, MP for the county since 1828, led him to champion the cause of parliamentary reform. This was an issue where his interests coincided with those of the town, for the reform proposals of 1830-32 involved the inclusion of Presteigne in the Radnor Boroughs constituency, which would enhance its status and give many in the town the vote for the first time.

As Roy Adams demonstrates, Sir Harford's stance on the issue brought him unprecedented popularity and for a time in early 1831 he may have had ambitions of standing for the county seat. On the defeat of the first Reform Bill he was deputed by a county meeting of freeholders in November 1831 to present an address to the king regretting its demise. In the same month an address, signed by Thomas Beaumont, the bailiff of Presteigne, and a number of leading tradesmen, was printed and circulated locally, expressing the gratitude of the signatories to Sir Harford for the attention he had paid to the interests of the town and to the cause of parliamentary reform. The passing of the Reform Act in June 1832 was celebrated in Presteigne by a 'Reform Festival', involving a procession complete with a band and banners, the distribution of bread, meat and cider to the townspeople and a celebratory dinner at the Radnorshire Arms for dignitaries of the town and county.

Given Sir Harford's fiery and argumentative temperament and his sometimes high-handed manner, (he was on one occasion rebuked by his fellow turnpike trustees for using their supply of road stone to repair his estate roads), it is not surprising that his intervention led to a marked rise in the political temperature in the locality. In the course of the campaign for parliamentary reform he had played a leading role in the formation of the Greycoat Club, which had the ostensible object of promoting the interests of the Radnorshire cloth industry, but which was in reality a Whig front organisation. Its major triumph was to win for the Whigs the close, ill-tempered and expensive county election of 1835, during the course of which £447 was spent in 'treating' Whig supporters in Presteigne alone. Nor was the ill-feeling confined to the narrowly political sphere, for a literary society, set up in Presteigne in 1837 on the founding of the library, broke up within a few years in a welter of rancour and factional squabbles.

Though in the heat of the moment Sir Harford could sound like a revolutionary—in 1830 in the course of a speech in favour of parliamentary reform he remarked that, 'When, as in France, kings forget their duties to the people, they should be reminded of them'—he was essentially an old-fashioned Whig who believed that the interests of property had to be defended against an overpowerful government and against the mob. His stance on social issues may be judged from the leading part he played in the attempt to establish a Society for the Protection of Game in 1816 to curb poaching. Again, in 1819 he ensured the establishment of a rigorous regime in the new gaol for he believed that 'it was not the object to render it more comfortable than was consistent with a due regard to the health of the prisoners.'

Sir Harford was not always involved in the local issues. He was conspicuously silent, for example, during the campaign to safeguard 'cottagers' rights', led by Cecil Parsons, the Presteigne lawyer and banker, when the purchasers of several crown manors in Radnorshire sought to eject long-established squatters from the holdings. Nor did he attend the celebratory dinner at the Radnorshire Arms in 1837 when Parsons was presented with silver plate to commemorate his victory in court. His supporters' celebrations, involving processions, fireworks and a bonfire led to a summons alleging 'riotous behaviour.'

The contentious nature of politics in the town in the second quarter of the century is well illustrated by the bitter controversies surrounding the appointment of guardians and officers of the Presteigne Poor Law Union set up in 1836. All such appointments were widely canvassed and bitterly contested, none more than the post of medical officer, where the rivals were Dr William Whitcombe, a kinsman of Sir Harford Jones Brydges and Henry Ince, backed by Cecil Parsons. Sir Harford initially used his position as chairman of the Union to install Whitcombe, who was also medical officer for the Kington Union, much to the chagrin of Parsons and three other guardians, who favoured Ince, the local practitioner. After questioning Whitcombe's ability, in spite of his impressive qualifications, to cover two Unions, Ince was appointed in 1838. The matter did not end there, for a letter to the *Lancet* alleged that in the Presteigne area three unqualified practitioners were employed as Union medical officers. At Presteigne 'an old army surgeon, whose infirmities incapacitated him from the performance of his duties, has appointed another old man as his deputy, who has for some years practised as a chemist, druggist and a cow and horse doctor.' This clearly cast some doubt on the suitability of Ince and his deputy, Vincent Cooksey, another Presteigne practitioner, and in February they were replaced by a John Downes Owen. He did not last long however, being dismissed in September for neglecting a pauper, and Ince and Cooksey were reinstalled. Whitcombe returned to the attack in 1843, concentrating on Ince's age and Cooksey's lack of formal qualifications. There seems to have been some justification behind

Whitcombe's allegations for Cooksey was soon dismissed again (for the use of improper language to a pauper). The Presteigne authorities acknowledged that Ince did little more than complete the local returns, which suggests that his supporters were motivated by little more than factionalism and narrow local allegiance.

By the 1840s the social and political tensions in the area seem to have eased and when a Chartist delegation visited the town in 1840 'these misguided men were told to leave Presteigne as soon as possible if they had any value for their bones' according to the *Hereford Journal*. Even so, poverty was still widespread in the locality, for on the occasion of Queen Victoria's wedding in 1840, soup and bread were distributed to more than two hundred poor families in the parish. Age and ill health saw Sir Harford Jones Brydges gradually withdraw from public life and his heir, who succeeded to the baronetcy in 1847, Sir Harford James Jones Brydges was a more private man with little taste for politics and public controversy. The political temperature fell with the Walshes holding the county seat virtually unchallenged over the next few decades, and the Lewises in the case of the Borough seat between 1847 and 1863. A measure of prosperity was beginning to return in agriculture and the prospects for the town brightened as attendances at the May Fair and Wardens Wake reached unprecedented levels in the early 1840s. It may have been renewed optimism which led to the abandonment of the proposal to build a Union Workhouse in Presteigne to house fifty inmates.

The Rebecca Riots of 1842-43 saw serious disturbances in Rhayader, where smallholders, with blackened faces and some disguised in women's clothes, destroyed the hated turnpike gates, disorder at Glasbury and fear of trouble at Knighton which led to the stationing of troops in that town for several months, but had no real repercussions in Presteigne. A group of young practical jokers, masquerading as Rebeccas, terrorised the keeper of the Corton tollgate into hiding under his bed, but were put to flight by Martha, the keeper of the Lower Gate on Broadaxe Lane.

The County Gaol
Sir Harford Jones Brydges had envisaged a spartan regime in the new gaol and its fittings and furniture were certainly in keeping with this sentiment. The debtors' rooms were furnished with a wooden bedstead, a flock mattress, two blankets, a rug, table stool and a pewter 'utensil' or chamber pot. The ten felons' cells were unheated, and furnished to hold two prisoners, containing two iron bedsteads on blocks, each with a straw mattress, two blankets, a rug and a 'utensil.' The ten cells in the House of

Correction were each intended to house one inmate, and were furnished to the same standard as the felons' cells. The day rooms each had a ten foot table and two benches, all fixed to the floor. The felons' day room, in later years at least, had the grim legend 'Remember, your sins will find you out' painted on the wall. The prisoners were allowed to use the day rooms, subject to good behaviour, between 7a.m. and 7p.m. in summer and between 8a.m. and 7p.m. in winter. Unlike the old gaol, the three categories of prisoner were segregated, as were the sexes, female inmates being housed in the first-floor cells, using one of the sick rooms as a day room after 1823, with one of the 'airing yards' being reserved for their exclusive use.

Convicted prisoners wore 'party coloured' uniforms. Male prisoners were issued with a jacket, trousers, shoes, two shirts and two pairs of stockings, while female prisoners were issued with a dress, a shift, shoes and two pairs of stockings. Every effort was made to ensure that the prisoners were kept fully occupied. Prisoners sentenced to hard labour broke stones between 9a.m. and 1 p.m. and between 2p.m. and 5p.m. and were each expected to break a ton of stone daily. Female prisoners worked in the kitchen or in the laundry. The routine included cleaning their cells each morning and whitewashing the premises every six months.

Initially the prisoners' diet was little better than in the old gaol, $1\frac{1}{2}$lbs. of bread per day, but in 1828, following a petition from the prisoners, a more substantial and varied diet was introduced:

Monday and Tuesday: Soup, 1lb. of bread, 2lbs. of potatoes, and salt.
Wednesday and Friday: Herring, 1lb. of bread, 2lbs. of potatoes, and salt.
Thursday and Saturday: 1lb. of bread, 2lbs. of potatoes, and salt.
Sunday: Meat, 1lb. of bread, 2lbs. of potatoes, and salt.

In 1848, after two prisoners were found to be suffering from scurvy, the diet was again revised to include gruel, milk, cheese and oatmeal, with quantities of food increasing with the length of time the prisoner had been confined in the gaol.

During the 1820s the number of prisoners in the gaol was much higher than in the closing decades of the eighteenth century and since legislation had reduced significantly the number of debtors liable to imprisonment, this probably reflects the increasing social tension of the period. Even so, the data of Figure 20, based on incomplete runs of duplicate weekly returns submitted to the Home Office, suggests that the gaol was rarely more than half full.

Year	Av. no. of prisoners	Max. no. of prisoners
1824	11	17
1825	11	20
1826	7	11
1827	8	12
1828	8	12
1829	5	8

Fig. 22: Weekly average and maximum number of prisoners held in Radnor County gaol, 1824-29
(Source: Radnor Quarter Sessions Records)

The new premises brought little improvement initially as far as security was concerned, for escape attempts were frequent in the 1820s. In 1824 six felons tried to escape by breaking through the wall of their day room, but were foiled by the gaoler, the subsequent inquiry finding that the mortar in the wall resembled ash in its consistency, enabling the stones to be removed with ease. In April 1835 six felons, including Peter Chandler, the son of Sarah Chandler, overpowered the gaoler, took his weapons and broke out. Two visiting magistrates, James Barnes and John Whittaker, happened to arrive at the gaol on horseback at that moment, and Barnes, with the help of some townspeople secured the two ringleaders, while the other prisoners made for the woods beyond Letchmoor Lane. Whittaker forded the Lugg and with the help of Mr Bodenham of Letchmoor Farm and his labourers cut off their escape, rounded them up and returned them to the gaol. In May 1828 two prisoners tried to escape over the wall while the gaoler and his assistant were at the May Fair, but were foiled by the gaoler's mother in law, armed with a blunderbuss. In June 1829 two prisoners escaped by breaking through the roof of a day room, only to be recaptured, and in July 1829 a further escape attempt was reported by the gaoler.

With such a record, the authorities became very sensitive on the subject of escapes, and even a casual threat to attempt an escape was sufficient to earn a prisoner a lengthy spell in irons. The supervising magistrates were authorised by the bench to take any measures they deemed necessary to improve security, but they had few suggestions beyond placing loose bricks on top of the walls surrounding the felons' yard. After 1829 there seem to have been few escape attempts, possibly because the newly appointed gaoler, William Paytoe, was an ex-prizefighter who, under the pseudonym 'Young Broome', had reputedly fought Tom King, the Champion of All England, and certainly had a formidable local reputation.

Until the 1850s the gaol was wholly controlled by the local Bench which delegated authority to a committee of five visiting magistrates, who met monthly to inspect the gaol, examine the journals and reports of the gaoler, chaplain and surgeon, audit the accounts, and interview and punish prisoners who had broken regulations. The Bench also appointed the gaoler at a salary of £65 and later £80 per annum. It was specified that he should be a married man, preferably without children, but if this was not the case, his children were to reside outside the gaol. The gaoler's accommodation at the gaol was to be furnished by the county in order to avoid any damage or loss to the apartments on the change of gaoler. The gaoler's wife, later given the title of matron, was to supervise the female prisoners, a role that was unpaid at first, but in 1841 with a salary of £8, later increased to £12 per annum. In 1841 the gaoler was given the title of governor, but his salary remained unchanged until 1861 when it was increased to £100 per annum. At first turnkeys were only appointed to assist the gaoler on a temporary basis, when the gaol was unusually full, or if the gaoler was absent, as in 1822, prior to the first and last execution at the gaol, when the gaoler was away searching for a hangman. From 1848 a turnkey was employed on a permanent basis at a wage of 11s. per week. The post does not seem to have been an attractive one for in spite of wage increases, one turnkey followed another in rapid succession. In 1852 no fewer than three men occupied the post and in the following years the post was often filled on a temporary basis, and sometimes on a part-time basis.

On the opening of the new gaol the existing gaoler, John Evans, who had been briefly dismissed following Sarah Chandler's escape, was confirmed in office. He was succeeded in 1828 by his nephew, the ex-prizefighter, William Paytoe, who was succeeded by his son Thomas in 1844. By 1847 the administration of the gaol was the subject of some in-fighting amongst the magistracy and after Thomas Paytoe's death at the end of 1847 the divisions came into the open. Early in 1848 the sheriff, Henry Miles, appointed William Went as gaoler against the wishes of the majority of the county magistrates, who appointed their candidate, Henry Verdon, the former superintendent constable of Knighton, as keeper of the house of correction at a salary equivalent to that of the gaoler. Went only lasted a few months before being dismissed for charging a prisoner 5s. for the use of a bed and was succeeded by Verdon. The dispute over the gaolership seems to have had political overtones for Went's cause was championed by the Tory *Hereford Journal*, while the Whig *Hereford Times* attacked him fiercely. Verdon held the post until 1870, though frequently in breach of the regulation that the gaoler should have no interest in any contract for the supply of goods to the prison, since his son, also Henry Verdon, secured contracts at various times to supply the gaol with potatoes, medicine, stationery and to provide photographs of the inmates for prison records. His successor, Thomas Calloway, had previously been the chief warden at Brecon gaol. When Calloway died in 1877, it was clearly only a matter of time before the Home Office closed the gaol and William Seally, a former chief warder at Dartmoor and head of the prison department of Trinidad and Tobago, was appointed governor on a temporary basis.

The fabric of the gaol had never been satisfactory, in particular, many of the rooms were damp as, it was alleged, the roof tiles had not been laid properly, and there were no coping stones on the walls. With increasing claims on the county's limited resources, expenditure on maintenance was minimal, and by 1849 the gaol was described as one of the worst in Wales. With central government exercising increasing supervision over prison standards, in 1857 £168 was spent on up-grading the gaol to ensure its future. The Prisons Act of 1865 imposed a further burden on the county, for if the gaol was to continue, additional staff would be required, a crank or treadmill installed for prisoners sentenced to hard labour, and the interior of the gaol remodelled to provide larger cells, each ventilated, heated and lit, and a bell system installed. In addition the roof needed replacing and the drainage system and water supply improved.

J.F. Perry, the prison inspector, calculated the capital cost of all this at £2,000, with running costs increasing by £300 to £820 per annum. In view of the fact that the average number of prisoners in the gaol over the last five years had been thirteen, and that Radnorshire's prisoners could be accommodated at Hereford County Gaol at a cost of 10s. per week per prisoner, he recommended the closure of the gaol.

Though two prominent Presteigne residents, Cecil Parsons and William Stephens, believed that a more modest expenditure could bring the gaol up to the required standard, the Home Office was adamant and in order to retain the gaol and thus assuage local pride, £2,235 was spent on an additional exercise yard, a crankhouse and upgrading the cells. Even so, the Home Office was not satisfied, for the new cells were still far below the minimum acceptable size. Moreover, the number of prisoners in the gaol in the 1870s never approached the anticipated daily average of thirteen, reaching only 8 in 1872, 5 in 1873, 9 in 1874, 8 in 1875 and 9 in 1876. Thus instead of an anticipated average annual cost of less than £54, the

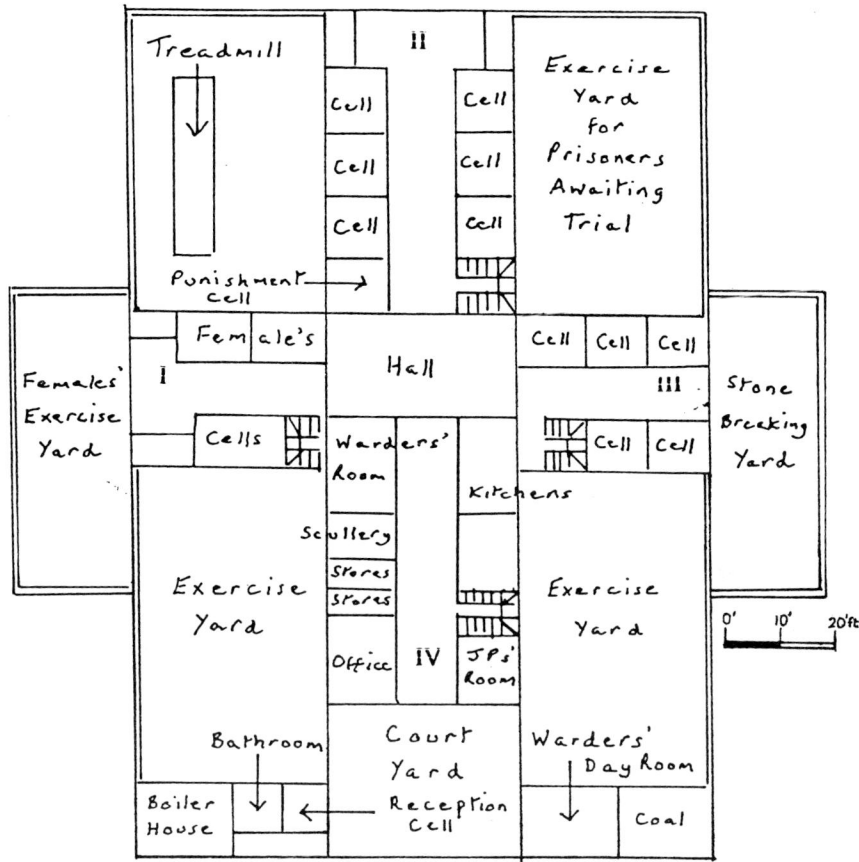

Fig. 23: The ground floor plan of the remodelled County Gaol, 1869. On the first floor, above Wing I were 3 debtors' cells; over Wing II were 7 prisoners' cells; over Wing III were 5 prisoners' cells, over Wing IV were the governor's quarters, over the hall lay the chapel and above the reception area was the infirmary (Source: Quarter Sessions Records)

annual average cost per prisoner 1873-75 stood at rather more than £81, exclusive of interest charges.

As the county failed to secure contracts to house prisoners from other prisons at a fixed weekly charge, the county gaol was clearly not a viable proposition, and with the passing of the Prisons Act in 1877, its future was uncertain. Even so the county authorities, urged on by the town, made every effort to retain it, for they feared that the loss of the gaol would soon be followed by the loss of the Assizes. However they had to

Radnor County Gaol c.1880
For a few years after its closure the old gaol served
as the town's police station

bow to the inevitable, for on 1 April 1878, on the first possible day he could do so, the Home Secretary closed the gaol, the prisoners being transferred to Hereford County Gaol. The blow was softened by the closure of other county gaols in Wales, at Beaumaris, Cardigan, Mold, Montgomery, Haverfordwest and Dolgellau, and by the closure of Hereford City Gaol. But even so, it was the first stage in the erosion of Presteigne's claim to be the county town and seat of government for Radnorshire.

CHAPTER VII

High Victorian Presteigne

For much of the third quarter of the century Presteigne enjoyed a spell of prosperity, but this rapidly faded with the onset of the agricultural depression in the 1870s, whilst improvements in communications, in particular the coming of the railways, ended the relative isolation of its hinterland which, to an extent, had sheltered the town from competition. With its trade declining and its industrial base almost completely destroyed, the town also lost its function as the seat of local government for the county. Within Radnorshire the centre of gravity was shifting from the eastern margins as improved communications and an inflow of capital led to the development of Llandrindod Wells as a spa town, and the gradual abandonment of subsistence farming in the heartland of the county. Inevitably the transfer in economic power was accompanied by a shift in political influence and by the end of the century Presteigne had lost many of its local government functions to Llandrindod Wells. Even so it remained the seat of justice for the county and retained its status as the county town, though this was increasingly difficult to justify as the town declined.

The Mid-Century Recovery
In the later 1840s Presteigne staged yet another modest recovery which lingered on, in an attenuated form, into the later 1870s. Its beginning was marked by sharp increases in the size of the crowds at the town's two most popular events, the May Fair and Warden's Wake, in the 1840s and 1850s. The population of the town rose steadily after 1841, to peak in 1871 at 1713, a figure not to be reached again until the closing decade of

the twentieth century. The town's housing stock also grew over the same period, reaching a total of 389 houses in 1881, by which time the recovery was grinding to a halt and thirty-five houses, 9%, of the total were unoccupied.

The town's recovery was closely associated with the change in the fortunes of the local farming industry in the 1850s and 1860s, which saw the population of the surrounding rural area, Discoed, Rodd, Nash, Little Brampton, Stapleton, Willey and Combe rise by 13.4% between 1851 and 1861. Even in 1871, when farming was once more facing problems, the population of this area was still 11.5% above the 1851 figure. The town's recovery was based on the re-assertion of its traditional roles as market town, service centre and processing centre for the products of its hinterland. In addition, the town's businesses may also have gained from the burst of railway construction in the area, firstly the Leominster-Kington line which opened in 1856, the Knighton-Llandrindod line completed in 1865, and finally the spur from the Kington line at Titley Junction to Presteigne which opened in 1875.

One stratagem adopted to maintain and possibly increase the volume of trade in the town was to increase the number of fairs or special markets held during the year. At the opening of the century the town had two fairs, both of which had their origins in its original market charter and were regranted in 1482: Warden's Wake on 20 June, at first a pleasure and livestock fair; and St Andrew's Fair, held originally on 30 November, but after the change from the Julian to the Gregorian calendar in 1752 and the subsequent eleven day adjustment, on 11 December. In 1809 a pleasure, hiring and livestock fair on 9 May was added, and in 1812 and 1819 respectively, the Candlemas Fair on 8 February and the Michaelmas Fair on 13 October were introduced, both cattle and horse fairs. The mid-century recovery saw the introduction of more fairs. In 1838 the Michaelmas fair became a two day event with 12 October reserved for the sale of sheep, and during the the 1850s two other fairs were added, that of 13 August in 1850 and the April Fair, held on the first Monday in the month, in 1857.

The third quarter of the century saw a revival of optimism in the town and a new entrepreneurial spirit which led to the formation of new businesses and the expansion in the scale of operations of existing concerns. Thus the period 1840-80 saw the establishment of the spittletree (spade handle) factory at the Barley Mow, which built up a thriving trade with the metalworks of the Black Country; a nail-making works at the rear of Newell's ironmonger's shop on Broad Street; a brickworks near Radnor

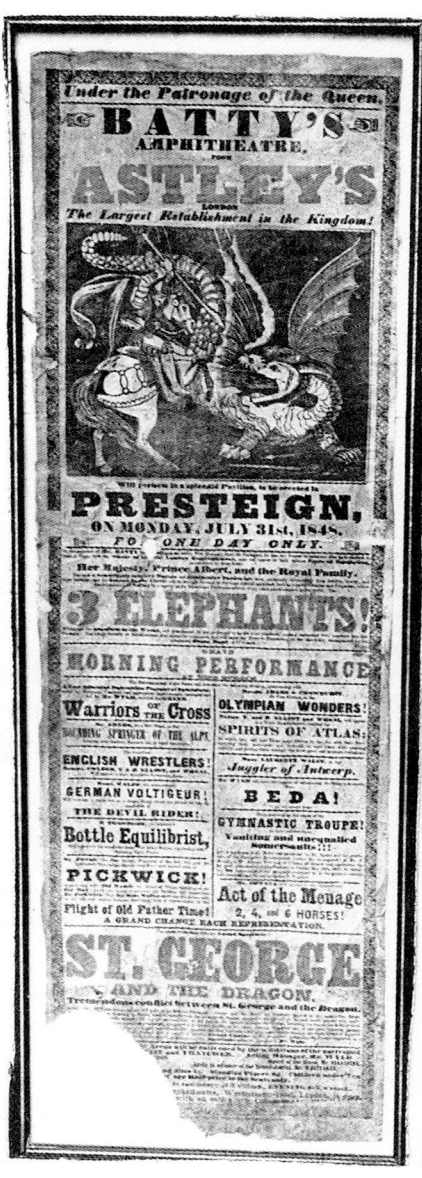

*The circus comes to town
31 July 1848*

Farm; the opening of the Capital Stores on High Street; several straw hat manufactures at the rear of the High Street, Hereford Street and possibly on Harper's Lane; and an extensive cooperage at Green End. The malt houses at the Barley Mow, Hereford Street and Back Lane seem to have increased their scale of operations, as did the tannery near Lugg Bridge, for whereas it possessed thirty-three tanning and curing pits in 1824, by 1878 these had increased to 124. The scale of activities in the timber yard in Broad Street had also increased, to the point that in 1863 a correspondent in the *Hereford Times* of 25 April complained bitterly of 'trucks and timber carriages continuously left under the churchyard wall night and day.'

Facilities in the town were also improved. In 1839 the street had been lit by oil lamps, though this does not seem to have lasted long for in 1851 Presteigne's streets were said to have been in total darkness. However, following the opening of the town's gas works in 1857, gas lighting was introduced in 1859. Another improvement came in 1870 with the introduction of the telegraph system. Care was also taken to maintain the town's dual role as the seat of justice and administrative centre of the county. Proposals to transfer the Assizes to Hereford were fought off every decade or so, whilst the lodgings were improved to counter the complaints of the

The waterwheel of the bark mill at the Tanhouse

judges, such as those of 1855 and 1867. Gas lighting was installed in 1860 (at first only in the kitchen and the servants' hall), and central heating in 1871. In 1857, when the Radnorshire Constabulary was formed, the Shire Hall became the police headquarters of the county, partly at least because of its proximity to the border, as the post of chief constable was initially a joint appointment with Herefordshire.

The town also gained from the revival of the militia in 1852 in the form of the Royal Radnor Rifles, for Presteigne became the corps' headquarters with the permanent staff based at Garrison House, purchased by the county in 1855. The troops' twenty-six days annual training took place near the town, with the parade ground first at Broadheath and later in a field over the Lugg Bridge, and the rifle range at the Butts, to the south-west of the Burgage. The presence of the Radnor Rifles in the town not only enhanced its status, but also produced additional business, later estimated to be worth £2,000 a year to the town.

Much of the credit for the recovery must go to the drive and enterprise of four men: John Weaver, Thomas Lewis, Cecil Parsons and Sir Richard Green Price. Weaver, the landlord of the Barley Mow, in addition to his inn, had extended the scale of his malting business, established the spittletree factory, and was instrumental in expanding the Nash limeworks and quarry in conjunction with his partner, James Mackenzie of Hill

Farm. The scale of his activities meant that he employed nearly forty workers, housing them in the rows of brick cottages built on the site of derelict houses next to the Barley Mow and on what became known as Gas House Row opposite. He died in 1882 at the age of 49, his obituary in the *Hereford Times* of 4 November commenting, '... if his place is not taken by some competent successor, there will be a loss in the town which will be felt keenly both by the working classes and trade generally.'

Thomas Lewis, whose family had founded a timber business in Hereford Street and the Radnor Farm brick works, was also a substantial employer, building up the tannery and timber businesses in Broad Street. He acquired several properties, including the Old Rectory and Moor Farm. But he subsequently over-extended his activities and was declared bankrupt in 1878, though he later paid his creditors in full.

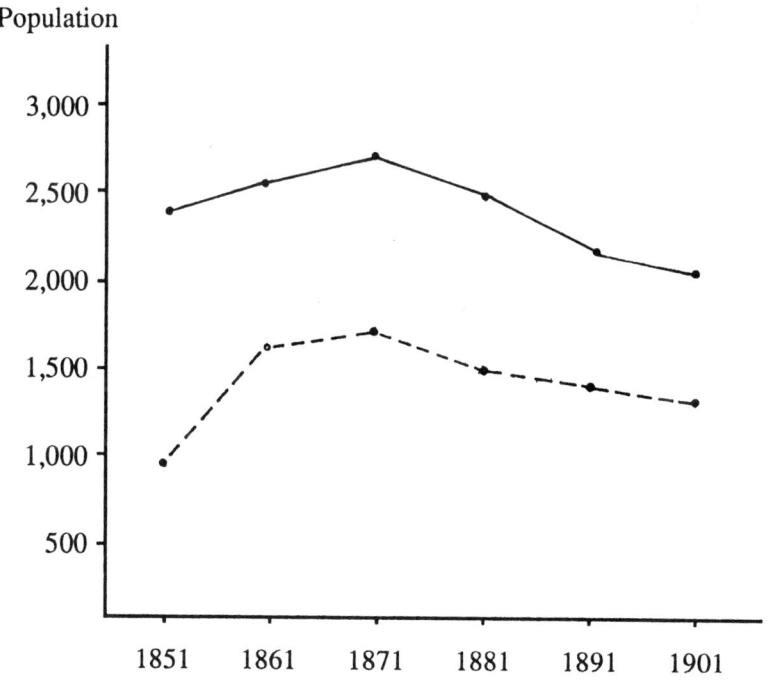

Fig. 24: The Population of Presteigne and the surrounding area
------ *Town Population* ——— *Town and surrounding area Population*
Surrounding area: Norton, Discoed, Rodd, Nash and Little Brampton, Willey, Stapleton and Combe
(Source: Printed census data, 1851-1901)

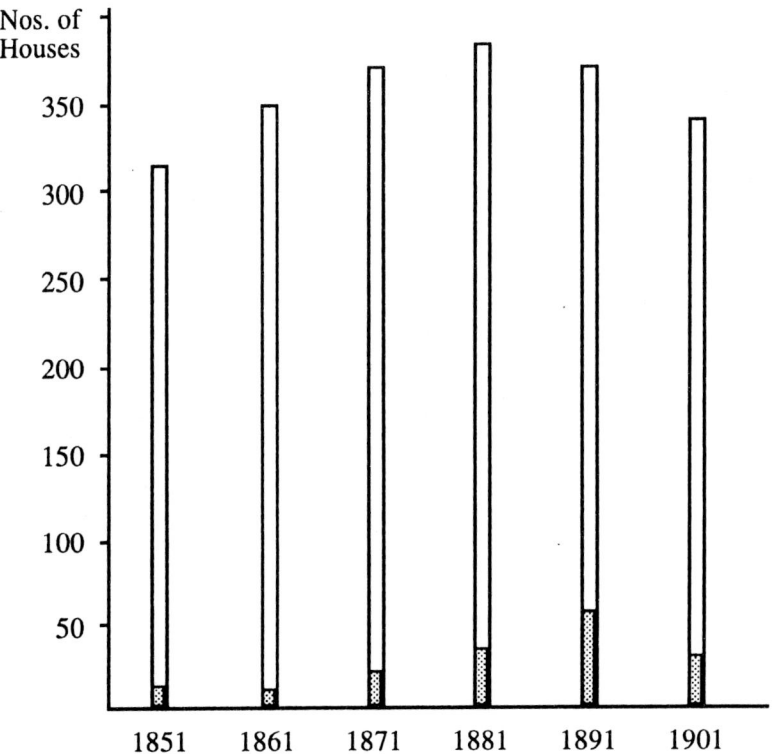

Fig. 25: Presteigne's Housing Stock, 1891-1901
▨ *Unoccupied houses*
(Source: Printed census data, 1851-1901)

In 1837 the formidable Cecil Parsons, probably with the backing of his distant kinsman Walter Wilkins, established the Radnorshire Bank in premises in Hereford Street, on the site now occupied by Lloyd's Bank. Until the later 1870s, when the Midland Bank opened a branch in Broad Street, Parsons' bank was the most important source of credit for the businesses of the town. Given his intimate local knowledge, his shrewd intellect and forceful personality, the mid-century recovery probably owed much to his business acumen. In the closing years of his life he was county treasurer, so he and another Presteigne solicitor, William Stephens, who was clerk to the peace, were important links between the town and the county establishment. Parsons died in 1876 at the age of 90.

Richard Green, as he was originally known, was a Knighton solicitor who had played an important part in modernising that town and in the

Norton Manor c.1920, the seat of Richard Price, Sir Richard Green Price and Sir Powlett Milbank

construction of the Central Wales line between Craven Arms and Llandovery. He had inherited the Norton Manor estate from his uncle, Richard Price, in 1861, assuming the additional surname of Price by royal licence. On moving to Norton he transformed the village; he was largely responsible for the enclosure of 720 acres of farmland, much of it open field arable; he also built Norton vicarage and the Gables for members of his family, arranged for the restoration of Norton Church by Sir Gilbert Scott, and built a new school and houses for his estate workers in the village. He also played an important part in overhauling Presteigne's commercial infrastructure, taking a leading role in the formation of the company which built the Assembly Rooms and Market Hall in 1865 and in promoting the Presteigne-Titley Junction line in the early 1870s.

Richard Green Price was elected as MP for Radnor Boroughs in 1863 initially as a 'Liberal Conservative', a stance which did not meet with the approval of the *Hereford Times*. He held the seat for the Liberals until 1869 when he made way for Lord Hartington. He was created a baronet in the 1874 dissolution Honours List. After being narrowly defeated for the county seat in the election of that year, he won it for the Liberals in 1880. He declined to stand in 1885, and stood reluctantly in 1886, when he narrowly lost, probably on the issue of Irish Home Rule. He was able to use his influence as MP to improve the town's postal services. In his dealings with the town he was always sensitive to the position of the

Broad Street in the late nineteenth century showing the Shire Hall and Market Hall on the left, by an unknown artist

Jones Brydges as lords of the manor, and was careful to yield precedence to them where necessary. Thus it was Lady Brydges who laid the foundation stone of the Assembly Rooms in 1863.

The construction of the Market Hall and Assembly Rooms was the most ambitious project undertaken by the town in the period and best illustrates the renewed optimism of the townspeople. The town was very aware of its lack of market facilities and, by the 1850s, of its lack of social facilities. Thus in 1856, when Mrs Sophia Evans provided the town with a public library and reading room, the local correspondent of the *Hereford Times* remarked: 'We have now but one wish unsatisfied, and that is to see a public building in the town able to afford accommodation at lectures, concerts or any other social gatherings.'

In 1862 the Presteigne Market Hall and Public Room Company was set up under the chairmanship of Richard Green Price, with a share capital of £1,500. The site, that of the old post office, was purchased for £400 and the new building, designed by Thomas Nicholson, the Hereford architect responsible for many of the buildings in the growing Llandrindod Wells, was completed at a cost of £1,300. However, the company had been unable to to raise all its capital by the sale of shares and a mortgage of £500 was raised from Elizabeth Abley on the security of the building by the trustees Captain James Beavan, John Lewis and William Price. The open arcade area of the ground floor served as a market hall on Wednesdays and fair days, while the Assembly Rooms above, capable of holding 250 people, served as a venue for many of the town's social and cultural functions. The venture was at first successful and employed a manager to supervise the lettings, but the initial enthusiasm soon faded and by 1880 it was failing to pay its way.

The construction of the Kington-Leominster and the Craven Arms-Llandovery railway lines had enabled Presteigne's rivals to capture parts of its hinterland. To the south, Titley and the surrounding area was even more firmly within Kington's sphere of influence, while to the west, Llangunllo and the upper Lugg valley had been captured by Knighton. At the dinner held in November 1865 to celebrate the opening of the Market Hall, Richard Green Price, who, with his son Dansey, held many directorships in local railway companies, was put under some pressure over the possibility of a line to Presteigne. At least two such schemes had already foundered; that of 1859, which proposed a line from Presteigne along the Lugg valley and then on to Penybont, and a scheme of 1863 which had envisaged a line from Marston on the Kington-Eardisley line via Presteigne to connect with the Knighton-Llandrindod line.

Given the influence of the Green Prices in local railway circles, it was only a matter of time before Presteigne got its line, though few would have envisaged that it would have taken four Acts of Parliament before it was attained. In the main, the delay stemmed from bitter rivalry between the Kington-Eardisley and the Kington-Leominster companies and their respective backers. In 1871 the Kington and Leominster company obtained an Act authorising the construction of a line from a point near Titley station on the Kington-Leominster line to Presteigne with a terminus near the county gaol, a distance of 5 miles 22 chains, though later the line was extended to locate the station near the Burgage, nearer the centre of the town. The cost was estimated at £40,000 and the GWR guaranteed interest payments in return for an agreement that it should operate the line and receive 60% of gross receipts.

The contract to construct the line was awarded to a London firm, Perry and Co., and the first sod was cut at Presteigne on 24 January 1872 by a daughter of Richard Green Price. The event was celebrated by a lunch at the Assembly Rooms and the distribution of bread and meat to the poor. 300 navvies were employed on the construction of the line which involved twenty bridges and many embankments and cuttings, some of them substantial. Matters were not helped by the collapse of the bridge at

Presteigne railway station c.1880

Forge Crossing in 1874, for according to Dansey Green Price, the contractors refused to proceed unless they were paid an additional £5,000. All the bridges on the line were redesigned and strengthened to such effect that when the line was inspected in September 1875, the inspector commented that the bridges had been made unnecessarily strong. The final cost of the line was £50,750 and Dansey Green Price later claimed that he and his father had borne the entire cost. This had been the informal arrangement with the Kington and Leominster company, but their subsequent dispute with the company suggests that this claim was an exaggeration. Even so, it is clear that the Green Prices had borne the great bulk of the financial burden.

The line opened on 9 September 1875 with the usual ceremonies; the inaugural train bringing distinguished guests, processions complete with a band, the town's three friendly societies with their banners and the Sunday School scholars of the town's churches, the distribution of bread, meat and coal, and a celebratory lunch at the Castle Inn. As with the earlier proposals, some saw the line as part of a larger and ambitious scheme linking South Wales and the Midlands with Aberystwyth, but J.B. Sinclair and R.W.D. Fenn view Sir Richard Green Price as much more realistic, seeing the line as a feeder in an essentially local system and thus

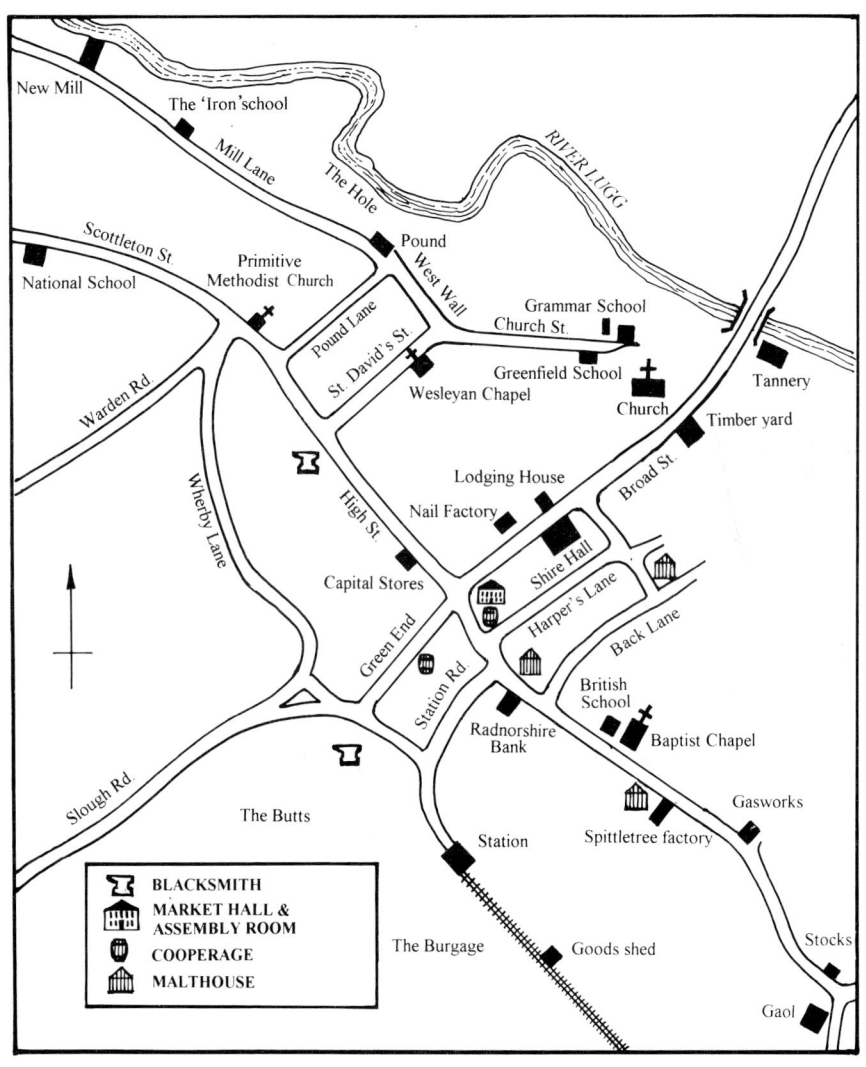

Fig. 26: Presteigne's Mid-Victorian Landscape

serving purely local needs. In his speech at the celebratory lunch Sir Richard certainly concentrated on the immediate local benefits—the reduced price of coal and the improved access to distant markets for the products of the area.

The line facilitated bulk transport and within a few years the Old Radnor Company of Kington and the Field Company and the Radnorshire Company, both of Knighton were established in the town, competing with local firms in the supply of coal, lime, animal feedstuffs, fertilisers and seeds. As early as 1882 some in the town had come to realise that the railway was a mixed blessing as far as the town's businesses were concerned also opening them up to wider competition. By the turn of the century an auction yard had been established close to the goods shed where the weekly cattle market was held, while the field beyond Appletree Orchard became the venue for the livestock fairs, previously held in the streets of the town.

Farming Patterns in the Presteigne Area, 1850-1914

The tithe commutation schedule of 1845 shows that in the mid-nineteenth century arable farming was still an important element in the local farming pattern. It seems likely that the area was still largely self-sufficient in bread corn, while the demands of the local malting industry encouraged the maintenance of a substantial acreage under barley. The greater emphasis on arable in the Presteigne township probably reflects its greater proportion of land under 500 feet compared to the parish as a whole.

	% Arable	% Grassland	% Woodland	% Common
Presteigne parish	33.3	47.8	11.7	7.2
Presteigne township	39.5	43.2	10.6	6.7

Fig. 27: Land utilisation in the Presteigne area, 1845
(Source: Parish Tithe Commutation Schedule)

The increase in the population of the rural area around Presteigne between 1851 and 1871 suggests that the local farming industry shared in the prosperity of the 'Golden Age of British Farming', though supporting evidence is largely anecdotal. Close proximity to the agricultural lime of Nash coupled with extensive land drainage probably led to increased yields and heavier stocking levels, while mechanisation tended to increase productivity and widen profit margins in the technically efficient mixed farming which predominated in the lowland parts of the parish. However, the period of prosperity barely lasted two decades; outbreaks of sheep scab and foot-and-mouth epidemics in the 1860s and 1870s led to serious, if shortlived, difficulties for pastoral farming, while the arable sector, faced with increasing competition from overseas producers as a result of improvements in communications, found grain prices falling to levels at which it could not compete. Wheat prices fell by 51% between 1871-75 and 1894-98, whilst the livestock sector saw price falls of 25% in the same period, with wool prices falling by 50%.

One response to the crisis was to cut costs by shedding labour and reducing wage levels. At Willey and Lower Kinsham in 1871, the fall in population in the previous decade was ascribed to migration in search of work. At Brilley, above Kington, the fall in population in the same period was attributed to migration to South Wales 'where higher wages can be obtained.' Tenant farmers gained some relief with rent abatements, such as that of 10% negotiated by the tenants of the Boultibrooke estate in 1882. However, such measures were short-term expedients and the long-term solution was to adjust local farming patterns to meet the new situation.

Some indication of such adjustments can be gained from an analysis of the parish agricultural returns to the Board of Agriculture. Since these were voluntary, they are inevitably incomplete, but by using mid-decade three year averages to minimise random fluctuations, general trends in land utilisation and cropping and stocking patterns can be established. There was a marked shift from arable to pasture, with the proportion of arable land reported falling from 37% in the mid 1870s to 24% in 1905-07, with permanent grassland rising from 62% to 74% in the same period. (This actually overstates the proportion of arable, since in the earlier decades the rough grazing went unreported and is thus excluded from the analysis.) The shift from arable was accompanied by a sustained shedding of labour, for between 1871 and 1901 the population of the rural areas surrounding Presteigne fell by 22.6%.

Within the shrinking arable acreage there were marked shifts in cropping patterns. While the proportions devoted to barley, root crops and clover and temporary leys remained relatively stable, there was a dramatic change from wheat cultivation to that of oats, with the proportion of arable land under wheat falling from 22% in the mid 1870s to 6% in 1905-07, while the proportion devoted to oats rose from 11% to 23% in the same period. The shift from wheat reflects the increased competition from cheap imported supplies, while the greater emphasis on oats reflects the growing importance of pastoral farming in the locality and the desire to cut costs by relying to a greater extent on farm produced animal feedstuffs. The continuing emphasis on barley cultivation, which continued to occupy 15 to 20% of the arable acreage, is more difficult to explain since by the 1890s the local malting industry had disappeared. Possibly it was a cash crop, destined to supply large scale malt producers in the Midlands and South Wales, alternatively it may have been cultivated to provide animal feedstuffs.

Pastoral farming had always played an important role in the local economy and by the beginning of the nineteenth century, according to Clark and Davies, the Hereford breed of cattle was locally predominant. The emergence of prominent Hereford breeders in the area in the mid-nineteenth century: James and Thomas Rea at Monaughty, William Tudge at the Great House, Llangunllo, John Rogers of Pilleth, Aaron Rogers at the Rodd and Benjamin Rogers at Doluggan and then at The Grove, Pembridge, suggests that the general quality of the local livestock, at least in terms of potential, must have been high, for all used locally bred Herefords in addition to stock from more famous strains in their breeding programmes. As a result of their efforts local Hereford herds gained a worldwide reputation and James Macdonald and James Sinclair in their *History of Hereford Cattle* describe Aaron Rogers' 'Gratefull' and 'Sir Archibald' as 'two of the finest show bulls ever seen'. The foot-and-mouth epidemics of 1865-67 and 1870-76 undoubtedly hit local farming hard, for in Radnorshire there were 186 cases reported in the first quarter of 1870, 324 in the third quarter of 1872 and 344 cases in 1873. The movement of cattle was seriously restricted and local markets ceased to function during both epidemics, though the transport of unaffected beasts to slaughterhouses via the railway was permitted. Again, only diseased animals were slaughtered, rather than affected herds, and by 1866 the Presteigne Mutual Cattle Insurance Company had been formed to minimise the financial impact of the epidemic on its members. The society employed its own butcher and if a member's livestock were infected, he slaughtered the entire herd, burying the infected carcasses, while those of the uninfected beasts were sent off to the meat markets, thus giving the farmers some return.

The incidence of disease in both sheep and cattle makes it difficult to interpret trends in pastoral farming from the returns since the figures relating to the 1870s may be abnormally low. Between the 1870s and 1905-07 stocking levels may have fallen, since though the totals of both sheep and cattle reported increased, the increase was not in proportion to the increase in the permanent grass acreage, which suggests a greater emphasis on quality or a shift towards a low cost, more extensive type of farming. The trend in cattle rearing seems to have been towards marketing stock at a younger age, thus the proportion of beasts under two years increased steadily throughout the period, from 32% of the total reported herd in the 1870s to 46% in 1905-07. This would have the effect of increasing the farmers' cash flow and also reflected the growing demand for smaller and leaner joints on the part of consumers. The trend in sheep farming is less clear, partly no doubt because the sheep rearing regimes in the upland and lowland areas of the civil parish would differ, a difference obscured in the aggregated return of flocks. There would seem to have been a growing emphasis on the production of wethers rather than lambs at the turn of the century, since the proportion of sheep over one year, other than breeding ewes, rose from 21% in 1895-97 to 30% in 1905-07. The demand in the meat trade was for mutton rather than lamb, and by keeping wethers for three to four years the farmer could maximise his income from wool sales while still satisfying the demands of the meat trade.

Matters Religious
Some indication of the religious affiliations of the townspeople and of the extent of church attendance is afforded by the religious census of 1851. Church attendance, at 75%, was higher than the average of 71% for small towns and rural areas as a whole in England and Wales. Unlike Wales as a whole, the established Church commanded the allegiance of the majority of worshippers in the town—43% compared with the 20.5% of the Primitive Methodists, the 8.3% of the Baptists and the 2.8% of the Wesleyans. This analysis is based on two assumptions; that attendances at the churches on the day of the census were no higher than usual, and that no-one attended more than one service on that day. Since neither assumption is entirely realistic, it seems likely that the analysis overstates the level of church attendance in general and, in particular, the level of support enjoyed by the Primitive Methodists, the most vigorous and evangelistic of the non-conformist churches, and which had both the largest number of Sunday School scholars, and placed the greatest emphasis upon regular church attendance.

W.H. Howse suggests that the parish church was not always well served by its rectors in the second half of the nineteenth century. Reverend Oliver Ormerod, rector between 1841 and 1880 obtained a licence of non-residence in 1847 and was absent from the parish in the

1850s and for long periods in the early 1870s. However, some of these absences may well have been occasioned by ill health, for in 1874, when he returned to the parish the local press announced him to be 'rehabilitated in health.' His successor, Reverend A.W. West, rector between 1880 and 1893, was also chancellor of Kildare Cathedral for at least part of his incumbency, which led to his periodic absence from the parish. Towards the end of his incumbency his effectiveness was hampered by age and infirmity. Both men also seem to have always been in some financial difficulty, although this was not exceptional, for in his evidence to the Commission of Inquiry on the State of Education in Wales in 1847, the curate of Presteigne remarked that 'It is proverbial for the rector to be in difficulty', concluding, 'an active, religious rector might make Presteigne a pattern instead of a by-word in the diocese.' In his diary, Francis Kilvert tells how Ormerod used to place his pocket knife on the offertory plate, saying that he had no change, while the curate had to sue West in 1888 in order to obtain his stipend.

However, the parish was by no means as neglected as this might suggest, for it was well served by a series of enthusiastic and hardworking curates. Typical of these was Reverend Charles Bowen, curate between 1837 and 1841. He built up the Sunday School, started in 1836, to the point where it rivalled the Primitive Methodist Sunday School in size, and campaigned vigorously, if unsuccessfully, in 1840 for the establishment of a National School in the town, suggesting that such a school could occupy the first floor of the new Market Hall which was being mooted at the time. He was also a thorn in the flesh of the medical officers of the Presteigne Union in his efforts to ensure adequate medical treatment for those on poor relief. He was widely esteemed in the parish and when he left in 1841 he was presented with silver plate at a farewell dinner.

The rectors of the last decade of the century were much more committed than their immediate predecessors. Reverend R.H. Cuthbert, presented to the living by his father-in-law, Reverend Edward Fowle, in 1893, was an enthusiastic High Churchman who re-established the patronal festival and rapidly won the respect of the town. On his death in 1898, the patron initially announced that he was to take the living, but in the end appointed the curate, Reverend H.L. Kewley as rector, a position he was to hold until his death in 1940. An enthusiastic and energetic clergyman, he served the parish and the town well. He was the driving force behind a successful evangelistic campaign at the turn of the century and played a leading part in the musical life of the town, for in the first decade of the twentieth century he revitalised the choral society and the town band. As curate he had played an important part in the founding of St Andrew's Football Club and always took a keen interest in the Jubilee Boys' Club, based in the parish room. His popularity may be judged from the fact that when he and his bride returned from their honeymoon in 1907, they were met at the station by a decorated wagonette and drove to the rectory through streets decorated with flags, bunting and flowers, to the peal of the church bells. He also played an influential role in the civic life of the town as a town councillor and a leading member of the local Conservative party.

Again, the restorations of the fabric of the church in 1854-55 and 1889-91 suggest a real commitment on the part of the parishioners, for such restorations involved considerable expenditure, not only of money, but also of time and energy. The 1854-55 restoration involved the removal of the galleries over the Lady Chapel and the arches of the northern aisle together with the eighteenth century paintings of Aaron, Moses, Time and Death over the northern arcade and the replacement of the old high pews. Mrs Sophia Evans donated the stained glass window of the chancel at this time and that west of the font rather later. According to the *Hereford Times* in 1895, she was also the 'pious old lady' responsible in 1855 for the placing of the fragments of fifteenth century stained glass in the east window of the Lady Chapel. The restoration of 1889-91, supervised by the rural dean, Prebendary C.E. Maddison, during the illness of the rector, stemmed from the bequest of £1,000 by Thomas Pugh in 1887 for the purpose, on condition that work began within two years. The roof, which was very dilapidated, was repaired, the obelisks removed from the tower, the lych gate of 1710 demolished, the 1855 pews replaced by chairs, the present pulpit installed, as was the rood screen, the latter in memory of Sophia Evans and Thomas Pugh. The total cost of this restoration was £5,031. This restoration revealed the early Norman elements in the wall of the northern aisle, whilst a further restoration in 1928-29 uncovered the magnificent medieval timber roof of the chancel and the fragments of medieval wall paintings over the northern arcade.

Of the non-conformist churches, the Wesleyans were the first to establish a footing in the town, *c.*1810, building their church in St David's Street by 1818 at the latest. Quarter Sessions records show that by 1830 the church had sixteen members, though this figure probably underestimates its strength, since it does not include committed adherents who were not full members. Even so, the religious census of 1851 shows it to be the least well supported of the town's churches, though it seems to have attracted a larger following in later decades for in 1870 the building had to be enlarged to accommodate a congregation of 210. The building fell into disuse after the branches of the Methodist Church reunited in 1932, and the building was then used as a storehouse until its demolition in the 1970s.

The Primitive Methodists gained a following in the town in 1820, with their first Presteigne member, Mrs Grace Newell, being admitted in 1821. By 1830, Quarter Sessions records show the 'Ranters' as having sixteen members, though church records show that when their first church was built in Harper's Lane in 1833 membership stood at sixty. By the 1840s, supported by the other non-conformists, the Primitive Methodists had begun to hold evangelical camp meetings on the Warden each year on the Sunday before Warden's Wake. In 1846 the *Hereford Times* reported that 200 children and several hundred adults had processed through the town singing hymns on their way to the Camp Meeting. Such meetings continued to be held on the Warden until at least the 1940s. Week night services were also held in private houses in outlying communities such as Gumma, Discoed and Norton, and also at Willey and Combes Moor before churches were built at those places in 1869 and 1865 respectively. By 1860 the Primitive Methodists had outgrown their Harper's Lane premises which seated 300 and in 1861 a new church was built at a cost of £887 in Scottleton Street and which was said, optimistically, to seat a congregation of 400. A schoolroom was added in 1888 at a cost of £350.

The Baptists were first active in the town in the early 1820s, the first baptisms taking place in the Lugg near the tanyard, which was owned by a sympathiser, Robert Lewis. Services were first held at the home of Thomas Thickens at 52, High Street, and later on the first floor of a storehouse at the rear of Newell's ironmongery business on Broad Street. In 1830, Quarter Sessions records show the Baptists as having eight members, again probably an under-estimate, for when in 1845 a Baptist church was built in Hereford Street, on a site bought from Robert Lewis, it had seating for a congregation of 260. Most of the money was raised through the good offices of Thomas Jones, the manager of the Radnorshire Bank. By 1851 the church had an attendance of at least 130 adults and scholars and clearly attracted a larger following in the next few decades, for in 1885 the church was enlarged and vestries and a school room added. By this date another church had been built at Stansbatch, served by the Presteigne pastor, and weeknight services were being held at Roddhurst, Nash, Dolley Green and Stapleton.

The Baptists shared the evangelical spirit of the Primitive Methodists and the two churches co-operated closely, holding joint revival services from 1859 and temperance meetings which started in 1847. In 1857 they formed Presteigne Temperance Society, which led to the setting up of a Band of Hope the following year, and by 1859 the movement claimed that there were 300 total abstainers in the town and the surrounding rural areas. In the 1880s the two churches were active in sponsoring the Blue Ribbon temperance movement. Both churches were to a degree 'gathered churches' expecting a high degree of commitment from their members and strong views, uncompromisingly held, could lead to internal dissension. On at least two occasions in the second half of the century Baptist pastors left after disagreements with sections of their congregation, while Primitive Methodist church records show that much was expected of its members. In 1842 one member was rebuked 'on the subject of visiting his grandfather on the Sabbath Day, when he ought to be attending to other things', while in 1847 a young woman was informed that 'on the day that she shall be married to that man she shall cease to be a member.' Later a member was disciplined for 'wasting his time in public houses' and for playing dominoes in the Bull. Since the churches saw themselves as competing for the patronage of the uncommitted, there seems to have been little in the way of ecumenical feeling.

Political feeling ran high in the town in the late nineteenth and early twentieth centuries, and with such issues as the Disestablishment of the Welsh Church coming to the fore, the very close identification of leading local non-conformists with the Liberal cause and of Reverend Kewley with Conservatism did not help matters. A measure of interdenominational rancour seems to have survived the First World War, for the proposal to erect a new lych gate to the churchyard as a war memorial foundered on the opposition of some 'not connected with the parish church', to use W.H. Howse's tactful phrase.

Presteigne Schools in the Nineteenth Century
Whatever the shortcomings of the mid-century grammar school, it maintained its close connection with the parish church, for its pupils were still expected to attend service at the church on a Sunday, irrespective of their parents' religious affiliations, much to the chagrin in 1851 of Thomas Jones, the Baptist deacon.

The state of the grammar school for much of the century is best summarised by an extract from James Bryce's report on the school in 1866, published in the report of the Schools Inquiry Commission in 1870. 'It has lain for a long time past in an abject and almost useless state. In 1847 the Welsh Education Commission described it as grossly inefficient, the boys ignorant, the master incompetent, the trustees negligent ... In 1866 it was somewhat yet not greatly better.' Bryce concluded that the school 'differs little from an ordinary National or British school, and where it differs, differs for the worse.'

Robert Phillips, headmaster between 1821 and 1849, was described in 1847 as 'in mind and body utterly unfit for his post' and Reverend Charles Blackburn, headmaster between 1854 and 1869 was, according to W.H. Howse, little better. The trustees, all men of standing, rarely visited the school, which in 1856 was described as 'almost unfit for a stable or cowhouse', while financial administration was also lax. The provision of a new school building in 1860 as a result of a bequest from Edward Lee James, improved matters a little, but in 1870 it could still be reported that 'the management of the school's affairs has been conducted with great remissness for a long time.'

The 1870 report galvanised the trustees into action, more stringent rules were drawn up for the administration of the school and a new, effective headmaster, F.J. Woodward, was appointed. Academic standards improved dramatically and the school roll rose to sixty-six, including thirty boarders, many of whom boarded at Woodward's house, The Vyne. However in 1878 the trustees suddenly dismissed Woodward, in spite of public protests. The reasons for his dismissal are not clear; at that time political feelings in the town were running high, and in one of his notebooks Howse indicates that Woodward was known to have entertained a visiting Primitive Methodist preacher, an action which the trustees probably considered highly inappropriate for the headmaster of what was still considered to be a Church school.

The trustees appointed in Woodward's place Charles Green, according to Howse 'one of the worst headmasters the school ever had', and by 1883 the school roll had dropped to five. Shortly after Green's appointment the old trustees had been replaced by a more broadly based board of governors who acquired Garrison House as the residence of the headmaster and boarders and tightened control of school management. Even so, Green remained as headmaster until 1883, when he was replaced by Reverend Thomas Newbery, described by Howse as 'a good scholar and a strict disciplinarian', under whose leadership the school once more prospered.

The Welsh Intermediate Education Act of 1889, intended to create a national system of education in Wales, supervised by the county councils, had the paradoxical effect of depriving the town of its grammar school from 1894 until 1898, an outcome which caused some disquiet in the town. The new school, built on the site of the old gaol which had been used for a while as the town's police station after the gaol's closure, cost £2,500 and was partly funded by the town which provided £750, £450 of which came from the sale of the old school in Church Street, and the balance raised by public subscription. Its running costs were met by the county council, which appropriated the old Beddoes endowment. The new school began with seventeen pupils, remaining a boys' school until 1902 when twelve girls were admitted. It also had a new headmaster, A.H. Smith, who remained at the school until 1927, since Reverend Newbery did not apply for the post as he did not approve of non-denominational schools. The authorities were well aware that the change in the school's status had not been welcomed by some sections of public opinion and at the formal opening of the new school by the Duke of Devonshire on 15 April 1899, Alderman Coltman Rogers, the chairman of the county governing body, referred to the 'smothered hostility' on the part of some and sought to disarm it by stressing the continuity between the new school and the Beddoes foundation, a theme to which he returned on the school's first Speech Day.

The shortcomings of the grammar school, and the fact that it catered only for boys, meant that there was scope for other schools to function in the town. In the second half of the eighteenth century the eccentric recluse Thomas Legge of Willey had maintained a charity school in the town at his own expense, providing the scholars with clothing and finding apprenticeships for them, while in 1797 at least one other private school was active in the town. By 1818 three other schools were also functioning; a writing school with fifty pupils, thirty of who were paid for by Thomas Beebee of Willey Court, a kinsman of Legge's, and two 'dame's schools' which between them had forty-five pupils. The report of the 1847 Commission into Welsh Education listed three 'private adventure' schools in the town offering little more than reading, writing and arithmetic. The largest was that of Reverend D. Evans, the Baptist pastor, the others being those of Thomas Price, a retired labourer, in St David's Street and of a Mrs Davies in High Street.

These were by no means the only private schools in the town in the mid-nineteenth century, for trade directories show that an Ann Still kept a school in Church Street between 1830 and 1858, while the 1844 directory lists schools kept by Ann Forester in St David's Street and by Annette Laping in Broad Street. Later directories show schools kept by Thomas Threlwall in Broad Street in 1858 and by Letitia Weatherstone in West Wall in 1868.

Other schools in the town with some aspirations to gentility, catered for girls and accepted both day and boarding pupils, offering in their curricula French, music, dancing and deportment. One such school was functioning at Harford House in the 1860s, kept by Miss Blackburn, the sister of the grammar school headmaster; while in the 1880s a similar establishment was to be found at 6, Broad Street, kept by a Miss Georgiana Newark, and in 1885-86 a Miss Wood was running the grandly named Presteigne Ladies' College. All three enjoyed a considerable reputation in their day, though the most established of this type of school in the town was that kept by Miss Elizabeth Hayes in Broad Street between the mid-1860s and the later 1880s. It was still functioning in 1891, though by this time in Hereford Street.

However, the future of such schools was bleak, for within a decade or so of the Welsh Intermediate Education Act of 1889 girls were admitted to the county secondary or intermediate schools, first at Llandrindod and then at Presteigne where the first twelve girls were admitted in September 1902. Such a decision was not taken by the county authorities without some pressure from the leaders of the local community, notably Lady Brydges, Mrs Corbett, Mrs Debenham, Reverend Kewley and Mr W.A. Pugh. The £400 capital costs of the alterations to the school to accommodate thirty girls were met locally, the local steering group having to provide the county authorities with forty local guarantors before they would embark upon the scheme.

Two free schools were established in the town in the mid-nineteenth century, both with a Church background. Greenfield, (now the church hall), was built and endowed as a girls' school in 1850 by Mrs Sophia Evans in memory of her husband. It could accommodate sixty pupils and functioned until 1929. The 'Iron School' off Mill Lane, was built in 1865 and maintained by Lady Brydges. It was a mixed school which could take sixty pupils and was initially described as a Church School. After the establishment of the National School it functioned as an infants school until its closure in 1892.

An attempt had been made by the Church to establish a National School in the town in 1835-36, but it proved impossible to raise sufficient funds and subscriptions were returned to the donors. The proposal was revived in 1840 but came to nothing. Energetic curates established a Night School in 1856 and a Ragged School in 1863 catering for children of the poor, from which Lady Brydges' school developed. In 1868, largely through the initiative of the Baptists, a British School was built in Hereford Street, on a site that had been acquired in 1863, with accommodation for 100 pupils.

The 'Iron School' after its removal from Mill Lane to Boutlibrooke

This appears to have stung the Church into action: Sir Harford James Jones Brydges donated a site on Scottleton Street and a National School to accommodate 127 pupils was built in 1869, and extended in 1892 to cater for infants.

Though for much of the century there had been no shortage of schools in the town offering a basic elementary education, there was still sufficient illiteracy to warrant the Working Men's Club, founded in 1886, holding literacy classes for several years after its inception. That this should be so, provides an insight into the attitude towards education on the part of the poorer sections of the community in the days before it was compulsory or free. A degree of literacy was increasingly regarded as desirable, if not essential, but sheer economic necessity meant that attendance at school rarely extended beyond two or three years at best, and was usually determined by the seasonal demands of the farming industry. Old attitudes lingered on after school attendance to the age of ten became compulsory in 1880, for school log books show markedly higher absence rates at lambing time and during the harvest, and the hearing of summonses for non-attendance of children at school tended to form a significant proportion of business at Petty Sessions in the 1880s.

The Social Environment of the Later Nineteenth Century

Though Presteigne society was strongly hierarchical and paternalistic in character, in the third quarter of the century at least, the social life of the town could be much more boisterous and much less deferential than one might expect of a Victorian country town. A certain amount of disorder seems to have been tolerated on such occasions as the May Fair and Warden's Wake, possibly as a safety valve, but anecdotal evidence suggests that the town was not as orderly at other times of the year as press accounts of the round of six-monthly tenants' dinners, the meetings and walks of the town's societies, the activities of the local churches and of the other functions of its polite society might imply.

For the tradesmen, clerks and skilled craftsmen of the locality, social life centred on the activities of the friendly societies which, in return for a small weekly payment, provided sickness and funeral payments, and which claimed a combined membership of more than 800 by the 1880s. The oldest of these was the New Club, founded in 1805 following the demise of the Old Club, the others being the Oddfellows, which founded a lodge in the town in 1841 and the Foresters, established in the town in 1865. One other, the Globe Inn Friendly Society founded in 1857, flourished more briefly. Lady Brydges was largely responsible for the foundation of a women's friendly society in 1878, the Presteigne Female Benefit Society, which concentrated not on social activities, but upon welfare, for it provided a means of saving for 'a rainy day.'

The most important occasion in the year for each friendly society was its 'walk' day when the members, in full regalia, carrying the society's banners and accompanied by a band, walked in procession to church. After the service the members returned to the inn which served as the society's headquarters for dinner, when some members on occasion became too 'convivial', and the day was rounded off by sports and dancing. The New Club held its walk on 20 June, Warden's Wake, while the Oddfellows' walk took place at first on 1 March and later on August Bank Holiday Monday, with the sports being held at Boultibrooke in conjunction with the Horticultural Society's Flower Show held there from 1854 until the later 1860s, again for a few years after 1880, and from 1906 until just after the First World War. The Foresters, whose procession was the most colourful, first held their walk on 29 May and later on Whit Monday. Held as they were on public holidays, the walks inevitably attracted large crowds, many of the spectators joining in the festivities with enthusiasm.

Two other annual high days in the town were the May Fair and Warden's Wake, both of which had became mainly pleasure fairs by the third quarter of the century. The May Fair, on 9 May, saw the streets filled with hawkers, booths, sideshows and roundabouts, and attracted large crowds and also pickpockets and cardsharps, the latter specialising in a game known as 'Pricking the garter', which seems to have been an early version of 'Find the lady'. In 1852 eight cardsharps and a number of pickpockets from as far afield as Bristol and Worcester were arrested and in 1874 it was thought necessary to send out the town crier to warn of the presence of pickpockets. Inevitably the town's inns did roaring business and the day usually ended noisily as 'elevated' revellers made their way home. In theory the revelry of Warden's Wake should have been confined to the Warden, which was crammed with sideshows, shooting galleries, drinking booths, cheapjacks' stalls and, where, in earlier days, bare knuckle prize fights were held, the day ending with sports and dancing. Again the day usually finished with disturbances, with the fighting sometimes spilling over into the town. The introduction of superintendent constables in 1844 and of the Radnorshire Constabulary in 1857 saw an attempt made to curb the disorder associated with such occasions.

The superintendent constables at Presteigne were Alexander Beatty, then James Dixon, and finally John Ball. James Dixon threw himself whole-heartedly into the job for, in 1851, after a burglary at Greenfields, the home of Mrs Sophia Evans, he pursued the burglars to within three miles of Birmingham before arresting them. In the same year, two men, who had not paid fines imposed on them for being drunk and disorderly, were put in the stocks, erected in 1844 opposite the gaol, for six hours. Such zeal provoked a little resentment in some quarters, for as the curate explained of the townsfolk in 1847: 'like most others, but perhaps in an unusual degree, they are averse to arbitrary measures.'

Matters seem to have come to a head at the Warden's Wake of 1857, when, according to the *Hereford Times* of 27 June, there was rioting in the streets of the town from midnight until 3a.m. in which 'the new police were roughly handled', and P.C. Daniel Thomas was nearly killed by a stone hurled by a rioter which left a dent in the door post of the Duke's Arms. The hostility shown to the police seems to have stemmed from the local constabulary's uncompromisingly strict attitude towards poaching.

In 1856 the *Hereford Times* of 18 October described Presteigne as a 'noisy, riotous and drunken town', and from time to time one can obtain glimpses of aspects of social life which the town's establishment preferred to ignore. Thus, in 1842 the town contained at least one 'house of ill repute' which seems to have survived into the 1850s. Bare knuckle prize fights continued to be held well into the second half of the century, while illegal cockfighting also continued into the early twentieth century, notably at a sawpit near the Burgage. This sport was popular not only with the humbler sections of the community, but also with some of the pillars of local society, including one senior churchman and a retired senior military man.

'The Hole', on the bank of the Lugg near West Wall, was a notorious spot for gambling, drinking, fighting and other disreputable activities which led at least one Primitive Methodist minister to hold an open air service there in an attempt to persuade the habitués of the errors of their ways. In his manuscript notebooks W.H. Howse records the reminiscences of some of the older inhabitants of the town relating to those days. Thus one old lady, born in 1868, recounted a conversation overheard by her father in the Castle in the early 1860s: 'Let's go to the Blue Boar boys, there's fiddling, dancing and Hell's delights!' The Blue Boar, on the site of the present Farmers' Arms, was one of the town's more livelier inns, very popular with the pedlars and hawkers during their visits to the area. An old man, recalling the 1870s, commented: '... there were sixteen or seventeen public houses in Presteigne open from 6a.m. until 11p.m. without a break; brawls were frequent, especially on Saturday nights, when it was seldom that there was not a free fight in one part of the town or another.'

In fairness to Presteigne however, it was not unusual in this respect, for as W.C. Maddox notes, the most common offences in Radnorshire at this time were drunkenness and drunk and riotous behaviour, and during one quarter in 1870 there were 95 cases of drunkenness and 130 cases of drunkenness with 'notorious behaviour' in the county.

To some extent such rowdiness and disorder was a reaction to the unremitting toil and the state of social deprivation in which the poorer sections of the community lived. Working hours were long for all, and until 1876 shop assistants in the town did not finish their days work until 9 or 10p.m. Thus the *Hereford Journal* commented in July 1876: 'In no town is the indoor confinement of shopkeepers' assistants so close and so severe as in Presteigne.' That there was a substantial degree of poverty in the town was tacitly admitted by the more prosperous sections of the community, for a society wedding was almost always marked by the distribution of bread, meat and drink to the poor, while on the occasion of a public celebration such as Queen Victoria's wedding or the coming of the railway, it was the custom for the expenses, including the provision of bread, meat and beer or cider for the poor, to be borne by the local gentry, professional men and tradesmen, who 'entered into a subscription' for the purpose. Private charity was also much in evidence in the town, particularly during the winter months: the parish magazine of February 1870 announced the distribution of thirty-six tons of coal amongst the needy, while in the Decembers of 1881 and 1882, the local press announced the distribution of beef among the poor by Mrs Otway, 170 families being the recipients in 1881; and the distribution of coal among needy families by Sir Powlett Milbank, Thomas Pugh and John Griffiths of the Moor. Even as late as 1911 loaves of bread were being distributed to poor widows at the conclusion of the morning service at the parish church. Nor were such charitable works confined to the very wealthy: between 1838 and 1840 a clothing club, financed by small weekly contributions of a penny or so on the part of well-wishers, purchased clothing for the poor, while at the turn of the century a coal club was operating on the same principle.

The populace at large did not always have the respect for the town's establishment which the latter thought it deserved and the guy burned on the town bonfire on 5 November sometimes bore a striking resemblance to a local dignitary who had recently offended public opinion. The successful campaign waged by Cecil Parsons against Sir Harford James Jones Brydges and Lady Langdale to keep the Warden in the town's hands in 1870 enjoyed widespread and sometimes vociferous popular support. Perhaps the most striking demonstration of popular disapproval of a local dignitary came in November 1884 when, against the wishes of her father, the daughter of a prominent Presteigne lawyer who was the clerk of the peace, the coroner and a church warden, married the curate. The couple returned to the town after their marriage to be met by a great welcome from the townspeople. When they next attended the parish church, at the conclusion of the service the unpopular organist played the 'Dead March' from 'Saul.' Though he later maintained that this was to mark the death of the postmaster general, public opinion in the town took it to be directed against the young couple and the following evening a procession, carrying an effigy of the organist, gathered at the Assembly Rooms. Led by a fife and drum band and to the accompaniment of shrieking and groaning, the crowd of 300 or so made their way to the organist's house in Broad Street and demanded that he should show his face. When he refused to do so the crowd proceeded to Grove Meadow where the effigy was burnt with the band playing the 'Dead March' and the crowd cheering. The organist subsequently summonsed the ringleaders and three young men of the town were bound over in the sum of £20. The police sergeant was demoted and moved away from the town, as was the police constable, for countenancing the proceedings. Later the curate was charged with habitual drunkenness, but the case was dismissed by the ecclesiastical court meeting at the Radnorshire Arms, and the curate and his wife were driven back to their lodgings in triumph.

However, by the closing decades of the century much of the vitality seems to have ebbed from communal life. In 1879 the number of farm workers hired at the May Fair had dwindled away and attendance had dropped, and while the traditional rope pulling on Shrove Tuesday, said to predict the price of wheat during the year, continued into the late 1890s its popularity had waned. Warden's Wake continued to be celebrated but it was only a pale shadow of its former self. After the demise of the New Club an attempt to revive the Wake in 1907 failed, though for a few years thereafter the town band gave a concert on the Warden on 20 June to commemorate the day of the Wake. To some extent this loss of vitality was a reflection of growing non-conformist influence in the town, though the major factor was probably the increasing difficulties faced by agriculture and therefore by the town's businesses which led to falling incomes and wages, growing unemployment and a sharp fall in the population of the town and the surrounding countryside.

Against this sometimes turbulent background, the establishment presided over the social life of the town which, prior to the opening of the Assembly Rooms in 1865, tended to centre on the Radnorshire Arms, the Shire Hall and a large room to the rear of the Duke's Arms known as the Volunteer Hall or prior to 1865 as the Assembly Room. The opening of this hall in 1860 led to the Duke's Arms replacing the Radnorshire Arms for a decade or so as the most prestigious hostelry in the town. A flavour of the social life of polite Presteigne society can be gained from Fig. 28 which lists the main functions which took place in the town between July and December, 1880.

The social event of the season was the County Ball, known as the Hunt Ball in the 1890s. The press report on the event in 1880 paints a glowing picture of the occasion:

> 'This aristocratic Ball (which was one of the most successful ever held in the town) was held on Tuesday the 28th inst. in the Assembly Rooms Presteigne. The room having been very elaborately and artistically decorated with evergreens etc. by the Misses Green Price, the Misses Green, Miss Evelyn (Corton), Mr Harris and others to whom much credit is due for their untiring zeal.
>
> 'There was a very large and brilliant assemblage. Dancing commenced at 10 o' clock and lasted until an early hour in the morning. A most efficient Cheltenham string band had been

engaged and an excellent programme was gone through in a manner which left nothing to be desired. Mr G. Thomas, the host of the Castle Hotel provided the supper, which was laid on the table with much taste and skill ...'

Such an event provided a pattern for other balls held in the town, often held at the same venue, and few finished before 4.30 a.m. while some went on until 5.30 a.m.

The closing decades of the century saw political feelings running high in the town. As a representative of the Charity Commissioners noted on his visit to the grammar school in 1877: 'Politics are very hot at Presteigne .... Whatever of a public nature was proposed, the first question asked was, 'Who proposed it?' and parties ranged themselves for or against it as they agreed with or dissented from the politics of the proposer ...'

Although the town at this time was predominantly Liberal in sympathy, the Conservative Party, led locally by William Stephens, Captain Otway and later Sir Powlett Milbank of Norton Manor, was gaining increasing support and in 1886 a local branch of the Primrose League, an association set up in memory of Disraeli, was formed in the area in order to broaden the base of Conservative support. As noted above, the dismissal of Woodward as headmaster of the grammar school may have been the result of a local political squabble and local press reports show considerable political rancour in Presteigne: the lengthy absence of Sir Richard Green Price while convalescing in the south of France led to Conservative charges that Radnorshire was in effect disenfranchised, while the purchase of the Duke's Arms by Captain Otway led to the Liberals claiming that this was a Conservative plot to deny them the use of the inn which had been previously their unofficial headquarters in the town.

The emergence of such issues as Irish Home Rule, and particularly Tariff Reform and the Disestablishment of the Welsh Church certainly polarised political opinion. Though the issue of Home Rule for Ireland was said to have cost Sir Richard Green Price the 1886 election, unlike the other two issues it had no direct bearing upon the interests of the local electorate. The landed interest, with its livelihood threatened by imports of cheap foreign foodstuffs, tended to favour the placing of duties on imports as advocated by the Tariff Reform movement, whereas the commercial classes believed it would push up prices and wages and lead to retaliation. Disestablishment was favoured by the non-conformists who resented paying tithes to a church which they did not support, and was opposed by the majority of Churchmen.

Thur., 1 July	Summer sitting of Quarter Sessions opened.
Wed., 7 July	Cricket match, Presteigne 129; Builth 42 and 45.
Mon., 12 July	Temperance lecture at the Baptist chapel.
Sun., 18 July	Sunday School Anniversary services at the Baptist and Primitive Methodist chapels.
Mon., 19 July	Primitive Methodist Sunday School tea and sports.
Tues., 20 July	Baptist Sunday School tea and sports.
Thur., 22 July	Summer sitting of Assizes began.
Mon., 2 Aug.	Oddfellows' Walk. Ludlow Brass Band followed by sports at Boultibrooke.
Mon., 16 Aug.	Presteigne Schools Treat—pupils' procession, tea and sports.
Tues., 28 Sep.	The County Ball at the Assembly Rooms.
Thur., 30 Sep.	Cricket Club Dinner at the Assembly Rooms.
Fri., 1 Oct.	Presteigne Sunday Schools' procession, tea and sports. Harvest Festival services at St Andrew's Parish Church and the Primitive Methodist chapel.
Sun., 10 Oct.	Baptist Harvest Festival services.
Mon., 11 Oct.	Baptist Harvest Festival Tea at the Assembly Rooms.
Tues. 12 Oct.	Livestock Fair.
Wed., 13 Oct.	Livestock Fair. Sanger's Moving Waxworks Exhibition.
Thur., 14 Oct.	Discoed Church Harvest Festival.
Tues., 19 Oct.	Missionary meeting at the Primitive Methodist chapel.
Thur., 21 Oct.	Autumn sitting of Quarter Sessions began.
Fri., 22 Oct.	Second day of Quarter Sessions. Race meeting at Broadheath.
Sat., 23 Oct.,	1st Radnorshire Volunteers' shooting competition at the Butts.
Tues., 2 Nov.	Rent dinners for Boultibrooke tenants at the Radnorshire Arms and for the Corton tenants at the Castle.
Wed., 17 Nov.	Presteigne Amateur Christy Minstrels' Show at the Assembly Rooms.
Wed., 24 Nov.	Missionary meeting at the Wesleyan Methodist chapel.
Sat., 11 Dec.	Livestock Fair.
Wed., 22 Dec.	Christmas Poultry Show.
Fri., 24 Dec.	Ist Radnorshire Volunteers Christmas Shoot.
Fri., 31 Dec.	Foresters' Dinner at the Duke's Arms. Watchnight services at St Andrew's Parish Church and the Primitive Methodist chapel.

Fig. 28: *Social Events in Presteigne, July-December 1880*
(Source: Mr E. Newell's copies of his press reports, by kind permission of Mrs Cherry Leversedge)

The parliamentary elections of the 1890s and 1900s in Radnorshire were almost invariably close, with majorities of 79 in 1895 and 14 and 42 in the two elections of 1910, which tended to raise political passions still further. Thus in 1895 a doggerel verse in vogue ran;
'Mr Gladstone in a carriage,
Frank Edwards in a gig,
Milbank in a donkey cart,
Walsh upon a pig.'

Since Sir Powlett Milbank, backed by the Hon. Arthur Walsh, later the third Lord Ormanthwaite, defeated the sitting member for Radnorshire, Frank Edwards (later Sir Francis Edwards), he had the last laugh.

The 1904 Education Act, which provided for the provision of public funds for Church schools, generated a degree of controversy in the town as elsewhere, for it meant that non-conformists, through the payment of rates, would contribute to the maintenance of Church schools. The Passive Resistance movement sought to mobilise non-conformist opinion against the measure and in Presteigne H.J. Sparey and R.A. Pugh were soon to the fore in this campaign. In the Urban District Council elections of 1903 candidates in Presteigne stood either as 'Church' or 'Non-conformist' candidates rather than under political party labels. However, from press reports it seems that only two Presteigne 'passive resisters', William Davies and H.F.Morris, had goods distrained for withholding part of their rates, compared with twenty-one at Knighton, nineteen at Llandrindod Wells and fifty-two at Rhayader.

The issue of Tariff Reform provoked a flurry of activity on the part of the Presteigne Liberals. In 1910 Free Trade meetings were held on the Warden, the Young Liberals were meeting at Silia, the home of J.H. Wale, a prominent local Liberal and non-conformist, and Conservative posters advertising a Unionist fete at Norton Manor were defaced with 'Only children in arms admitted'.

Initially local attitudes to the attempt to find coal on Folly Bank were determined by political considerations for Aaron Griffiths, the promoter, was a prominent local Liberal, and the 'Battle of Harley Hill' of 1912 also had political overtones for the encloser of the hill, who had to compromise by erecting stiles to give access to the public, was the prominent local Liberal, J.H. Wale. Local political divisions were still deep in 1914, for the three retiring Liberal members of Presteigne UDC found themselves opposed at first by no fewer than seven Conservatives, though only two of the latter actually contested the election, and then unsuccessfully.

Cultural and Sporting Life

For much of the century cultural and sporting activities were the preserve of the wealthier sections of the community, since most of the townsfolk had little leisure time apart from the club walks, the fairs, other public celebrations and, after 1871, bank holidays. Even as late as 1888 the *Hereford Journal* could comment on the Foresters' Walk in Presteigne, 'to many in that district this is the only day of absolute enjoyment in the whole year'. Not until the 1890s did some in the town secure a five-and-a-half day working week: for the shop assistants this came in 1894 when it was decided that the town's shops should close at 2p.m. on Thursdays, although for the remainder of the week they stayed open until 7p.m. in winter and 8p.m. in summer.

Throughout the first half of the century book clubs and libraries were functioning in the town, references to such institutions occurring in the local press in 1816, 1837, 1840 and 1847, though membership seems to have been by invitation tending to make them socially exclusive, catering only for the town's elite. The library and reading room given to the town in 1856 by Mrs Sophia Evans and that set up in the Assembly Rooms in the later 1860s were intended to serve the general public, but given the limited literacy of much of the town's population and that neither library was free, both tended to have a middle class clientele. The Debating and Literary Society which functioned for a few years after 1895 and again in about 1910 also had an overwhelmingly middle class membership. The Reading Room and Working Men's Club set up in 1886 was taken over by the town's shopkeepers and clerks, and although it survived until at least 1929, by 1906 it was held that it was no longer fulfilling its original purpose.

From at least the middle of the century the town had a strong musical tradition which, to an extent, cut across social class. By 1822 the town had its own band, which by the 1840s was flourishing to the extent that in 1844 it was able to purchase new instruments and a few years later membership was large enough to start a juvenile brass band, The band continued to function until the later 1890s and was re-formed in 1905 by Reverend Kewley, surviving with breaks during the war years until the mid 1960s. By 1853 at the latest the town also possessed a string orchestra and for two spells in the 1880s and 1890s, a fife and drum band. From its inception in 1863 the town's Philharmonic Society, under the leadership of Charles Blackmore, the bugle major of the Royal Radnor Rifles, was giving concerts in the Shire Hall, the Radnorshire Arms and the Assembly Rooms, and its traditions were carried on in the 1880s and 1890s by the Music Society. By the middle of the century both the

Baptist and Primitive Methodist churches had their own choirs and during the 1850s and 1860s the choir of the parish church was beginning to establish a reputation in diocesan circles, probably reaching its peak under in the 1870s under the direction of Charles Green. A choral society was formed in 1885, but by the late 1890s it had run into financial difficulties, from which it was rescued in 1902 by Reverend Kewley, functioning thereafter intermittently until at least the early 1950s.

The Assembly Rooms, the normal venue for the concerts of the choral and music societies, also saw performances by professional touring groups such as the Drawing Room Opera Company in 1874, the Roberts Harpists, the Stanley Ward Players and Hinde's San Francisco Christy Minstrels, all of whom visited the town in 1882. There was a strong tradition of amateur light entertainment in the town throughout the second half of the century. The Juvenile Entertainers of 1848 were succeeded in 1860 by the Ethiopian Serenaders and the Amateur Christy Minstrels formed in 1868. The latter society continued to function into the 1890s, giving a series of concerts in the winter each year, and was revived in the early 1900s by Reverend Kewley. The minstrels were in the main young men of the town, clerks and shop assistants, but the Amateur Dramatic Society founded in 1866 and revived in the 1890s, the Penny Readings of the 1870s and the Popular Entertainments of the 1880s also drew from the local gentry families, notably the Greens and the Otways.

The gentry also took the lead in most sporting activities in the town. Richard Price of Norton Manor was the patron of Presteigne's race meeting, held annually from 1839 and his interest was shared by his nephew and heir, Richard Green Price, and the latter's son, Dansey. The meetings were held at Broadheath and continued into the 1880s, with a break between 1852 and 1864 as a result of serious disorder at the 1851 meeting. Hunting, in all its forms, was always popular with the gentry: the locality had a pack of harriers from at least the third quarter of the eighteenth century until the late 1850s, its own otter hunt from 1814 until 1838, while hare coursing remained popular throughout the nineteenth century. Packs of beagle hounds were also kept in the locality from time to time in the first half of the century. At first Presteigne did not have its own pack of fox hounds and during the 1820s and 1830s local enthusiasts had to rely on the occasional visits of Walter Wilkins' pack. But in the 1840s Thomas Ricketts of Combe House maintained a pack and in the 1850s Captain James Beavan started the Presteigne Hunt, from which the Radnorshire and West Herefordshire Hunt developed in 1869, with the Green Price family playing a leading role. The family also were the patrons of the Archery Club of the 1860s and the Polo Club of 1874 which played its matches on Broadheath. The Green Prices and the Evelyn family of Corton were also largely responsible for the formation of the Golf Club in 1897 which had its course first at Paradise and then at Broadheath from 1907 until the club's demise in 1915.

Quoits and skittles were always popular pastimes in the town's inns throughout the nineteenth century and beyond, and bowls also had a wide following in the town, which at one time could boast of three greens—on the Warden, at the Radnorshire Arms, and behind the Oxford Arms in Broad Street. In the first half of the century bare knuckle prize fights, usually held on the Warden, also attracted large crowds. One of the most gruelling was the 'severe pugelistic contest' of July 1814 between John Edwards, husbandman, and Thomas Beaumont, meal-man, for this contest lasted one hour and forty minutes, ending in the 40th round when Beaumont sprained his wrist in a fall and was unable to continue. As we have seen, cockfighting remained popular in the area throughout the century, despite being made illegal in 1835.

The first recorded cricket match in the town took place on Thursday, 18 July 1844 at Broadheath, when the recently formed Kington side defeated Presteigne by 4 wickets and 10 runs. This may well have been the Presteigne club's first match for the *Hereford Journal* attributed the large crowd of spectators to the novelty of the game. However, the Cricketers' Arms on Broadheath opened in 1838, which suggests that the area already had associations with cricket and that the 1844 match may have represented a revival of the sport in the area rather than its introduction. Later the club may have played at Corton, for there is a reference to 'the old cricket field at Corton' in the *Hereford Journal* of 1874. During the 1870s the club enjoyed mixed fortunes and may well have ceased to function for a while. By the 1880s matters had improved and the club, now with a ground at Grove Meadow, began to enjoy a period of success which lasted until the outbreak of war in 1914. During the 1880s the team included three members of the Green Price family and three members of the Evelyn family, several of these being of county standard, and the club provided the nucleus of the Radnorshire XI. During the 1890s the Australian test player Trumble turned out for the club on his visits to Stapleton House, while in the years before 1914 the club also employed a professional.

The sons of the local gentry, having been introduced to soccer at public school, also played a role in popularising the game in the locality. Thus the football club, formed in November 1879 under the presidency of Captain Otway, included in its team which defeated Leominster Scarlet

Runners 5-1 in January 1880 two members of both the Green Price and Evelyn families. One member of the latter family, E.C. Evelyn, went on to win a Welsh cap in 1887, being a member of the team defeated 4-0 by England at the Oval, though by this time he was playing for Worcester Crusaders. The phraseology of the press report announcing the formation of the 1879 club suggests that it was not the first soccer club in the town and indeed, when T.G. Britten, whose family farmed at Stapleton Castle, won the first of his two Welsh caps against Scotland in 1878, Football Association records show him as playing for a Presteigne team.

In 1883 the town also had a youth team, the Presteigne Blue Stars, who played at Greenfield. By the early 1890s the town had two senior soccer teams, Presteigne Town and Presteigne Rovers, but for the remainder of the decade the history of the sport in the town is far from clear. Local tradition suggests that by the mid 1890s the Rovers had ceased to exist and that after financial difficulties had led to the winding up of the Town team in 1896, Reverend Kewley formed the Presteigne St Andrew's club in 1897. However, this is not entirely borne out by local press reports. The Rovers club certainly seems to have folded by the end of the 1893-94 season, but reports in the *Hereford Journal* suggest that three soccer clubs were active in the town in the 1894-95 and 1895-96 seasons— Presteigne F.C., Presteigne Town F.C. and Presteigne St Andrew's F.C., with some players turning out for all three teams and Reverend Kewley playing for both Presteigne and Presteigne Town. However, some of their fixtures suggest that prior to 1897, the St Andrew's club may well have been only operating at a junior level. By the opening years of the twentieth century both Presteigne Town and the St Andrew's clubs were active, but by the beginning of the 1906 season the latter was the only senior soccer club in the town.

The proliferation of football clubs in the 1890s, drawing team members from all social classes in the town was, like the formation of the Cycle Club in 1891 and tennis and hockey clubs in 1907, a consequence of the spread of the five-and-a-half day working week and the gradual reduction in the length of the working day, which together gave the working man the time to engage in leisure pursuits. This also probably explains the introduction of successful and popular ambulance and nursing classes in 1898 and the establishment of organisations in the town catering for the social and recreational needs of the youth of the town. Prior to the turn of the century these had been met by the Sunday Schools and to some extent by the friendly societies. In 1897 Miss Debenham formed the Diamond Jubilee Boys' Club which later on was to meet in the parish room which had been fitted out as a gymnasium and in 1899 a branch of the Girls' Friendly Society was set up in the town. A Boys' Brigade unit was formed in 1902, as was a Boy Scout troop by 1909, though the Girl Guides were not active in the town until 1912. The specific social and recreational needs of the women of the town, however, continued to be virtually ignored, for beyond the nursing class and cycling club mentioned above, there existed for them only the church and chapel women's meetings such as the Mothers' Union, formed in 1894. Cycling seems to have been one new leisure activity which appealed to the young ladies of the town, for lady cyclists featured prominently at local bicycling gymkhanas and in the parades and processions which formed part of the celebrations to welcome home local volunteers from the Boer War in 1901 and the coronation of Edward VII in 1902.

The Decline of the Late Nineteenth Century
During the closing decades of the century the town's population fell rapidly and by 1901 it stood at 1,245, a fall of nearly 28% since 1871. The town's housing stock also fell, but even so the proportion of houses unoccupied remained quite high—9% in 1881, 17% on 1891 and 9.5% in 1901. By 1898 a town councillor could comment, without contradiction that Presteigne 'had been dormant and almost dead for years.' The decline seems to have stemmed from two factors, the agricultural depression and the loss of its role in local government to Llandrindod Wells.

Throughout the century commercial directories had attributed much of Presteigne's prosperity to its role as county town. However, by the closing decades of the century, many of its administrative functions had disappeared or had been usurped by Llandrindod Wells. The process had begun in 1876 with the amalgamation of the Royal Radnor Rifles with the Brecon Militia and the transfer of training and of the depot to Brecon. In 1878 the gaol had been closed and the Presteigne Poor Law Union dissolved, its Radnorshire components being absorbed by the Knighton Union and its Herefordshire townships by the Kington Union. In 1889, by a narrow majority, the newly formed County Council decided to make Llandrindod Wells its headquarters, and in 1899 the Standing Joint Committee, the police authority, followed suit. In terms of employment and reduction in the town's trade, the direct impact of these changes was small for Presteigne remained the normal venue for Quarter Sessions and Assizes, but the impact in terms of status was considerable in the long run.

However, it is apparent that the decline of the town mainly stemmed from the agricultural depression which had led to a sharp fall in the popu-

The auction field near the goods shed c.1900

lation of the surrounding rural area of nearly 23% between 1871 and 1901 and a decline in the incomes of farmers and landowners. Both of these would have a marked impact on the volume of trade in the town and led to a reduction in the number of businesses and to a reduction in the scale of the undertakings which survived since the level of activity would not encourage further investment. The livestock markets of the town had always been in the shadow of those of Kington and Knighton which steadily eroded Presteigne's influence in the more distant parts of its hinterland, while the railways gave farmers of the area access to markets further afield such as Leominster, Hereford and Craven Arms. In an attempt to retain the existing level of trade in the livestock markets the number of fairs was again increased. In 1880 a sheep fair was introduced on 21 September (though it did not attract the attention of the local press correspondent), which subsequently became a horse fair, and in the 1890s a November fair was added. Other fairs were held from time to time in an attempt to revive the town's flagging trade, and by the end of the century it was not uncommon for there to be eleven or twelve fairs during the course of the year. However, since this expedient was followed by all the market towns in the area, it probably had little impact.

In the meantime the town's industrial base had disintegrated. Malting, Presteigne's staple industry, was ruined by the Malt Tun Act of 1880 which introduced changes in taxation which favouring large-scale concerns, and the town's last malthouse ceased to function in 1892. The spade-handle factory continued operations in the 1880s but had closed by the early 1890s, as had the tannery, the saw-mill, the brickworks and the nailmaking business, while the large cooperage at Green End saw its business shrink dramatically. Undoubtedly their decline had been hastened by the coming of the railway which also led to the decline in business of the town's shoemakers and dressmakers in the face of competition of mass-produced goods. The railway also enabled the great houses to deal with the London shops on a regular basis rather than with local craftsmen and retailers, thus providing another grievance to be aired in the local press.

The situation was best summed up by M.A. Hayer and M.L. Heppel writing in 1911 of their visit to Presteigne, during the course of which they encountered the parish clerk: 'He told us he was a cooper by trade and used to work almost all night and day in cider time, and employed journeymen too, but now he had almost nothing to do. There is not half the cider made and the zinc manufacturers have robbed him of the other kinds of work. No-one wants wooden washing tubs now. It seems rather sad how the village trades are dying away. The ready-made clothes have slain the village tailor, and the ready-made boots the village shoemaker; it is inevitable but it is sad, and plays its part in driving the country people into the towns.'

The decline in the town's commercial fortunes is well illustrated by the fate of the Market Hall and the Assembly Rooms in the closing decades of the century. By 1880 the company was in arrears in its payments to the mortgagor, Mrs Elizabeth Abley, and in 1882 with the company virtually defunct, court action led to the property passing into her hands. It fared no better and in 1897 was offered to the town for £550, little more than the original mortgage, as a fitting means of commemorating Queen Victoria's Diamond Jubilee. However the town was unable to raise this sum and the Jubilee was celebrated by the formation of the Boys' Club. In 1903 Presteigne UDC purchased the building for £450 and ran it as a municipal concern, but with the town's trade continuing to decline, in 1909 part of the hall was used to house the town's fire engine, though the Assembly Rooms continued as the venue for many social functions until the opening of the Memorial Hall in 1953, and served as the town's cinema until 1964.

CHAPTER VIII

The Struggle for a Future

After some attempt to halt the slide in its fortunes prior to 1914, for much of the first half of the twentieth century Presteigne seems to have accepted a degree of stagnation as inevitable, apart from brief flurries of optimism surrounding the opening of the new auction yard in 1926 and the realisation in 1944 that victory and peace were on the horizon.

In Search of a New Direction
The turn of the century had seen the town continue to decline: its population fell by more than 8% during the decade 1891-1901 and by a similar proportion in the following decade, to stand at 1,141 by 1911. The surrounding rural area also lost population, though not to the same extent, falling by 3% between 1891 and 1901 and by $4^1/_2$% in the following decade. Against this background the comment of Edwin Davies in 1905 that 'the town does not present an appearance of much business activity' comes as no surprise. By 1909 some visitors viewed the town as rather a quaint backwater. One, intrigued by the use of the town crier to announce a railway excursion, the town's lack of Sunday trains and of a telephone system, and the unavailability of the London newspapers before 11a.m., remarked that the only intrusive sound to be heard was the horn of an occasional motor car, which was 'still the cause of a little excitement and some speculation.' Certainly at that time Presteigne had by no means come to terms with the car, for by the end of 1909 only nine cars and nine motorcycles had been registered in the town by the Radnorshire authorities. The first motor vehicle to be registered was the motorcycle of W.H. Virgo in January 1905, while the first cars registered were those of Dr

The Assembly Rooms and Market Hall in the early twentieth century

Debenham and A. Lewis, both of which were registered in January 1906. A speed limit of 6 mph had been imposed in the town in 1904 between Greenfield Turn and Boultibrooke bridge.

This slow decline in its fortunes was not accepted passively by the town and its leaders, notably Richard Rogers, the town's first county councillor and the chairman of the Urban District Council since its formation in 1895 until his retirement in 1900, and later Reverend H.L. Kewley, the energetic rector, and Philip Davies, the auctioneer. The modernisation of the town's infrastructure continued. Mains sewers serving Broad Street, St David's Street and Church Street had been constructed in the late 1880s, with a tank and filter beds at the Tanhouse, and land irrigation at Whitewall Farm to deal with the sewage for the remainder of the town. The whole system was flushed twice a day with water pumped from the Lugg by the old water wheel at the Tanhouse. The town relied for drinking water on its wells and since the water level was no more than twenty feet or so below ground level the risk of pollution from the piles of horse manure stacked outside the town's stables was ever present. Matters improved in 1904 with the establishment of a mains water supply, the work of the Presteigne Water Company, set up in 1903 with a capital of £2,500 in £10 shares. The scheme involved pumping pure spring water from Colebrook Meadow and New Mill Orchard to reservoirs on the Warden. The waterworks were opened by Lady Brydges on 13 June 1904.

The Shire Hall and Broad Street in the early twentieth century

The waterworks also enabled the town's sewers to be cleansed twice a day from flushing tanks built at the New Mill.

However, a substantial proportion of the town's houses remained unconnected to either the mains water supply or mains sewage until the late 1930s, and diphtheria, endemic in the town since 1897, continued to cause concern, with twenty or so cases reported annually in the years before the First World War. A further important public health measure was the establishment of an isolation hospital beyond the Warden in 1903 following a case of smallpox at the lodging house on Hereford Street. A further improvement to the infrastructure came in 1910 when the town had its first telephone exchange, predicted to be 'of immense benefit to the town', though by 1919 it only had twelve subscribers.

An attempt was made to regain some of the functions associated with its role as the old county town. In 1894 the UDC sought to persuade the authorities to establish a permanent militia camp in the locality and in 1907 the proposal to build new county council headquarters in Llandrindod Wells was used to try to win back for Presteigne its role as the seat of local government for the county. In May of that year a public meeting was held in the Assembly Rooms, chaired by Sir Powlett Milbank, and a resolution was passed to the effect that '...the existing Shire Hall and county buildings at Presteigne are everything that is required for the needs of the county and any further outlay upon new buildings would be a waste of public money.'

However, such attempts ignored the shift in local political and commercial influence away from the eastern fringes of the county and the town had to be content with small triumphs—the decision to locate the new County Secondary School at Presteigne rather than at Knighton, and fighting off proposals to shift the Assizes from the town in 1905 and 1910.

The one bright spot was the rise in the prices of all farm products except wheat between 1894-98 and 1910-14, particularly marked in the livestock sector, which saw price rises of around 20% in the period and by 1907 a sheep market had been built on Hereford Street, enabling the auction yard near the railway station to be devoted to cattle sales. While Knighton and Kington possessed larger hinterlands and superior road and rail facilities, this did much to slow down the town's decline as a market centre and to keep alive the weekly market in that part of the Market Hall not used to house the town's fire engine.

Not all the proposals aimed at restoring Presteigne's fortunes looked to the past. Many ideas were floated by the Presteigne Traders' Association,

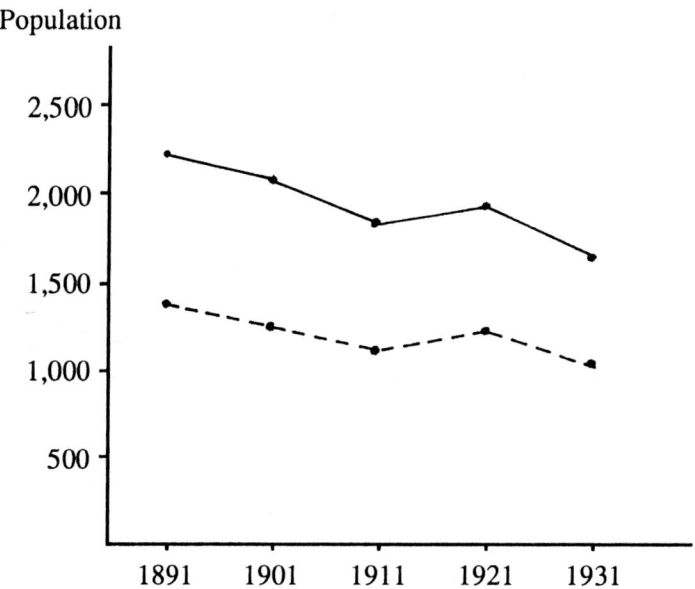

Fig. 29: The Population of Presteigne and the surrounding area
------ *Town population* ⸺ *Town and surrounding area population*
Surrounding area: Norton, Discoed, Rodd, Nash and Little Brampton, Willey, Stapleton and Combe
(Source: Printed census data, 1891-1931)

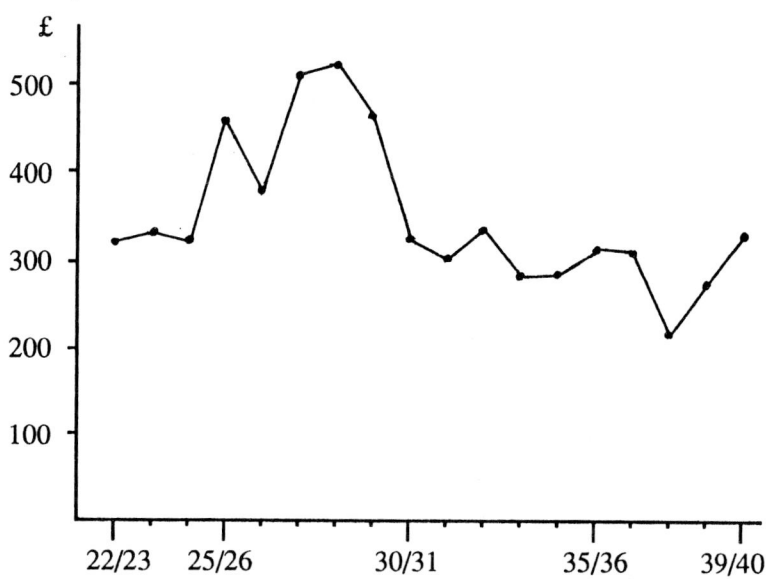

Fig. 30: Annual Outdoor Relief and Transitional Unemployment Expenditure in Presteigne during the Financial Years 1922/23 - 1939/40
(Source: Knighton Poor Law Union records)

founded in 1908, which, according to the *Hereford Journal* in 1910 'made almost too many suggestions for the comfort of the UDC.' Many of the ideas called for the council to take the lead and the statutory constraints on its expenditure were not always understood in the town. Thus in 1898, inspired by the sudden rise to prosperity of Llandrindod Wells, the discovery of a mineral spring at Stocking Farm and of a saline spring at Combe led to the suggestion that Presteigne should seek to develop as a spa. However, the UDC found that it could not spend public funds on an analysis of the medicinal qualities of the town's springs. When a group of public-spirited townsmen funded such an analysis the report was unfavourable, and hopes that the town might 'eventually beat the great Llandrindod' came to nothing. In 1905 the proposal to advertise Presteigne as a health resort also foundered, though in the following years tourism was increasingly seen as a source of income and before 1914 the Presteigne Development Association was advertising holiday accommodation and publishing weekly lists of visitors to the town.

The successful floating of the Presteigne Water Company in 1903 and of the Presteigne Laundry Company in 1913 suggests that local capital

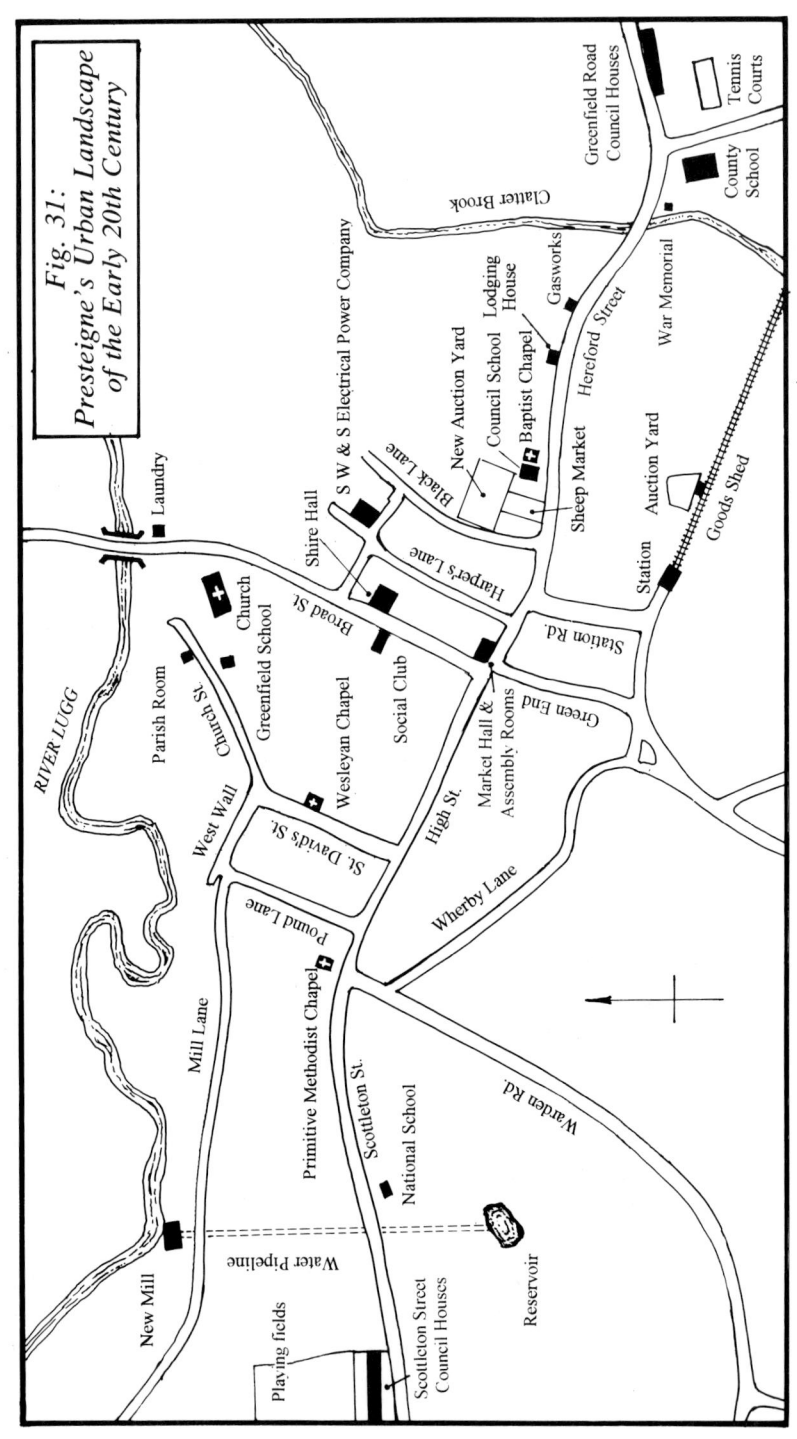

Fig. 31: Presteigne's Urban Landscape of the Early 20th Century

was available for investment in enterprises, thanks to the recovery in farm incomes. The return on capital so invested was rather better than that offered on deposit accounts with the commercial banks, and in the years preceding the outbreak of war in 1914 two locally funded attempts were made to find coal to the south of the town. Though geologically impossible, since the local strata consists of Silurian and Old Red Sandstone rock, with the nearest Carboniferous coal-bearing strata more than twenty miles away in the Clee Hills, the presence of limestone outcrops had given rise periodically to speculation that coal was present. In the opening decade of the nineteenth century Charles Rogers of Stanage had sunk a shaft in what became known as Coal Pit Field to no avail, giving rise to a local tradition, mentioned in the *Radnor Express* of 21 March 1912 that 'one of the miners left his hammer on a good bed of coal' and that the venture had foundered on the opposition of the Clee Hills coalowners.

In 1910-11 Philip Davies had sunk a shaft 350 yards to the east of Caen Wood, but this was abandoned at a depth of forty feet. The attempt to find coal received a fresh impetus with the arrival on the scene of Aaron Griffiths of Willey Lodge. In 1911 he had purchased the twenty-six acres of Folly Farm from the executors of F.L. Evelyn's Kinsham Court estate for £743 and in the following year had purchased the adjoining Nash Wood. When walking over his newly acquired land he found pieces of coal scattered over a relatively large area and recalled a local tradition that coal had once been worked in the nearby Sandy Parks. The many excavations in the area led him to conclude that these were open-cast workings, abandoned when the surface seam had been exhausted. A trial bore was sunk to a depth of nearly 900 feet amidst growing optimism and in March 1913 the Radnor Coal Syndicate was set up following an announcement that three seams of excellent coal had been discovered. Aaron Griffiths was more circumspect and advised would-be investors 'to limit your subscription to a moderate or small amount.'

According to the *Radnor Express* and the *Hereford Times* the shares were taken up with enthusiasm, though the company records show that by mid-April only 826 shares had been sold, 400 of these to three individuals. Local opinion was divided, some were justifiably sceptical, while the views of many were coloured by political and sectarian allegiances. Since Aaron Griffiths was a prominent Liberal, the *Radnorshire Standard*, Conservative in sympathy, initially poured scorn on the enthusiastic reports of the venture contained in the Liberal *Radnor Express*.

Thus in March 1912 the *Standard*, resorting to ridicule, reported the finding of a nugget of gold at Green End and of the discovery of a gold field under the cabbage patch. With disestablishment of the Welsh Church a burning issue of the day and Aaron Griffiths a staunch Primitive Methodist, the *Standard* could not resist a dig at local nonconformity: 'We understand that the Presteigne chapel people could hardly listen to the sermon last Sunday, their thoughts were so full of "coal".'

With the sinking of a drift shaft into the side of Folly Bank and growing local optimism, the *Standard* changed its stance. However, at the end of June 1913, after the negative report of 'a well-known coal expert' from Lancashire, the two directors of the Syndicate, both 'outsiders', recommended that the venture should be wound up. But an extraordinary general meeting of shareholders decided to continue and three local men, Aaron Griffiths, R.A. Pugh and Reverend H.L. Kewley were elected as directors, the registered office of the syndicate was transferred to Presteigne, and another local man, Samuel Young, became company secretary. The town had closed ranks in the face of outside scepticism.

The tempo of activity then quickened since it was essential that commercially viable seams should be proved as soon as possible if sufficient capital was to be raised to ensure the continuation of the venture. The sudden death of Aaron Griffiths from peritonitis on 23 September 1913 was a severe blow, for he had been the driving force behind the venture and had met the initial expenses out of his own resources. Folly Farm and Nash Wood had been heavily mortgaged and he left a personal estate valued at nothing. By the end of 1913 the financial situation was such that the company only survived by the sale of postcards and pottery souvenirs. Though in January 1914 what were mistakenly thought to be the first signs of a leading of coal was discovered, the company had resorted to settling its debts by the issue of paid up shares. Towards the end of March, with still no sign of coal, work at the drift was halted, though the men offered to carry on without pay, but since no buyer could be found, the company was wound up in November 1915.

The failure of the venture seems to have provoked no resentment in the town towards the promoters, for many believed that it had failed as a result of a whispering campaign on the part of the South Wales coal-owners which had starved the enterprise of capital. Orthodox geological opinion had been hostile from the start. T.G. Cantrill commented in *The Geological Magazine* of November 1917, '... a more hopeless district in which to sink for coal could not have been found if deliberately sought for.' Though the promoters had gained the support of some unnamed

The trial bore for coal at the Folly, 1912

geological and mining experts, their judgment was primarily based on what they took to have been earlier coal workings in the locality and pieces of coal on or near the surface. Cantrill identified the workings as abandoned quarries from which outcrops of limestone had been extracted in previous centuries and found remains of several kilns in which the limestone had been burned to produce agricultural lime, arguing that the coal found on the surface was the result of accidental spillage. Another geologist, Professor Watts, elaborated on this, telling how an old quarryman in the area had explained that it was the practice for coal carted from the Clee Hills for use in the kilns to be buried in the old limestone workings to prevent its deterioration. However such explanations do not account for the confident assertions made by Aaron Griffiths and his successors that coal seams had been discovered. Given their undoubted integrity, for they were all local men with considerable public reputations, self-deception would seem to be the most likely explanation. Layers of black shale are occasionally found in Ordovician and Silurian strata, and it would be all too easy for laymen, willing their venture to succeed, to convince themselves that such shales were the eagerly anticipated coal seams.

The possibility of restoring Presteigne to prosperity was the constant theme of press comment on the venture, though some locals feared that the discovery of coal would 'spoil the picturesqueness of the neighbourhood.' The opinion of the majority however, was summed up by the *Radnor Express* of 13 March 1913: 'If all goes well and they find a working seam, what does it mean for Presteigne? Why work. And plenty of it and work brings the money too, no matter how dirty the jobs may be.'

The hopes and objectives of the Radnor Coal Syndicate are perhaps best summed up in the obituary notice of Aaron Griffiths in the *Express*: '... his main object was finding work for the people of Presteigne, so that it may be the means of raising Presteigne out of the rut of lethargy it appears to have irretrievably fallen into ...'

Presteigne soldiers leaving for active service, August 1914

The Impact of the First World War
In August 1914, following the outbreak of war, D Company of the Herefordshire Regiment of the Territorial Army, formed in 1908 and consisting of men from the Kington and Presteigne localities, was mobilised along with the rest of the battalion under the command of Colonel Drage of the The Rodd. The battalion subsequently served at Gallipoli and in Egypt and Palestine, winning a mention in dispatches for the landing at Suvla Bay. Prior to the introduction of conscription in 1916

Corton House Red Cross hospital, 1917

most of the local volunteers joined the Herefords or the King's Shropshire Light Infantry, though some were subsequently drafted to other regiments and corps as a result of the heavy casualties of trench warfare on the Western Front. Even so, of the forty-four men of the parish killed on active service between 1914 and 1918 and whose names are recorded on the War Memorial, twelve were serving with the KSLI and nine with the Herefords.

The people of Presteigne were given some insight into the horrors of trench warfare on the western front through the presence at Corton of a Red Cross hospital which opened on 29 October 1914 and closed in July 1919. Initially it had twenty beds but its capacity was increased after the summer of 1916 to twenty-eight beds and six emergency beds. Until 1917 it operated under the supervision of the 3rd General Western Hospital, Cardiff and thereafter was attached to Shrewsbury. Local management was in the hands of a committee chaired by Reverend Kewley, with Miss Evelyn as commandant, Dr Lower as medical officer, Mrs Hudson as lady superintendent and Miss Hamer as quartermaster. The hospital had a staff of eighteen VADs (members of the Voluntary Aid Detachment), orderlies and domestic staff. The first patients admitted were ten Belgian soldiers and the hospital was reserved initially for Belgian casualties, the first British casualties being admitted in May 1915. By the time that it closed in 1919 the hospital had treated 760 casualties. In 1917 it had begun to specialise in amputation cases with Miss Hamer in charge of the manufacture and fitting of artificial legs. From January 1919 the hospital dealt exclusively with such cases, in all supplying 261 artificial legs.

For her work in connection with the hospital Miss Evelyn was awarded the OBE, whilst Miss Hamer, Miss Coates, Mrs Smith, Mrs Lower and Mr A.M. Wilson, received official recognition for their contributions. The presence of the hospital gave people an opportunity to make some immediate contribution to the war effort, entertaining the patients with concerts, providing occupational therapy—notably embroidery and wood-carving, and providing hospitality for those convalescing. The 'boys in blue' were virtually given the freedom of the town, and at least one young lady of Presteigne met her future husband among the patients at Corton hospital.

The war brought an unprecedented degree of control over every aspect of ordinary life, with food, fuel and petrol supplies strictly regulated. The farming sector found its production and marketing patterns closely supervised, and under the pressure of the War Agricultural Executive, the acreage under wheat in Presteigne increased significantly, from an average of 6.5% of the arable acreage between 1905 and 1907 to 10.5% in between 1915 and 1917. The drive to increase food production took place against a background of a shortage of horses and labour, particularly after the introduction of conscription, and with the Allies preparing for the 'Big Push' in 1917 the exemption of farm workers became increasingly difficult to secure. Given such a shortage, farm workers' wages rose rapidly, from 18s. per week in 1914 to 30s. in 1918 and 44s. in 1921. With food in short supply, farm product prices doubled between 1914 and 1920, producing great hardship for those families where the breadwinner was on active service. Thus the Norton parish meeting in March 1917 made an appeal to able-bodied men to assist those women whose husbands were serving in the army in cultivating their gardens.

The demands of the war effort also led to a marked expansion in forestry as its timber resources were exploited, on a scale probably not seen since the Napoleonic wars, to provide pit props needed as coal production was expanded. Initially in 1917 felling centred on Nash Wood, Caen Wood, North Wood and Harley's Wood, Slough Road being virtually destroyed by timber carriages, and during the post war boom of 1919-21 felling was extended to Norton, Stapleton, Cole's Hill, Cascob and Bleddfa. Much of the felling was carried out by the official Timber Supply Department, though private firms such as the Monmouth and South Wales Pitwood Association were also involved, usually on short term contracts. The scale of the operations may be judged by the application to the UDC

A timber waggon passing the Bull Hotel, c.1920

made in February 1919 by the Timber Supply Department for permission to use Broadheath as an unloading station for an aerial railway bringing timber from the surrounding hills. In the event this was not built, though a railroad or tramway was built to enable the felled timber to be transported from Cole's Hill.

The conscription of older age groups in 1917-18, combined with the increased demand for labour by the farming and forestry industries exacerbated the labour shortage. To some extent this was made good by the increased use of local female labour, the Women's Land Army and foreign labour, notably from Portugal, while troops unfit for overseas service were drafted in to work in forestry, as were young men from the South Wales coalfield, the latter causing some resentment as local men in older age groups were called up for military service. Problems of accommodation meant that prisoners of war were not used by the local farmers, though thirty or so were employed at their Dolyhir works by the Old Radnor Trading Company. The escape of two prisoners from Dolyhir on 3 August 1918 caused some excitement. However, they gave themselves up two days later, when they were seen trying to cross the road between Nash Wood and Corton by convalescing soldiers at the hospital who marched them to Presteigne police station. PS Higgins was out on duty when they arrived, but his wife locked them in the cells after giving them bread and cheese and cups of tea.

The coming of peace on 11 November 1918 was initially greeted in the town with disbelief, as the report in the *Radnor Express* of 14 November makes clear: 'The news of the signing of the Armistice was received at Presteigne by means of private telephone messages before the official announcement appeared, and, for some time the people hardly credited it. When the official intimation appeared at the Post Office, the inhabitants made haste to display flags and the town was soon gay with them. The Boys' Band, under Conductor George Morgan, played about the streets and added to the general festive nature of the occasion.'

On 14 February 1920, following a dinner at the Volunteer Hall, the former servicemen of the parish were each presented with a silver chain and a medal by Miss Evelyn, and in the same month the Conservative Club at 9 Broad Street was converted into a non-political social club to provide the ex-servicemen with a rendezvous in the town. On 24 October 1920 the War Memorial was unveiled by Mr J.S. Arkwright, following a parade of ex-servicemen from the Assembly Rooms, led by the town band conducted by Reverend Kewley.

The returning servicemen formed a 'post' of the Comrades Association which soon had a membership of 110, with a civilian, Mr W. Thomas, as commandant. At the end of July 1920 the Comrades Association was wound up and replaced by a branch of the British Legion, with Captain Walsh as commandant and Colonel Drage and Miss Evelyn as vice-presidents. The Comrades and the Legion played an important part in the life of the community in the early 1920s, organising the Whit Monday carnival and sports, establishing a savings bank and undertaking welfare work such as providing war widows and their dependents and others in need with tickets to obtain free food from the town's shops at Christmas. They also formed an effective political lobby in the town which the authorities could not afford to ignore. The secretary of the British Legion, Mr W. James, was elected to the UDC and played an important part in pushing through the building of the town's first council houses and in securing preferential treatment for ex-servicemen seeking work.

However, by the mid 1920s the public spirit engendered by the war had evaporated in the rigours of the post-war slump. By 1923 there were complaints that the War Memorial was neglected and untidy and in 1924, after the debts of the war memorial committee had been wiped out by public subscription, the maintenance of the memorial was taken over by the UDC. By 1925 the local branch of the British Legion had ceased to function and remained in abeyance until the autumn of 1931.

Farming in the Presteigne Area between the Wars

With 23% of the town's working population occupied in farming in the inter-war years, the fortunes of the town remained closely tied with that of agriculture. By 1920 the boom was over and thereafter, until at least 1937, agriculture was in difficulties, with marked crises in 1921-23 and 1928-33. By 1923 farm product prices had fallen to almost 50% of those of 1920, and with the exception of wool, prices drifted downwards for the rest of the decade, with the arable sector worst hit. In the crisis of 1928-33 sheep farming was not affected until relatively late, wool prices falling sharply in 1930 and sheep prices collapsing in the local markets in the second half of 1931. However, by September 1933 the local press was reporting a sharp recovery in ewe prices at the Kington and Knighton sheep sales and by 1937 farming was back in a rather precarious equilibrium, helped by the de-rating of agricultural land and buildings, the introduction of subsidies in wheat and beef, and the development of marketing schemes for sugar beet, potatoes and livestock. It is against this background of volatile market conditions that the shifts in local farming patterns must be viewed.

Land utilisation in the Presteigne area saw a shift at the margin towards permanent grass, the acreage devoted to this rising by rather more than 4% between 1905-07 and 1935-37, at the expense of arable and rough grazing acreages, which both fell by 2% or so during the same period. The trend towards pastoral farming can also be seen in changes in the cropping pattern in the arable sector. The proportion devoted to oats rose from 23% to 31% and to clover and temporary leys increased from 32% to 38% between 1905-07 and 1935-37, mainly at the expense of the barley acreage which fell from 17% to 4% of the arable acreage over the same period. The proportion devoted to wheat fluctuated, by 1925-27 it had fallen to 3.5%, only to rise to 7% of the arable acreage by 1935-37, probably as a result of the introduction of the subsidy on wheat, and possibly at the expense of barley. The early decades of the century also saw the introduction of two new crops, oilseed rape during the wars years, and sugar beet in the 1930s, both grown on a small scale and neither accounting for more than 10 to 15 acres in any year.

Within the livestock sector the inter-war years saw significant shifts in emphasis. The total number of horses kept in the locality fell sharply after 1905-07, reflecting the fall in demand for horses for transport. The number of horses kept for farm work declined rather more slowly, from an average for the parish of 63 in 1915-17 to 57 in 1925-27 and 50 in 1935-37, which suggests that even in the later 1930s tractors were the exception rather than the rule in the Presteigne area. The total number of cattle kept in the inter-war years remained stable at about 650, compared with the average of 820 in 1905-07. This numerical stability however obscures two clear trends—a shift away from dairying, and a marked increase in the the number of beasts over two years of age. In the sheep sector the trend was towards lamb production, reflecting the increasing demand for smaller, leaner joints as consumers' preferences shifted from mutton to lamb.

The stock was also kept on a greater acreage of pasture, meaning there was a fall in stocking levels. This reduction may in part reflect a fall in farmers' working capital in the difficult trading conditions of the inter-war years, but may also indicate a greater emphasis on the quality of livestock reared in face of increasing competition from imports. Beef may also have been seen as comparatively profitable, in response to the beef subsidy available in the 1930s. Nevertheless, the price of store cattle and wethers continued to decline after 1933.

Presteigne stock market had gained a good reputation in the early 1920s, attracting buyers from south Wales, Wolverhampton, Birmingham and Manchester and buoyant trade led to the opening of a new cattle market in the Back Lane, behind the sheep market off Hereford Street, in December 1926. By March 1927 it was claimed to be 'Radnorshire's Best Fat Stock Mart' and in its report on the Presteigne market on 2 March 1929 the *Hereford Times* commented: '...It is gratifying to find new buyers attending at every auction and the outlook for this stock district would appear to be most encouraging.'

However, as the economic crisis deepened in the early 1930s, the volume of trade fell sharply and by the middle of the decade Presteigne New Auction Mart Ltd was considering selling part of the orchard acquired with a view to expansion to the council for the erection of public toilets or for use as a children's playground. Hopes had risen briefly towards the end of 1934 when Presteigne was designated as a grading centre (where fatstock were graded for subsidy purposes), but by 1939 Presteigne Chamber of Commerce was asking the UDC to do its utmost to prevent the closing of the auction market.

The break up of the Norton Manor and Boultibrooke estates which began after the deaths of Sir Powlett Milbank in 1918 and Lady Brydges in 1923 seems not to have led to an increase in the number of farm units in the locality. Indeed, the number of farm holdings in Presteigne fell from 61 in 1905-07 to 38 in 1935-37, probably in response to the difficult farming conditions in the inter-war years. The number of holdings under

The new cattle market on the Back Lane, 1927

5 acres fell by 50% between 1915-17 and 1935-37, while the number of holdings between 5 and 50 acres fell by 25% between 1915-17 and 1925-27 and by a further 14.5% in the following decade, the fall being most marked in the 5 to 25 acres category. In the main the farms were worked by family labour and throughout the inter-war years the number of paid farm workers remained constant at 47 to 48. Labour costs were reduced, however, by recruiting male workers under 21, and employing more female and casual labour. Anecdotal evidence suggests that costs were further reduced by cutting back on routine maintenance such as hedging, ditching and the repair of farm buildings.

Life and Work in Presteigne during the Inter-War Years

In his report to the UDC in 1955 Dr David Walker, the medical officer of health, commented 'A notable figure has said that this town only exists by virtue of what it does not spend, not on what it earns.' This was probably more true during the inter-war years than at any other time in the century, for stagnation was the characteristic of the period. The population of the town rose from 1,141 in 1911 to 1,172 in 1921, probably reflecting the short-lived boom in forestry, but by 1931 it had fallen to 1,102, which was also the estimated population in 1938. The population of the surrounding area fell more sharply over the period, from 752 in

1911 to 652 in 1931. The town's population was also aging, the proportion aged over 60 rising steadily from 12.9% in 1901, to 15.1% in 1911, 16.1% in 1921, and 17.3% in 1931.

An analysis of the town's housing stock reinforces the impression of stagnation, for the period 1919-39 saw only twenty-two houses built . Of these twelve were council houses, six in Greenfield Road, as a result of the 1919 housing scheme, were completed in 1922, and six built in Scottleton Street under the 1936 scheme, were completed in 1938 and subsequently named Wilson Terrace after the donor of the site, A.M. Wilson. Since the housing stock, which had totalled 345 in 1901, was estimated at 330 in 1939, some sub-standard housing had been demolished or put to alternative use between the wars. Even so, the quality of the remainder left much to be desired, for the 1939 housing survey found ninety-one houses—27% of the total—to be sub-standard, in spite of sustained pressure by the UDC to improve matters. For example, a survey in 1921 had found the water supply to many houses unsatisfactory, with sixty houses served by wells, whilst thirty cottagers still carried water by hand from the Well House spring in Broad Street. Action was taken so that by the early 1930s most of the wells had been condemned and the majority of houses had a mains water supply. Sanitary arrangements in the town were also improving. In 1937 at least twenty-four houses shared one WC between two houses and about fifty houses in the town were still served by earth closets, but by the outbreak of war in 1939, more than two-thirds of these houses had their own WC fitted.

The failure to provide more council houses stemmed from a variety of factors, not least the difficulty of acquiring a site acceptable to both the UDC and the Ministry of Housing which the owner was willing to sell, a factor which seriously delayed the implementation of the 1919 and 1936 schemes. Again, some councillors believed that given the low wage levels prevailing locally, few working families could afford the rents charged for such housing and certainly there were initially no applicants for the two larger houses on Greenfield Road; while in 1938 the rent for the Wilson Terrace houses was fixed at 6s. per week plus rates, a level beyond the means of many requiring such housing. Some councillors thought that a further decline in the town's fortunes was inevitable and that in the long run additional housing was not necessary. Finally, given the climate of financial retrenchment in the inter-war years, central government imposed stringent controls on local authority borrowing, while the UDC was under strong local pressure to keep expenditure and rates as low as possible.

The occupational pattern in the town changed little between the wars, three broad occupational groupings; agriculture, personal services and the professional and commercial sector providing more than 60% of employment, the proportions of the labour force remaining constant at 23%, 19-20% and 20% respectively in the censuses of 1921 and 1931. The labour force was predominantly male, 71% male in 1921 and 72% in 1931, with the proportion of the female population of working age in employment falling from 31% in 1921 to 27% in 1931. The female labour force worked mainly in the commercial and personal services sectors; in 1921 seventy-five of the 141 employed women and girls were in the personal services sector, forty-five of them in domestic service.

Since local wage levels were tied to those of farm workers, either formally, as was the case with county council roadmen, or informally as was the case with most manual workers, usually a few shillings higher in recognition of farm workers' payments in kind, the sharp fall in farm workers wages from 44s. per week in 1921 to 30s. in 1923 meant that most workers in the town found that their wages and standard of living fell markedly in the early 1920s. The reintroduction of a statutory minimum wage for farm workers in 1924 halted the slide and by 1931 the wage of an adult male farm worker had risen to 31s., only to fall back to 29s. 6d. by 1932, little more than the maximum transitional relief of 27s. 3d. for which an unemployed man with a dependent wife and two small children was eligible. Not until 1935-36 did local wage levels begin to move beyond those of the mid 1920s.

The extent to which unemployment posed a problem in the town in the inter-war years is by no means clear. The recovery in the fortunes of the town's livestock market in the 1920s, together with the generally steady trade reported in butter, eggs, poultry and rabbits at the weekly Wednesday market suggests that farm incomes did not fall as sharply as in some areas, thus assisting the survival of the town's businesses, most of which depended largely on family labour. Of the town's labour force in 1931, 77% were classified as 'operatives' or paid employees, the remainder were self-employed or working in family concerns. In such circumstances a falling off in trade was reflected not so much in a shedding of paid labour, but rather in a fall in profits, a less intensive use of family labour and a sapping of business confidence.

The shift in employment patterns in the farming sector noted in the previous section worsened employment prospects for adult male farm workers in the locality and probably explains the decline in the population of the surrounding rural area in the period between the wars. The ending of the boom in the forestry sector after the coal strike of 1921 also reduced employment in the locality, for although timber felling continued on an extensive scale until at least 1923-24, forestry never offered employment on the scale it had done in 1918-19 when the Pitwood Workers' Union had recruited more than a hundred members in the Presteigne area. In the town itself the 1920s saw job losses in the more traditional sectors of the local economy, for a comparison of the 1921 and 1931 occupational censuses shows the number involved in metal-working falling by a third to 18, probably as a result in cost-cutting in the farming sector, while the temporary closing of Nash quarry prior to 1931 saw the loss of a further nine jobs.

Throughout the period the employment situation was always fragile, for much of the available work in agriculture, road construction, building and the catering and hotel trades was highly seasonal. Even during the forestry boom of 1917-21, contracts were short term, for a few months at best. The end of a contract was often followed by a spell of unemployment, a situation which brought at least one timber haulier in the town to bankruptcy. Judging from expenditure on outdoor poor relief, cash payments made to those not maintained in the workhouse, which rose steadily throughout the 1920s, to peak in the financial year 1928-29 at a figure 62% above that of 1922-23, the employment situation in the locality deteriorated throughout the decade. Underemployment also became common for manual workers, whilst short spells of work interspersed with longer periods of unemployment becoming the norm for many.

As with the country as a whole, unemployment peaked in the early 1930s; the 1931 census showed forty-two people in the town unemployed, which had reduced to twenty-five by March 1933, though this was by no means a true indication of the extent of unemployment in the town. In such a situation the UDC formed an unemployment committee on which all the town organisations were represented. In addition to palliatives such as the provision of more allotments to supplement those set up near Greenfield in 1919 and the formation of a club for the unemployed, the committee suggested that the UDC should provide public work schemes such as bringing forward the planned erection of public toilets on Hereford Street and the construction of a children's playground, tennis courts or a golf course. However the UDC did not have the funds and even the building of the toilets had to wait until a loan had been obtained from the Public Works Board. Other suggestions included reopening the limeworks at Nash and even that the attempt to find coal locally should be renewed, a suggestion which brought a letter from T.C. Cantrill to the *Radnor Express* of 22 January 1925 to the effect that such an attempt would only 'incur fresh loss and invite further ridicule.'

Throughout the period the UDC was keenly aware of the need to protect employment in the town. Thus in 1922 when the contract to repair damage done to the streets by the heavy timber traffic was awarded to an outside firm, the UDC secured a promise that the firm would use local labour wherever possible, and similar arrangements were reached with the outside firms which secured the contracts to fence the new recreation ground in 1937 and to build the Scottleton Street council houses in 1938. Under pressure from the Development Association and the revitalised Chamber of Commerce, the UDC stopped letting the Warden for grazing in 1926 for a few years in an attempt to provide some facilities for the potential tourist trade, while in 1937, when the Nash quarry company re-opened the Folly Bank quarry, it gained the support of the UDC in spite of protests from the grammar school and nearby residents at the hazard to health posed by the high silica content of the resulting stone dust. Any proposal which threatened the commercial wellbeing of the town was resisted strongly by the UDC which protested at proposals to move the Assizes from Presteigne in 1937 and at plans to establish senior elementary central schools at Kington and Knighton in 1938, since these were seen as threatening the viability of the town's schools. Fortunately the slight recovery in agriculture, the extensive programme of road improvements initiated by the county council and the steady flow of orders for roadstone at Nash quarry seem to have been sufficient to reduce local unemployment to below crisis proportions in the later 1930s. Even so, in the summer of 1939 there was enough unemployment in the town to warrant a town councillor suggesting that those without work should be employed in the construction of dug-out air raid shelters.

During the 1930s poor relief expenditure in the town fell back, but initially at least this stemmed not from improving employment but from the cut in benefit levels of 15% and the application of the means test, which in Radnorshire led to more than half the claims for transitional unemployment payments being rejected or granted at reduced rates. Underemployment seems to have remained a problem in the locality throughout the 1930s; in the summer of 1933 a Cascob forestry worker worked for only two days in a period of three weeks and an Evenjobb farm worker for only two days in a four week period.

As in many small towns the economic uncertainties of the 20s and 30s produced a widespread belief in Presteigne that money and trade should

Presteigne railway station, c.1919

be kept in the town as far as possible. Thus tenders for goods and services under £10 were limited by the UDC to Presteigne businesses and wherever possible orders for roadstone were placed with Nash quarry. Perhaps the most extreme manifestation of this philosophy came in 1932 when, on the death of the medical officer of health, Presteigne's Dr R. Walker was appointed as his successor, one Presteigne councillor commented, 'Let's keep our money at home and give it to the ratepayers'.

This stance produced a very ambivalent attitude towards proposals to improve transport facilities. The abortive attempt in 1919 to establish a light railway between Presteigne and Llanbister Road, which could have linked Presteigne with the Central Wales line met with general approval, as did the establishment of local bus services with Kington, Knighton and Leominster and W.J. Bethell's proposal in 1932 to establish a 'radial' bus service, to bring passengers into the town from Deerfold Cross, Walton, and Whitton and Cascob. On the other hand, Mr Bethell's proposal of 1932 to run a service between Presteigne and Llandrindod and the Midland Red's proposal to run a service from Kidderminster via Leominster and Presteigne to Aberystwyth did not meet with universal support since some thought they would result in townspeople taking their custom out of the town.

This very defensive attitude must be seen against the background of the high level of long term unemployment which was becoming the norm

The Ministry of Labour Training Camp at the Slough

over much of the country during the early 1930s, the consequences of which were to be seen locally in the presence of the Ministry of Labour Training Centre, set up early in 1929 on the Slough Road. Its purpose was to 'harden' and retrain long term unemployed young men from the industrial areas, initially for forestry work in Canada, though by the end of 1930 this option had been closed and most of the trainees were returned to their home locality and the prospect of further unemployment at the end of a maximum of twelve weeks' training.

The training centre, which could accommodate about 150 trainees, consisted of a complex of prefabricated buildings including seven dormitory huts, a dining room and kitchen, a recreation centre, stables, offices and staff quarters. It was administered jointly with the Shobdon Training Centre by the commandant, Captain J.H. Owens, the deputy manager, Mr J. McGregor and the accountant, Mr A.E. Rendle, and was manned by a staff of about twenty clerks, orderlies, drivers and gangers, most of the latter having had some experience in the Canadian lumber business. The camp was run on military lines and the trainees, who seem to have come in the main from the South Wales and Lancashire coalfields, in addition to building roadways and felling and hauling timber, using Canadian techniques, were also employed on routine camp maintenance. The trainees, who received their keep and 4s. per week pocket money, were issued on their arrival with a working shirt, corduroy trousers, boots and waterproof clothing. The regime was spartan and the food, though usually

Top: The interior of Hut 6
Bottom: The YMCA Hut
both at the Ministry of Labour training camp at the Slough

The training camp entry in the Silver Jubilee Carnival, 1935

adequate, tended to be monotonous, and local tradition has it that on one occasion the quality of the food provoked a one day hunger strike. The recreational hut, run by the YMCA, could hold no more than fifty men, and despite the hard work and enthusiasm of the welfare officer, Mr Stanley John, a gifted musician from South Wales with family connections in the mining industry, who organised football and cricket matches, film shows, whist drives, cribbage and dominoes tournaments, debates and concerts, the lure of the local pub proved too much on most evenings.

It was normal policy to locate such centres some miles from the nearest village, and the proximity of the Slough Road centre to the town undoubtedly helped the establishment of friendly relations between the centre and the local community, particularly in the early years; cricket and football matches were arranged between the centre and local teams, trainees coached the Jubilee Boys' Club in boxing and football, and played for local football clubs. One Shobdon trainee, John Evans, playing for Presteigne St Andrew's, was signed by Hereford United in January 1935 and subsequently transferred to Arsenal. The management of the centre seems to have encouraged this policy of integration: the centre entered a team in the local knockout cricket competition and a detachment from the centre took part in the parade and service at the war memorial on Armistice Day in 1930, whilst local dignitaries attended the centre's Sports Day in August 1930, when the town band provided the music, and local musicians and singers featured prominently in the camp concerts. A particularly good relationship seems to have been established between the centre and the local Primitive Methodist Church, largely through the initiative of the minister, Reverend W.G. Cripps, who prior to leaving the town in the autumn of 1929, seems to have acquired the status of camp 'padre' and to have established the custom, which persisted until at least 1934, of providing refreshments and a social evening for trainees in the schoolroom after the service on Sunday evenings.

Police authorities seem to have regarded the establishment of the camp with some trepidation and the chief constable warned the locals to avoid any trouble with the trainees. In the event the trainees seem to have avoided brushes with the law. Press reports suggest that there were no more than three clashes between trainees and local young men and in the two cases that came to court it is clear that the local men had started the trouble. In the first of these cases in 1930, the chairman of the local Bench, Mr W. Thomas warned that 'if there was any feeling that these men [i.e. the trainees] were to be "shot at" it was to be dismissed.'

Even in the first years of its existence the presence of the centre was not welcomed by all. The close run election of 1929 for the Brecon and Radnor constituency had seen Conservative, Labour and Liberal candidates each, amazingly, secure more than 33% of the poll and when twenty-six trainees were included on the Presteigne electoral register in 1930 the Conservative Party agent successfully objected. As time went on the relationship between the centres and the local communities seems to have deteriorated. The novelty of the situation wore off and with an increasing element of compulsion in the attendance of the unemployed at such training centres, the attitude of the trainees may have become more resentful. When a Shobdon trainee was charged with stealing a cycle lamp in 1934 a police inspector stated that some of the trainees 'wandered about the roads making themselves a nuisance to the police and everyone else. They thought they could do what they liked.' In 1934 a young man at Presteigne, seeking to justify his attack on a trainee, contrasted the trainees unfavourably with those of the early years.

Another factor which may have hampered the forging of a sustained good relationship was the lack of continuity at the Presteigne centre. It functioned throughout 1929 and 1930, but then closed after protracted negotiations with the UDC over connecting the centre's sewage system to that of the town had failed to produce any agreement. Throughout 1930 there had been complaints of sewage polluting the Clatter Brook, but the Ministry of Labour clearly thought that the sum quoted to link the camp

The Ministry of Labour summer training camp, 1933

with the town's sewage system was excessive and transferred operations to the Shobdon camp, leaving the Slough Road centre closed. In 1932 the camp was functioning once more as an overflow camp for the Shobdon centre, but it closed down again in the autumn. In 1933 the centre opened once more on a temporary basis, with a summer camp close by where the trainees were accommodated in tents. The Presteigne centre was active again as an overflow camp for periods in 1934 and 1935, but thereafter its history becomes uncertain.

The UDC incurred some hostility over the closing of the centre at the end of 1930 since some businesses in the town had lost trade as a result. However the UDC was no stranger to controversy, for it had been closely involved in two of the three 'breezes', or public disputes, in the town in the 1920s and early 1930s. The first of these had occurred early in 1921 when the UDC had arranged for the felling of some of the trees on the Warden and some of the townspeople had carried away some of the lopped branches and tops to use for firewood. When the UDC threatened to prosecute anyone who did so in future, 'the mothers, sisters and widows' of men who had fought in the First World War stated their 'determination to assert their rights'. At the end of January 1921 nineteen townspeople, more than two-thirds of them women, were duly charged with stealing timber from the Warden at Presteigne Petty Sessions. Mr A.E. Careless, defending, shrewdly persuaded the Bench to accept the

The Presteigne townspeople charged with stealing timber from the Warden, 1921
Mrs Herrits, wearing a dark hat and coat, is in the centre of the front row

case of Mrs Prudence Emma Herritts, aged 77, as representative, thus ensuring public sympathy lay with the defendants. The UDC was unable to produce title deeds in support of their claim to own the Warden and the town crier, Mr Samuel Greenhouse, testified that people had taken wood from the Warden in the past including himself and possibly the wives of some councillors. PS Higgins testified that during the seven years he had been stationed in the town he had seen people taking wood from the Warden, while Mrs Herritts and Mr Wozencroft testified that they had done so for fifty years. Councillor Philip Davies admitted that townspeople had taken brushwood on past occasions, but that the UDC had usually sold larger loppings and tops as faggots, thus reducing the burden on the ratepayers. The case was dismissed on the grounds that the court did not have jurisdiction and although the UDC considered taking counsel's advice, it decided to let sleeping dogs lie, ultimately safeguarding its position by according the Warden the status of a park and issuing appropriate bye-laws.

The second controversy concerned the custom of holding the May Fair in the streets, with the larger stalls and roundabouts on Broad Street and

Presteigne May Fair, Broad Street, 1920

the smaller on St David's Street. Any suggestion that it should be sited on a field on the outskirts of town had always been resisted by the tradesmen of the town who feared that this would lead to a loss of business. In 1922 some residents complained of the fair 'being dumped in Broad Street' and in 1923 the UDC initially refused to let the streets for the fair, a decision opposed not only by the tradesmen but also by local public opinion. A protest meeting was held and in the UDC elections Philip Davies, a strong supporter of holding the fair in the streets, topped the poll, whereupon the UDC reversed its decision. However, motor traffic was growing steadily and in 1927 the chief constable insisted that sufficient space be left on the streets during the May Fair for vehicles to proceed and in 1928 the county council banned the erection of stalls and roundabouts on the public highway. Though the UDC was advised that such a bye-law could not apply to a customary fair of such long standing, for the next two years the main body of the fair was held on what is now Station Road, then a private road, by arrangement with the GWR, though this meant that the UDC lost much of its £15 letting fee, almost the equivalent of a penny rate. In 1930 the fair was back in Broad Street, attended by crowds much larger than had been the case in the immediate past, but in 1931 it was clear that the fair had outgrown the streets for the new Noah's Ark and Ghost Train were so large they they blocked the street completely and press reports stressed the risk to safety inherent in allowing such large structures in such a confined space and with such large crowds. It was reluctantly conceded that the fair should no longer be held in the streets, and thereafter it was sited on the Barley Mow Field, by the GWR goods shed.

The third controversy was sectarian and concerned the elementary schools of the town. Though there were three elementary schools in the town, they contained in all fewer than 200 pupils and the Radnorshire Education Committee wanted to use the opportunity offered by the retirement in 1924 of Mr W. Thomas, headmaster of the National School, to rationalise elementary education in the town and to prepare for the planned raising of the school leaving age. They proposed closing the Greenfield School, which catered for girls, and turning the other two schools into junior and senior elementary schools, favouring a scheme whereby the National School became a mixed junior school and the former British School, now administered by the county, a mixed senior elementary school. The managers of the National School were not enthusiastic since part of the cost of expansion to accommodate both girl pupils and more boys would fall on the Church authorities, while the Baptist minister, Reverend Watkin Jones, correspondent of the Hereford Street school, opposed the scheme since it would mean that the younger children of nonconformist parents would follow a Church religious education syllabus. In his view the scheme put forward by the education committee represented 'the third attempt in $17^{1}/_{2}$ years made by the Church people to capture the council school'. Though the views of his fellow managers were less entrenched, the opposition of both sets of managers meant that the county authorities had to abandon their plans, though in 1929 Greenfield School was closed and its pupils transferred to the National School.

In both controversies the stance of the UDC was determined in part by financial considerations, for given the perceived need to keep the rates as low as possible, the UDC's financial position was at best finely balanced. To raise funds, it sold the Isolation Hospital on Harley's Hill in 1922 and the old Pound in 1924, while to keep costs down the UDC for a time dispensed with the services of a salaried surveyor, his work being carried out by a committee of councillors. Nevertheless, the UDC was able to improve the town's infrastructure; in 1923-24, after the streets had been repaired, they were given a tarmacadam surface and in 1923 electric street lighting was installed after a trial between gas and electric lights outside the Assembly Room which attracted a substantial number of onlookers. In the 1930s the town sewage system was improved, though financial constraints meant an ambitious and long planned new system of sewage disposal had to be abandoned. Finally in 1934, at long last, the public toilets at the junction of Hereford Street and the Back Lane were completed.

In spite of the economic problems and uncertainties of the period, the inter-war years saw substantial improvements in the general amenities of the town. The first proposal to provide Presteigne with electricity came in 1919 when the Bishop's Castle Electricity Company suggested that the water power of the Lugg could be utilised in conjunction with a suction gas pump to generate electricity. The UDC considered that such a scheme was on too small a scale to provide both light and power and favoured joining the Hereford Corporation scheme which aimed to provide electrical power for neighbouring Herefordshire towns and villages such as Kington and Pembridge. This would have meant a delay of nearly a year and a group of local businessmen formed the Presteigne Electric Company, with Mr H.J. Sparey as managing director, which proposed a larger scale version of the Bishop's Castle Company's scheme, involving the use of two water pumps to power the generator. The government's regional electricity commissioner at first rejected the scheme, but the Presteigne company, with UDC support, successfully appealed, and in 1921 its generating plant was installed by the electrical engineers, Atkins and Paul of Knighton. The local company had a short life for in 1929 it was absorbed by the Staffordshire, Worcestershire and Shropshire Electrical Power Company.

Since at least 1930 some sections of opinion in the town had been pressing for a children's playground and the Silver Jubilee Committee of 1935, supported by the UDC, made the provision of such an amenity its major objective. Several sites were considered—part of the Barley Mow field, land at the Burgage, land behind the new Auction Yard, and the Warden—before the Orchard Field, at the junction of Scottleton Street and Knighton Road, was chosen. The UDC was considering the purchase of this when the owner, Mr A.M. Wilson, gave the field to the town in 1937 for use as a playing field, with ownership vested in the Charity Commissioners and management in the hands of a local committee consisting of councillors and members of the public. The project was now on a much larger scale than had originally been envisaged; in addition to a children's playground with swings and a see-saw, it was proposed to provide a bowling green, three grass tennis courts and football, hockey and cricket pitches. Lack of funds, however, meant that only one tennis court could be laid, the construction of the other two courts and the bowling green being put in abeyance. Although plans to provide a drinking fountain, a shelter and public toilets on the playing fields were drawn up in May 1939, the outbreak of war meant that their construction was also postponed.

The town had enjoyed regular weekly cinema shows at the Assembly Rooms since at least the autumn of 1918, power being provided, before the advent of mains electricity, by an oil or gas-driven generator. During the immediate post-war boom the cinema operated three evenings each week, though by 1929 this had fallen to once or twice a week. By 1931, with 'talkies' showing in 'a neighbouring town', probably Knighton, the Presteigne cinema closed, much to the alarm of the UDC for the cinema rent was its largest source of revenue after the rates. In November 1932 a fortnight long demonstration of 'talkies' at the Assembly Rooms led to the re-opening of the cinema, now equipped with a sound track. The cinema seems to have been regarded as the one potentially profitable investment opportunity in the town in the 1930s, and at least two attempts were made to establish another cinema. In 1932 efforts were made to form a syndicate of ten investors, each putting up £100, to finance the erection of a purpose-built cinema in the town, while in the later 1930s films were shown in the drying room of the old laundry. The UDC reacted with alarm at these threats to its revenue, taking care to comply to the letter with the requirements insisted upon by the chief constable in order to retain the cinema licence of the Assembly Rooms, upgrading the seating by the purchase of old seats from the Palladium Cinema, Hereford, and asserting its determination to oppose any application for a cinema licence from any other quarter.

The establishment of the cinema and the playing fields illustrate the unprecedented widening of the social and sporting amenities available for all age groups in the town during the inter-war years. The coming of peace saw most of the pre-war clubs and societies resume their activities, though few, apart from the football club, the town band, the Girls' Friendly Society and the organisations associated with the churches, functioned continuously throughout the period. The Choral Society, revived in 1921, saw several breaks in its activities as did the Tennis Club, while the Amateur Christy Minstrels, revived in 1920, had disbanded by the mid 1920s. The Hockey Club, re-formed in 1920, had varied fortunes, turning out mixed teams until the later 1920s, then lapsing for a few years before

Scottleton Cottage, Presteigne

emerging as the Ladies' Hockey Club. Even the well established Jubilee Boys' Club had a few years of inactivity between 1921 and 1923. Some pre-war groups took time to re-establish themselves. The Cricket Club was not playing regularly until 1926 and its future remained uncertain until 1932, when Captain F.O. Lewis gave a field, now the John Beddoes School playing field, for the joint use of the club and county school as a cricket ground. The Scout troop was not re-formed until 1929 and the Guides not until 1933.

The post-war period also saw the formation of a number of new sports clubs. The Bowls Club, formed in 1920, played at the Radnorshire Arms until 1927, then at the Oxford Arms before returning to the Radnorshire Arms in 1933, where it remained until 1952. In 1924 Dr Debenham formed the Harley Hill Golf Club, but this did not survive into the 1930s. 1925 saw the formation of the Badminton Club, which in 1928 took over the Volunteer Hall at the Duke's Arms and equipped it for badminton, before ultimately migrating to the County School gymnasium. In 1926 the Automobile Club was formed which, in addition to organising reliability trials and hill climbs, gradually assumed a wider significance in the social life of the town, for the town's first modern dance band the 'Syncopators' was formed by some of its members, initially to perform at the club's social functions. Under the auspices of the Automobile Club, the first vintage car rally, which has been held annually with the exception of the war years, was organised in 1938. Later the club organised the town's bonfire and fireworks display on 5 November.

Three other organisations established in the period also had a wider impact upon the town. The work of the British Legion in the earlier 1920s has been outlined above. The local branch ceased to function in the mid 1920s, but the revival of interest in the observance of Armistice Day in the town in the later 1920s, with businesses closing for half an hour to enable a fuller attendance at the service at the War Memorial, seems to have rekindled interest in the Legion and the local branch was re-formed in 1931, with the Women's Section being re-established in 1934. During the crisis years of the early 1930s it championed the cause of ex-servicemen and campaigned hard to alleviate unemployment. Toc H had flourished briefly in the town in the early 1920s and was successfully revived in 1933. It was essentially an enabling agency, its members seeking to assist other groups in the town to secure objectives of value to the community. It helped the town band organise its August Bank Holiday carnival, flower show and sports, which had replaced the Whit Monday sports as the town's major social event by the late 1920s, and was influential in securing the provision of public grass tennis courts on the Broadaxe cricket ground in 1934. Presteigne's Women's Institute, which held its first monthly meeting in April 1928, in addition to meeting its members' social, cultural and educational needs by taking part in music and drama competitions, and organising lectures on home nursing, cookery and needlework, also campaigned against rural deprivation, lobbying the authorities effectively to secure improved nursing services, water supplies and postal services in rural areas, and also the extension of public telephone facilities in the villages.

Other organisations flourished more briefly. In 1923 a Radio Club was established in the town and the achievement of a member in receiving a broadcast from Pittsburgh was considered worthy of a mention in the local press. However, with private ownership of radios becoming more widespread, the club was wound up in 1925. The political parties were very active in the town in the 1920s, setting up women's and youth sections, though the tempo of political activity died down after the formation of the National Government in 1931, which blurred the distinction between the parties for a while, though a local branch of the 'Imps', the Junior Imperial League, functioned sporadically in the town during the 1930s.

Though the range of social activities in the town had broadened, the general social environment became markedly less boisterous, partly at least as a result of economic uncertainty. In the late 1920s, Mr Whitmore Green Price, the chairman of the local Bench, could assert that a few decades earlier the court had tried more cases of drunkenness in a day than it now did in a year, maintaining in 1927 that Presteigne was now 'one of the most sober towns in Wales'. However his stance was not entirely objective, for the chief constable, supported by the town's churches and the local branch of the British Women's Temperance Association, was consistently campaigning to reduce the number of licensed premises in the town, claiming that nine (eight after the closure of the Cricketers' Arms in 1929) hotels and public houses were too many for the town's population of about 1,100. The Bench, probably seeking to defend facilities considered essential for Presteigne's role as a market town, successfully resisted the campaign, stressing that the town's licensed premises also served the population of the surrounding rural area.

Presteigne and the Second World War

For more than a year before the outbreak of hostilities the town had been preparing for war, with the emphasis on civil defence and the reception of evacuees. The town's police sergeant, PS Bailey, initially the only qualified civil defence instructor in the county, began to train his fellow police officers and members of the ARP (Air Raid Precautions) in first aid, anti-gas measures and in dealing with incendiary bombs. ARP equipment, gas masks and the six stretchers allocated to the town were stockpiled at the

Shire Hall, two first aid posts were set up and later a food decontamination depot was established at the Appletree. Particular attention was paid to heightening public awareness of the means of protection in the event of a gas attack. In July 1938 an anti-gas exhibition was held in a shop on the High Street and in October a demonstration of gas-proofing measures attracted an attendance of nearly 500 adults and more than 150 children. Early in 1939 the UDC circulated a broad outline of the proposed evacuation scheme to all householders, attracting a suggestion from the Chamber of Trade that the old Ministry of Labour training centre could be used to house evacuees. The UDC rejected this proposal, presumably because conditions there were considered too spartan, nominating instead the parish hall and the Assembly Rooms as evacuation reception and feeding centres, the latter later being replaced by the county school.

During 1938 and 1939 meetings, marches and exhibitions were held in the town on behalf of the Presteigne Troop of the 332 (Radnor) Battery Royal Field Artillery, the local Territorial Army unit, based at the Drill Hall in Hereford Street. On the outbreak of war the Battery was mobilised, serving in Northern Ireland, the south coast and subsequently in Normandy, the Low Countries and the Rhineland, finishing up at Hamburg in May 1945. With the exception of this unit, the introduction of conscription at the outset meant that servicemen of the area were scattered through the units of the armed forces, rather than serving in regionally-based regiments as had been the case in the 1914-18 war.

In the late summer and early autumn of 1939 the UDC abandoned its routine monthly meetings in favour or fortnightly, weekly and sometimes daily meetings as it sought to implement the flurry of instructions from government departments, to facilitate the activities of the ARP, Fire Services and later, the Local Defence Volunteers, and to co-ordinate the work of the voluntary organisations anxious to make a contribution to the war effort. Initially, competing claims and overlapping jurisdictions made the task of co-ordination difficult, for it took time to establish priorities and routine procedures. During the first week of August the UDC found volunteers to assist the police assemble gas masks which were issued to the public between 10 and 15 August, though infants' respirators and young children's gas masks were not available until April 1940. At the end of August the UDC issued instructions to householders to screen their windows and a few days later appealed for blankets for the evacuation reception centres, appointed a Fuel Officer and a local Food Control Committee, and arranged for the Fire Station to be manned around the clock. On 19 September the UDC was notified that street lighting was to end 'for the duration', pedestrians later being assisted at night by white lines painted along the edge of the town's pavements.

However, as the 'phoney war' continued, the initial sense of urgency waned. The twenty or so blankets collected for the evacuation centres were returned to their owners and the walls of sandbags erected at the junction of Broad Street, High Street and Hereford Street to protect the post office and Market Hall from bomb blast, but which hampered visibility, were removed after a couple of minor motor accidents and a number of near misses. In April 1940 the UDC, without success, asked the county Civil Defence Committee if the siren, reserved since the previous May for use as an air raid warning, might once more be used as a fire alarm.

In the second half of 1940, Dunkirk, the threat of invasion and the Blitz brought home to the town the reality of war. Fears of an airborne landing saw the removal of all signposts and of Presteigne's name from all notice boards, though it remained on the town War Memorial, while a proposal to stop the town clock in case it provided a guide to enemy aircraft was rejected by the UDC. In July 1940 the town's old fire engine and large piles of stone and rubble were placed on Broadheath to deny its use to the enemy as a landing ground, though these were removed in October 1940 at the request of the War Agricultural Executive Committee in order that it could be ploughed and sown with barley. Proposals to block potential landing sites in Norton made by the parish meeting were overruled by the military authorities who had taken over Norton Manor and took the view that such obstructions would hamper military training.

In March 1940 the Chamber of Trade had asked the UDC to use its best offices to secure the use of the old training centre on Slough Road as a military camp, but without success. After Dunkirk however, military accommodation was at a premium and military units were stationed at Norton Manor and at the old training centre, though the latter was utilised only briefly and was vacated by the autumn of 1940, thereafter serving as a War Agricultural Executive depot. Plans to use Broadheath as a training area came to nothing, though land belonging to Hill Farm and Paradise Farm was utilised for training purposes by the troops stationed at the training centre. The military also requisitioned several houses in the town as billets for the use of troops manning searchlights in the locality, and for a while there was also a temporary military camp at Greenfield.

Norton Manor, taken over by June 1940, housed military units until at least 1944. Much of the training took place on Stonewall Hill, where, on the afternoon of 28 February 1943, two Presteigne boys were killed and several others wounded, two fatally, in an incident involving an unexploded 3 inch mortar bomb, left on the hill after a training exercise. The party of nine boys had been walking on the hill 'raising rabbits' when one found the mortar, carried it for a while and then when he examined it with the other boys sitting close by, it exploded. The blast was heard by a soldier out walking on the hill who was able to give immediate first aid and then summoned assistance. There were three other such incidents in the county, at St Harmon in June 1942, at Newchurch in August 1943 and at Old Radnor in September 1945, though only in the latter case was there further fatalities.

The troops stationed in the locality did not always have the respect for the civil authorities which the UDC tended to expect. Speeding army lorries damaged shop blinds in the High Street, endangered pedestrians using Lugg Bridge and damaged the surfaces of Warden Road and Chapel Terrace. A large stone was placed on the corner of Globe House to protect the house from damage by army lorries turning down Chapel Terrace on their way to the refuse tip. Troops billeted in the houses requisitioned by the military authorities sometimes took a cavalier attitude to the blackout arrangements, much to the dismay of the local ARP unit, while after three fires at Norton Manor requiring the services of the town fire brigade in little more than three weeks, the UDC felt constrained to warn the military authorities that a charge would be made for the brigade's services in future.

Nor did the UDC always see eye to eye with the military authorities over the latter's requisitioning policies. In October 1940 when there were negotiations afoot to allow the requisitioning of the County School for billeting, transferring the pupils elsewhere, the UDC objected, pointing out that the newly-built central school in Knighton was empty and that the County School would not benefit from its endowments should it be moved away from the town. Again, when the military authorities requisitioned the Market Hall in January 1941 and used the upper and lower ante-rooms as offices, the UDC objected on the grounds that this prevented the use of the building for public entertainment and made it difficult to use the cellar, previously designated as one of the town's four public air raid shelters. Nor was the UDC privy to military information. Thus in February 1941 some of the councillors enquired of the town's military status in the event of an invasion, whether it was designated as an open or as a defended town, and though the matter was deferred until Councillor Lane Walker, an officer in the local Home Guard, could be present, he was unable to shed any light on the matter.

Within a few weeks of the war starting the first unofficial evacuees had begun to arrive in the town, in most cases female relatives and children coming to stay with kinsfolk. In mid-1940, with fears of invasion rising and the Blitz beginning, the clerk to the UDC was appointed chief billeting officer and the official evacuation scheme swung into operation. Most, though not all of the unaccompanied child evacuees came from the Bootle area of Liverpool, though since official records seem to have been lost, precise statistics as to numbers and their home locations cannot be established. The earlier influx of evacuees and the preference of some householders to take unofficial evacuees whose status could be easily established, rather than unknown and unaccompanied children, made for some difficulty in initially placing the latter and the UDC had to insist that they should be given precedence. Inevitably there were some problems in the placement of evacuees. Some householders arranged for the transfer of children billeted on them without reference to the billeting officer, while one teacher returned to Liverpool with a 'derogatory report' on the quality of some of the accommodation allocated to the children, possibly stemming from an idealised picture of rural life and being quite unaware of the extent of rural deprivation. In May 1941, when a child evacuees' parents visited one weekend, they threatened to take him away immediately if a better billet was not found before they returned home.

While the overall responsibility for the evacuees was vested in the UDC, their welfare was in the hands of the Womens' Voluntary Service (WVS). The plight of the evacuees, far away from their homes, in a rural environment which initially at least they did not understand, aroused widespread sympathy on the part of the townspeople who formed a welfare committee to look after their interests. The creation of a third body in the town with some interest in the welfare of the evacuees raised the possibility of competing jurisdictions and in an effort to prevent this the welfare committee operated under the aegis of the WVS with two co-opted councillors among its members. Even so there were complaints that the welfare committee trespassed on the work of the billeting officer and the county medical authorities.

A few in the town, possibly alienated by the unfamiliar accents of the evacuees and their more 'streetwise' and sometimes more assertive manner than their local counterparts, were less sympathetic. One councillor believed that too great an emphasis on the welfare of the evacuees on the part of the community would encourage some parents to wash their hands of any responsibility for their evacuated children. He clearly believed that the evacuees were responsible for some of the vandalism which was beginning to occur at the town's playing fields and in September 1941 roundly condemned the teachers for going on holiday instead of staying in the town to supervise the evacuees during the school holidays. One suspects that public opinion in the town resented his attitude, for on one Saturday evening in May 1941, when his wife had just returned from Hereford, he answered a knock on the door to find the billeting officer, a policeman and two evacuees, one of whom was to be billeted on him. He convened an extraordinary meeting of the UDC to protest, citing his wife's health and her contribution to the war effort as reasons to reverse the billeting officer's decision., but to no avail.

Though there was an influx of accompanied evacuees late in the autumn of 1943 which led the billeting officer to consider requisitioning, by the beginning of 1944 evacuees had begun to return home and his salary was reduced from £75 to £26 per annum. However, with the onset of V bomb raids in May 1944, many of the evacuees returned to their old billets.

Another war time responsibility of the UDC was the collection of salvage. Early in 1940 part of the market hall was set aside on Wednesday and Friday afternoons as a collection point for waste paper. The response may well have been disappointing for by April the Boys' Club, under the direction of Miss Evelyn, was undertaking a regular collection of waste paper throughout the town. For a time Miss Evelyn also organised the collection of scrap metal which was stored at the rear of the Market Hall, though this was subsequently undertaken by the UDC directly, sending the refuse cart around for the purpose on the last Wednesday and Friday in each month. Plans for the collection of bones as salvage for processing into bonemeal and for the manufacture of glue were dropped in view of the small quantity likely to be available and the health hazards involved in their storage. At the beginning of 1941 Mrs Newall of Corton was appointed as salvage warden, a post she held until the end of the war, with the WVS undertaking much of the work of collection.

During the second half of 1940 eastern Radnorshire experienced its first air raids of the war. That of 1 July on Gwernaffel may well have been targeted on the pipeline carrying Birmingham's water supply from the Elan Valley reservoirs, whilst that of 31 July near Llangunllo may well have been directed at the pipeline or at the nearby Knucklas viaduct, one of the most vulnerable points on the Central Wales line which carried anthracite from the western area of the south Wales coalfield to the West Midlands. The other raids were clearly more random, possibly the result of damaged enemy aircraft jettisoning their bombloads before heading

48th POW Camp, Clatterbrune

back to base, for the bombs fell well away from areas of strategic importance. Thus on 12 September five bombs fell in the Broadheath area, one on Lower Heath Farm, and on 25 September six bombs fell near the junction of the Knighton-Presteigne and Whitton roads, three of them on Jenkinallis Farm.

The raids caused no casualties, but seem to have jolted the town into taking civil defence more seriously, for a degree of complacency, if not laxity, seems to have been creeping into the observance of air raid precautions. At an air raid warning practice towards the end of August 1940 one fireman failed to turn up while some members of the ARP and Local Defence Volunteers (LDV) were censured by the UDC for lighting matches and smoking cigarettes during the exercise. At the same UDC meeting one councillor complained that during dances at the Assembly Rooms, cars were left with their lights on in Broad Street and Station Road. During September the approach to civil defence became much more rigorous: in future cars were to be left in the station yard during dances and the UDC asked the police to prosecute those who failed to observe blackout regulations. At the end of January 1941 the town was divided into six areas for civil defence purposes with specific teams to deal with fires started by enemy action, rescue and first aid.

The Local Defence Volunteers came into being on 15 May 1940 when the first volunteers were enrolled at the police station. By June, in a

Prisoners from the 48th POW Camp helping with the harvest

uniform of denim overalls the LDV had taken up its duties, receiving battledress in December, by which time it was better known as the Home Guard. By May 1942 B Company (Presteigne) of the 1st Radnor Home Guard, had a strength of 6 officers and 123 other ranks, and consisted of four platoons: No. 1 Presteigne, No. 2 Llandewi, No. 3 Whitton and No. 4 Discoed-Cascob. In addition to infantry training, military exercises and liaising with the police, ARP and civil defence, the Home Guard carried out a wide range of duties, thus freeing regular troops for service overseas. The Presteigne platoon manned the observation post of the church tower between 10p.m. and 6a.m. each night in three watches, tracking plane movements and noting any breaches of blackout regulations,. They also operated a nightly road patrol, stopping and checking the credentials of all road users, checking the blackout in rural areas and investigating any suspicious occurrences. The other platoons of the Company patrolled their areas on a daily basis, sometimes on horseback and operating road blocks.

Another military establishment in the town was the 48th POW Camp, built on land at Clatterbrune requisitioned from Captain F.O. Lewis in

1941, the prefabricated buildings being erected during the first half of 1942. The camp was built to hold 1,000 Italian POWs, but the population fell to 750 or so after the war had ended when German POWs, some of whom had been previously held in the USA, were kept in the camp. The prisoners were housed in four rows of huts, each of which held fifty men. The compound also contained a kitchen, mess room, hospital, canteen, recreation room and a hall used for concerts and film shows. The guard room, guards' living quarters, chapel, offices and stores were located between the POW compound and Greenfield Road.

The prisoners were provided with army type battledress, usually dyed brown with distinguishing coloured patches. Most were employed on farm work in the locality, transported from the camp under escort at 7a.m. and returning between 5 and 6p.m.. They were paid 14s. per week in 'camp money' which could be exchanged in local shops, and 14s. in cash or in credits. The daily routine of the camp was: 6a.m. reveille and breakfast; 12-1p.m. lunch; 6-7p.m. dinner; 10p.m. lights out. Leisure facilities were limited; a radio and a small library in the canteen, and occasional concerts and film shows. In 1944 the camp commandant sought permission from the UDC to use the Assembly Room for a weekly cinema show for the Italian POWs and from the Education Committee for the use of the county school playing field for soccer matches for the POWs, but both requests were rejected; not out of any deep hostility towards the POWs, but because the authorities would not sanction the use of these facilities on Sundays, the only free day for the prisoners. The German POWs had their own pitch at the camp where they played matches against local teams, and at least one POW played for Presteigne St Andrew's.

For the most part relations between the POWs and the camp authorities were good, though there were some passive resistance on a few occasions when the food provided was unpalatable. Only one prisoner tried to escape and he was recaptured within a few hours on Wapley Hill. Much to their surprise, the POWs found that their rations were more generous than those of the local population and some shared their coffee and sweet rations with civilians with whom they were on friendly terms. The prisoners had their own orchestra, concert party and dance band and their concerts at the Assembly Rooms, at Knighton, Builth, Brecon and Eardisley attracted large audiences.

Once the war had ended the camp regime was considerably relaxed; the POWs were allowed into the town during certain hours, though officially banned from public houses, while some were billeted outside the camp at hostels in Peterchurch, Talgarth and Eardisley. In 1946-47 the POWs were shipped home, the few troublemakers going first. Some prisoners, both Italian and German, preferred to stay, marrying local girls.

As in the rest of the country, the community devoted much of its energies to the war effort, joining in savings schemes, raising funds for the welfare of the forces and for Britain's allies. The War Agricultural Executive Committee sought to increase food production and under its auspices every available acre was devoted to this purpose: Broadheath was cultivated from 1940 onwards and in 1943 one of the County School's fields, Gaol Meadow, was ploughed and planted with potatoes. Anecdotal evidence suggests that the Committee's advice and directions were not always appreciated, for some farmers were reluctant to change their habitual pattern of land utilisation, believing that they knew the potential of their farm better than any committee.

War restrictions and regulations permeated every aspect of life, though food and fuel rationing bit less deeply than in urban areas. The area's orchards, gardens and hedgerows meant that fresh fruit and vegetables were relatively plentiful, while the meat ration could be supplemented by the occasional rabbit or trout obtained through a little judicious poaching, or more often through the network of family relationships and mutual obligations built up over the generations. This source could also yield a load of firewood and occasionally a piece of bacon, some eggs and even a little farmhouse butter.

Given the uncertainties of war, the monotonous austerity of wartime life, the presence of British and US servicemen in the wider locality and a Women's Land Army detachment based at Whitton, together with constraints on travel, local entertainment was at a premium. This hunger for entertainment was utilised to raise funds for war charities, the UDC organising the War Charities Committee to co-ordinate the activities of the charities and to apportion the proceeds between them. Under its auspices whist drives, concerts and dances were held, usually in the Assembly Rooms. The dances in particular attracted large numbers and although they ended at 11p.m. (until the later stages of the war), provoked complaints from at least one resident of Broad Street.

Accepting the demand for entertainment it is ironic that for the first year or so of the war the cinema at the Assembly Rooms was closed. Mr Brown, the tenant of the cinema, had given up his lease in April 1939 and prospective tenants had been deterred by the poor projection facilities and the UDC's reluctance to improve them. Early in 1941 the tenancy of the cinema was taken by Mr Hodges and Mr Hatfield, and with business booming the UDC raised the rent to the unprecedented level of £2 7s. 6d. per week. For the next few years shows were held on Mondays, Tuesdays, Fridays and Saturdays, with a Saturday afternoon matinee performance for a while. Attendances at weekend performances were so large that the more expensive seats were raised to enhance visibility. With the gradual transfer of troops out of the area in the closing months of the war, the boom was over and the cinema reverted to its previous pattern of two shows per week.

The war years also saw the establishment of two new enterprises, Botanical Drugs Ltd. and Charles Hill and Co., both of which were to play an important role in the post-war development of the town, although not under their original names. The outbreak of war had interrupted the import of medical supplies, notably digitalis, and to remedy this the government had encouraged the establishment of small processing centres. Dr R. Walker had set up such a centre in his garage at Warden Court, but by 1943 the business had outgrown its original premises and moved to a new factory built by Italian POW labour at the Burgage.

Edward Hill, a director of Charles Hill and Co. of Hall Green, a firm which produced zinc alloy castings, had come to know Presteigne on fishing holidays between the wars, and after his wife and children moved to the locality from Birmingham to escape the bombing, he decided, in 1941, to establish a 'shadow' factory in the town in the former S.W. and S. Electrical Power premises at the junction of Ave Maria Lane and Harper's Lane. After the building had been reconditioned and strengthened, the original labour force of ten, led by a foreman from the Hall Green works, began the production of zinc alloy castings, anti-tank mine fuses and machine gun bullets. In 1943 the factory was extended to house machinery sent from the USA under the Lend Lease scheme and the labour force gradually increased to eighty.

The two firms, both of which depended heavily on female labour, provided a long needed boost to the local economy, and the increase in purchasing power which this produced led to a revival of confidence in the future of the town in the closing years of the war. In 1944, under the 'Housing of the Working Classes Post-War Programme' the UDC planned to build at least forty council houses and a Town Planning Committee was set up consisting of the UDC and representatives of the British Legion, the Women's Institute, the Foresters, the Oddfellows and of Charles Hill and Co. to plan for a prosperous future once the war had ended.

Fifteen men of the district lost their lives serving in the armed forces during the Second World War and it was felt that simply recording their names on the War Memorial was not a sufficient tribute; it was decided that a memorial hall should be built. The project made little headway until 1950 when two prefabricated buildings were acquired at a disposal sale. This seems to have given fresh impetus to the scheme; £2,800 was raised by public subscription, the Presteigne branch of the British Legion donating £400, and the Welsh Church Fund made a grant of £2,300. The Memorial Hall was opened on 25 May 1953 by Lady Delia Llewelyn. The building and equipping of the hall cost some £6,500, but by April 1954 the deficit had been cleared and the Memorial Hall became the main venue for the town's social events.

Post-war Presteigne
The poor quality of much of the town's housing stock together with a sharp rise in population produced an acute housing shortage in Presteigne in the immediate post-war years. Between 1931 and 1951 Presteigne's population rose by 13.9%, with in-migration accounting for almost two-thirds of the increase. In contrast Radnorshire's population had fallen by 6.2% in the same period, with the county experiencing an out-migration rate of 10.7%. The rural area surrounding the town had shared the county's fortunes during the period, its population falling by rather more than 8% during the period 1931-51. Moreover the age structure of the town's population in 1951 was certainly the healthiest in Radnorshire and one of the most balanced in mid-Wales: nearly 25% of the population was under 15 and only 17% aged 60 and over. The increased housing need had been recognised by the authorities, for in 1944 the UDC had drawn up plans to build council houses once the war was over. After considering sites at Townend and Clatterbrune, part of Silia Meadow was bought, and between 1947 and 1953 fifty-eight houses and six old people's bungalows were built on Castle Road, so named in 1949.

However, by 1961 the population of the town had fallen from its 1951 total of 1,255 to 1,197, whilst that of the surrounding area fell by 16.7% in the same period. Even so, by 1960 it was clear that there was still a housing shortage in the town, the Chamber of Trade expressing its concern that this was leading to a drift away from the town on the part of younger people and pointing out to the UDC that many working in the town were having to live outside it. However the town's inadequate water supply and sewage system hampered further house building. The water company's capital resources were limited and there were few local springs which it could utilise to significantly expand the supply. As for

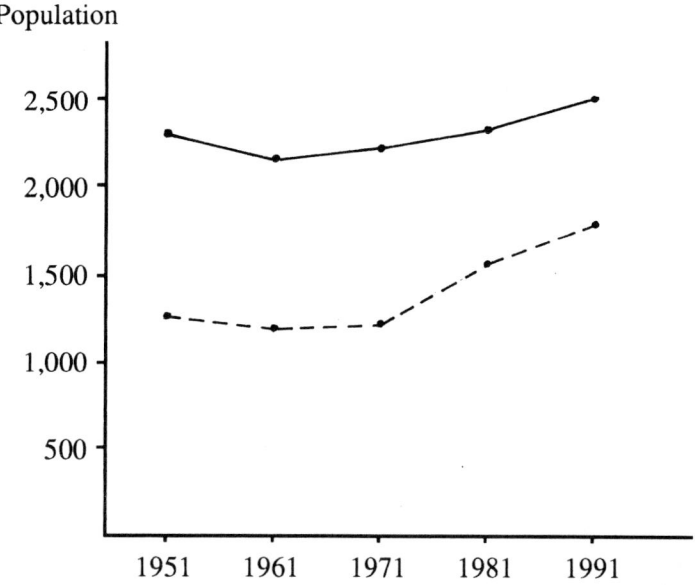

Fig. 32: The Population of Presteigne and the surrounding area
------ *Town population* ——— *Town and surrounding area population*
Surrounding area: Norton, Discoed, Rodd, Nash and Little Brampton, Willey, Stapleton and Combe
(Source: Printed census data, 1851-91)

the sewage system, Dr David Walker, the Medical Officer of Health, commented in 1955, 'I doubt if there is another Urban area in the country with a sewage plant like ours.'

By 1965 a new sewage treatment works had been established to the north-east of Clatterbrune and in 1967, after protracted negotiations, the UDC bought the water company and sold the concern to the Radnorshire and North Breconshire Water Board, gaining access to the latter's supply, a water main then being laid from Dolley Green to the reservoir at the Warden. Once these schemes were in hand, the UDC felt able to proceed with its housing programme. In 1964 the Townend site was bought and in 1966 plans were drawn up for a first phase of thirty houses and twelve bungalows, with part of the site reserved for an old people's home. A second phase of 26 houses, Western Avenue, was completed in 1971. A third phase of building was planned on the remainder of the Townend site, Appletree Orchard and Pasture, bought by the UDC in 1967, and part of the railway station land acquired in 1969. With local government reor-

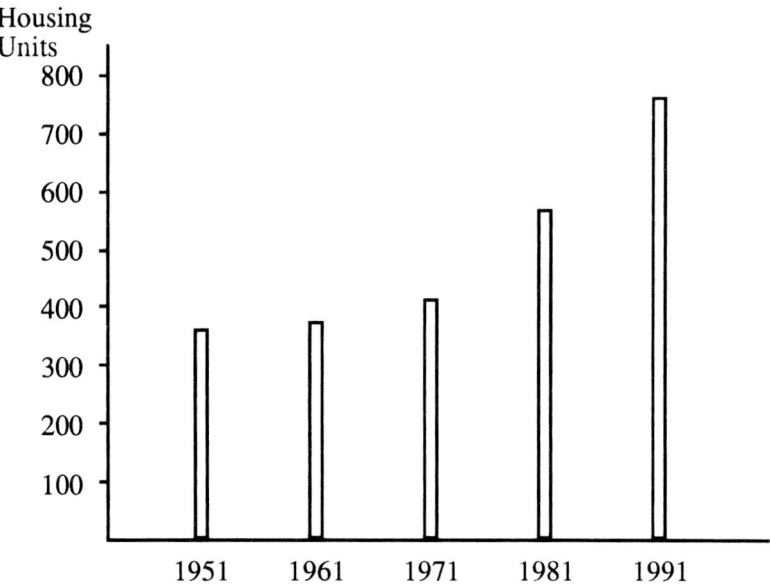

*Fig. 33: Presteigne's Housing Stock, 1951-91
(Source: Printed census data, 1951-91)*

ganisation in the offing, the UDC was unlikely to be in existence long enough to oversee the completion of a conventional council house scheme at Appletree Meadow, and it was decided to sell sixteen sites to council tenants wishing to build their own houses and others to people of working age, with an embargo on resale for a period of five years.

Significantly there was little private sector house building prior to the 1970s for it seemed to many that the town's future was highly insecure, a leading townsman commenting in 1960 that 'Presteigne may be losing the will to exist.' This pessimistic mood stemmed from the continuing erosion of the town's traditional roles and amenities. An early casualty was its market function. As early as October 1945 no livestock market was being held in the town and sporadic attempts to revive it met with little success. In 1954 the UDC planned the refurbishment of the auction yard and the market restarted in April 1957, but had closed within a year. The market restarted in 1959 but ceased to function in 1963 and following the sale of its fittings and fixtures in April 1964, the cattle auction yard was sold to Kaye Alloy Castings. The adjoining sheep market was acquired by the UDC and following the sale of the stockpens at the beginning of 1970, it was converted into a car park which also incorporated part of the playground of the old Hereford Street primary school.

When the Market Hall had been derequisitioned in 1944 the UDC had hoped to restart the weekly Wednesday market, but had met with little success and by 1947 the Market Hall was functioning as a vegetable shop. The Assembly Rooms above continued to house the social functions of the town until the opening of the Memorial Hall in 1953, but with the closing of the cinema in 1964 and the Fire Brigade moving to its new Fire Station on Back Lane, the building seemed redundant, particularly after the plans in 1968 to convert the Assembly Rooms into a social club for Kaye Alloy Castings came to nothing. A public meeting to discuss the future of the building in October 1968 was reluctant to demolish the building to the first floor or to demolish the whole building except for the clock tower and suggested that it could house a library or a museum with the ground floor used as an indoor playground, but could not formulate a financially viable alternative. By 1970 the UDC felt that the only alternatives were to demolish the building or to sell it, but with a best offer of £1,500 and reluctant to take the unpopular step of demolition, in 1972 the UDC decided to clear the Assembly Rooms and to put them in good and safe order and to refurbish and refit the former market hall as a shop.

The town's function as a seat of justice also came under threat. In 1947 a proposal to transfer the Assizes to Llandrindod Wells was fought off successfully, but in 1949, faced with an estimated bill of £2,000 to repair the Shire Hall, the authorities decided to transfer both Quarter Sessions and Assizes to Llandrindod Wells. The UDC mobilised local public opinion, public protest meetings were held, and a petition presented to the Lord Chancellor in order to secure a reversal of the decision. As a result of the Courts Act of 1970 however, the assize system was dismantled, and the last Assizes were held at Presteigne in October 1971, though magistrates' courts were still held at the Shire Hall for nearly two decades. The presence in the centre of the town of two largely redundant buildings could not but add to the impression of decline.

In the meantime Presteigne had also lost its rail link. At the beginning of February 1951 the rail passenger service on the Titley-Presteigne line was suspended, officially because of the coal shortage, and at the end of March this suspension became permanent, much to the indignation of the UDC which protested that '... this town, the capital of Radnor, is virtually isolated'. The UDC and Chamber of Trade enlisted the services of the local MP, Tudor Watkin, and of Lord Rennell of Rodd to fight the closure, but without success, and in the summer of 1964 the surviving skeleton rail freight service came to an end. Though initially local bus companies increased their services to Kington and Leominster, these

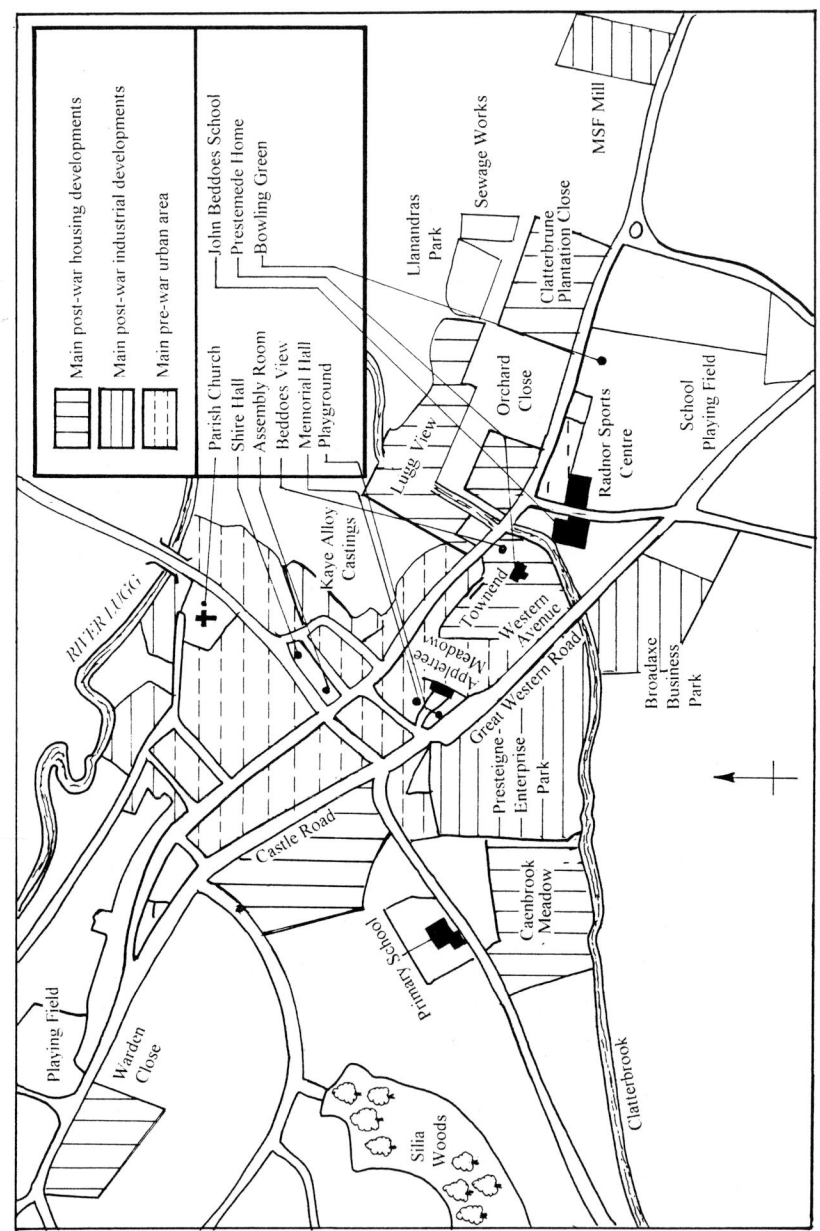

Fig. 34: The growth of Presteigne since 1945

were soon curtailed as a result of growing car ownership, reinforcing the impression of stagnation and decline.

The town's secondary school also seemed under threat immediately after the war, for in 1946 it was suggested that a new secondary school should be built at Knighton to which pupils at the County School should be transferred. Not surprisingly, this suggestion produced fierce protests from the UDC, Chamber of Trade and the staff of the County School. The proposal was dropped and the County School remained at Presteigne, with a new secondary modern school sited at Knighton. In the 1950s successive headmasters, Mr D.E. Redfearn and Mr T.G. Moses, together with W.H. Howse, made a determined effort to raise the school's status: its name was changed to Presteigne Grammar School; it regained the income from its endowments from the county authorities and a much greater emphasis was placed upon its long history, with Founder's Day celebrated annually.

Between 1959 and 1963 the school buildings were remodelled and a new hall built, and in 1964 the Local Education Authority decided to concentrate secondary education in east Radnorshire by closing the secondary modern school at Knighton and establishing a bilateral school at Presteigne, though in 1968 it was decided that a comprehensive school would be more appropriate to the needs of the area. After the old grammar school premises had been greatly extended, John Beddoes School received its first pupils in September 1970. In the meantime the town's educational facilities had been further enhanced by the building of a new primary school in 1963 on part of Silia Meadow to replace the town's two other primary schools and also Norton School.

The expansion of the school coincided with, or perhaps helped to encourage population growth. Presteigne saw a small rise to 1,215 in 1971, but that in the surrounding area grew by 11%, largely as a result of the marked population increase in Norton as it began to develop as a dormitory village. However, the age structure of the town had altered sharply, and by 1971 the 60+ age group accounted for 25% of the population, with the proportion of the population under 15 falling to 20.6% and the 15-44 age group falling by nearly 5%.

The post-war period saw the town beginning to broaden its industrial base. After the war Botanical Drugs Ltd. changed its name to Presteigne Produce Co. Ltd. and turned to the drying and processing of culinary herbs and vegetables and the packaging of figs, dates and brazil nuts. The firm relied in the main on female labour, and employed, at its peak, about a hundred workers, many of them part time, remaining in production until 1973.

In 1945 Charles Hill and Co. began to run down the scale of operations at their zinc alloy castings factory on Harper's Lane and in 1946 the business was bought by the West Bromwich firm of Kaye Alloy Castings. In 1951 aluminium pressure diecasting was introduced and gradually both the scale of production and the size of the labour force employed began to expand, and the premises were extended in 1951, 1962 and 1972. However, the process was far from smooth since, in the era of 'Stop, Go', demand for industrial components fluctuated sharply and this was reflected in the output and employment levels of the firm.

CHAPTER IX

Towards the 21st Century

Between 1971 and 1991 the population of the town rose by more than 40%, from 1,215 to 1,717. Norton's population rose even more sharply, by 72%, from 250 to 429. The population of the surrounding area, Discoed, Rodd, Nash and Little Brampton, Stapleton, Willey and Combe, increased more steadily, by 12% over the same period. Much of the population increase stemmed from inward migration, a significant proportion of which consisted of retired people, and the age distribution of population continues to be heavily skewed towards the over 60 age groups, which made up more than a third of the population by 1991.

The increase in population, together with rising expectations, has led to a steep rise in the town's housing stock, from 420 units in 1971 to 748 in 1991. Much of the new housing has been homes for sale, with three relatively large estates, Warden Close, Clatterbrune and Orchard Close being completed by the early 1980s, while the closing years of the decade saw a start made on two further developments, at Caenbrook Meadow and Plantation Close. Even so, the first two phases of Lugg View were built by Radnor District Council, the third phase being a housing association development, as was Beddoes View, completed in 1993. A less obvious aspect of the expansion of the town's housing stock has been in the form of flat conversions above retail premises in the centre of the town, as the ending of retail price maintenance, the generally high interest rates of the period and more frequent deliveries led to a reduction in the levels of stock carried so reducing the need for retail storage space. The increase in population and housing also necessitated further improvements in the town's sewage system and an increased water supply, with the Pilleth borehole becoming the source of the town's water in 1978, augmented by the development of a second borehole in the early 1980s.

Though the UDC and its successor the Town Council sought to encourage the development of light industry, such attempts initially met with little success beyond the building of the Midland Shires Farmers' mill and warehouse in the early 1970s, and John Beddoes School was the largest employer of labour in the town after Kaye Alloy Castings. Part of the problem in attracting industry to the town lay in the difficulty of access to the area scheduled for industrial development above Station Road, while growing car ownership was producing traffic congestion in the town centre.

In the mid-1960s Radnorshire County Council began to consider building a by-pass around the town, a proposal not initially welcomed by the UDC or Chamber of Trade since it was believed that this would simply hasten the town's decline. Though plans for a by-pass, the eastern section of which would utilise the old railway line, were drawn up in 1970 and planning permission for the project was obtained in 1974, the country's financial problems meant that the scheme was postponed for a few years. In 1978 the project was revived, the planning authorities arguing that it would enable 'lateral' development of the town, rather than ribbon development. By this time planning permission had lapsed, and after the plans had been modified to include an underpass for the use of children attending the primary school, planning permission was renewed and work began on the eastern section, to which there were no objections, late in 1979.

After a public inquiry into the western section which resolved means of access to the town centre, work on the relief road (the term preferred by the Town Council) was completed in 1984 and the new road was named the Great Western Road in 1986. Closely associated with the relief road scheme were plans to build a lorry park and car park. The lorry park at the top of Station Road was built in 1985, though ten years later, despite sustained pressure from the Town Council and Chamber of Trade, the town is still awaiting the car park.

The relief road gave access to the proposed industrial estate and by 1982 the first units had been built and let, the first occupants being a horse carriage builder, Mangar Aids (now Mangar International), an organ builder and a video distributor. By 1984 work had begun on further units to bring the total to ten and by 1989 the Development Board for Rural Wales was considering the extension of the site to develop the present Broadaxe Business Park. Though some concern was expressed in the later 1980s at the failure to let units to local people and at the amalgamation of units into larger premises, the presence of the industrial estate, now Presteigne Enterprise Park, considerably broadened the industrial base of the town. Two firms located there, Mangar International, which started as a cottage industry at Llanfihangel Rhydithon, and Labtech Ltd., which started as a small family business on the industrial estate in 1984, are now major employers in the town, both producing high value-added products.

The 1980s also saw a marked increase in the town's social, sporting and cultural amenities. In 1983 the Mid Border Community Arts Association was founded, based initially in the Shire Hall, with the objective of bringing more arts-based activity to the area. The major event associated with the MBCA has been the festival held each year at the end of August, with concerts held in St Andrew's Church and an art exhibition at the Shire Hall as the centre pieces of a highly varied programme. The first festival, held in 1983 was a relatively modest event, but with patrons such as Lord Croft, Sir Geraint Evans and Sir Sidney Nolan, it soon developed into a major regional event attracting many visitors to the town and necessitating its own infrastructure. The festival developed its own 'fringe' in the shape of the first Sheep Music festival on the Warden in 1992. The MBCA has also sought to provide a varied programme of events throughout the year, featuring local amateur and visiting professional writers, musicians and artists, and also seeking to involve younger age groups in its activities. These aspects of its work were greatly assisted by the conversion of the Assembly Rooms into a theatre/community arts centre, work on which began in 1990.

The other major innovation in the town's amenities came with the East Radnor Leisure Centre which opened on 9 January 1989. The first hint that the town had ambitions in this direction came in 1962 when there is a reference in the UDC minutes to a Sports Centre Committee. However, it was not until 1979 that the UDC heard that there was a possibility of a sports hall being built in the town, though this did not become a formal proposal until 1984. In mid-1987 a Sports Centre Action Committee had been formed, John Beddoes School and its Parent Teachers Association playing an important role. The committee pledged to raise £30,000 locally towards the cost of the project. By the end of 1987 nearly £18,000 had been raised and by the end of the next year, with the Town Council contributing £5,000, the target was reached.

Alongside such high profile projects, were other measures initiated by the Town Council to improve the town's amenities: play areas were provided at Lugg View and near the Memorial Hall, while the play equipment at the Playing Fields was updated and refurbished on several occasions. The Withybeds, acquired by the UDC in 1967 and left as a nature reserve, was subsequently leased to the Radnor Wild Life Trust and laid out as a small nature park and bird reserve, which opened in May 1990. In 1992 Went's Meadow, on the banks of the Lugg near Boultibrooke Bridge, was acquired and similarly leased to the Radnor Wild Life Trust. In 1994 Silia Woods was acquired and donated to the Woodland Trust, with public access to the woodland walks which were established there. During the 1980s Presteigne Town Council emerged as one of the most enthusiastic and successful recycling authorities in the region, handling bottles, cans of all types, paper, cardboard, textiles and hand tools.

The growth in the town's amenities over the past decade or so suggests that there has been a resurgence of confidence in the town's future, and the two royal visits to the town in the 1980s may also reflect this. On 11 September 1884 the Princess Royal opened the refurbished premises of Link Line, responsible for the production of a community tape magazine, while on 15 September 1989 she returned to the town to formally open the East Radnor Leisure Centre.

The last half of the twentieth century saw more changes in Presteigne than the town had experienced since the sixteenth century, and as the pace of change quickened in the 1980s, strains began to show as the delicate balance between development and conservation began to be tilted towards one side or the other. Thus controversy was very much in the air in the later 1980s. In 1988, with the leisure centre nearing completion, it was proposed that Broadaxe Lane be closed to through traffic, in spite of objections from Radnor District Council, the police, the fire service, the town council and a petition bearing 800 signatures. The decision provoked an outcry and in the end it was decided instead to install 'sleeping policemen' as a traffic calming measure, much to the relief of public opinion in the town. Towards the end of 1988 it was suggested that the High Street should have a one-way system, possibly extending into Hereford Street as far as Station Road. This again met with opposition, particularly from the Chamber of Trade, but after the scope of the scheme was reduced so that the one-way system was to extend no further than the junction with Broad Street, it was implemented, initially for a twelve month trial period.

The decision to seek grant-maintained status for John Beddoes School in 1989 divided not only the parents. but also the local communities, and after a controversy which generated much more heat than light, the proposal was decisively rejected by the parents. The last dispute of the late 1980s came over the proposal in 1989 to remove the magistrates' court from Presteigne to Llandrindod Wells as a result of the amalgamation of the petty sessional divisions. Local public opinion was firmly united in opposition to the proposal and matters were not helped by the injudicious suggestion on the part of a county councillor that on the closing of the court in the Shire Hall, some of the fittings and fixtures of the building might be removed to the County Council Chamber at Llandrindod Wells. The successful campaign against this suggestion reconciled public opinion in the town to the loss of the court, sweetened by the decision that the court room at the Shire Hall 'would be used as necessary' if the case load warranted it.

The slump of the early 1980s hit the town hard and matters were not helped by the area losing its Intermediate Development Area status in 1982. Unemployment rates in the Presteigne Planning Area rose to more than 15% in 1985 as Kaye Alloy Castings reduced its labour force by more than 50%. The slump of the early 1990s had considerably less impact upon the town and three major concerns, Kaye Alloy Castings, Mangar International and Labtech increased their labour forces in the first half of the 1990s, the latter extending into Broadaxe Business Park in 1994. The 10% sample survey of employment in the 1991 census suggests that the broadening of the town's industrial base in the second half of the century has had a profound impact on local employment patterns, for nearly 30% of the sample were employed in manufacturing, 18% in distribution and catering and 23% in the service sector, with less than 13% now employed in agriculture.

As in other small towns, the retail sector has felt vulnerable to competition from the supermarkets and superstores in the neighbouring larger towns. However, there has been no marked loss of retail floor space to non-retail use in the town and the number of retail units has increased since 1971. The town's retailers have been helped by the growth in the town's population, the broadening of its industrial base and the expansion of the town's amenities which has encouraged visitors. The Chamber of Trade has sought to encourage this latter feature, publicising major events in the town such as the Festival, the annual Sheep Music Festival, the vintage car rally held annually in October and in its promotion of Presteigne as 'The Town of Festivals', in conjunction with the Presteigne Promotion Association. In particular it has sought to broaden the town's appeal to visitors by organising non-arts based events such as the Quilt Festival of 1993 and the Science Fair of 1995.

The expansion of the town's amenities forms part of the most sustained effort in the town's history to develop tourism, and the current restoration of the Shire Hall to its 1870 condition represents the most ambitious project in such a programme. The townscape, with the Victorian shopfronts of High Street and the Georgian facades of St David's Street and Broad Street, together with the quiet cobbled courtyards, certainly has much to offer the tourist. So too the glorious countryside surrounding the town, which, in easy reach of the Welsh mountains and coast and the towns of mid-Wales and the Marches, has much to commend itself as a tourist base. However, some fear that an increase in tourism would destroy the quiet tranquillity which lies at the heart of the town's appeal.

Over the last decade or so Presteigne has enjoyed a relative prosperity such as it has not experienced since the mid-nineteenth century as a result of a series of decisions taken by a number of disparate individuals and bodies, rather than as a result of a coherent and all-embracing plan. The history of the town shows that the line between stagnation and steady growth is is a very fine one, and the false dawns experienced by the town in the past should serve as a warning against any complacency.

Bibliography

Abbreviations used: *TRS* - Transactions of the Radnorshire Society
TWNFC - Transactions of the Woolhope Naturalists' Field Club

Chapter 1
B.G. Charles: *Non-Celtic Place Names in Wales*, 1938
E. Ekwall: *English Place-Names*, 4th edition, 1960
R.W.D. Fenn: 'The Character of Early Christianity in Radnorshire', *TRS*, Vol. XXXVII, 1967, pp7-16; Vol. XXXVIII, 1968, pp62-8
M. Gelling (ed): *Offa's Dyke Reviewed, by Frank Noble*, 1983
J. Hillaby: 'Early Christian and Pre-Conquest Leominster', *TWNFC*, Vol. XLV, Part III, 1987, pp557-685
M. Lloyd Jones: *Society and Settlement in Wales and the Marches 500 B.C. to A.D. 1100*, 1984
S.H. Martin: 'Roman Coins', *TWFNC*, Vol. XXXIII, Part III, 1951, p275
F. Noble: 'Archaeological Finds in the Knighton Area', *TRS*, Vol.XXVII, 1957, pp62-71
W.R. Pye: 'A Further List of Roman Coins from Corton', *TRS*, Vol.XXXV, 1965, pp22-23
Lord Rennell: *Valley on the March*, 1958
Royal Commission on Ancient Monuments: Radnorshire, 1913
Royal Commission on Historical Monuments: Herefordshire Vol. III, North-West, 1934
C.S. Stanford: *Croft Ambrey*, 1974
The Archaeology of the Welsh Marches, 1980
C.S. Stanford (ed): *Guide to Prehistoric and Roman Sites in Herefordshire*, 1976

Chapter II

Bruce Coplestone-Crow: *Herefordshire Place-Names*, 1989
  'Further Information Concerning Combe Castle'.
  Herefordshire Archaeological News, No.66, Autumn 1996, p16
  'The Lordship of Kington', *Herefordshire Archaeological News*, No.66, Autumn 1996, pp25-9
J.T. Evans: *The Church Plate of Radnorshire*, 1910
M.A.Faraday: 'The Assessment for the Fifteenth of 1293 of Radnor and other Marcher Lordships', *TRS*, Vols. XLIII, 1973, pp79-85 and XLIV, 1974, pp 62-68
  'Mortality in the Diocese of Hereford, 1442-1545', *TWNFC*, Vol. XLIII, Part II, 1980, pp.163-74
P.E.H. Hair: 'Chaplains, Chantries and Chapels of North-West Herefordshire *c.*1400, Pt. 2', *TWNFC*, Vol. XLVI, Part II, 1989, pp245-88
Geoffrey Hodges: *Owain Glyn Dwr*, 1995
W.H. Howse: 'Early Grant of a Weekly Market to Presteigne', *TRS*, Vol. XXVI, 1956, pp43-46
A.W. Langford: 'The Plague in Herefordshire', *TWFNC*, Vol. XXXV, Part II, 1956, pp146-53
Ordnance Survey: *SO 3064-3164, scale 1:2500*, 1974
Philips and Co Deeds: Powys County Archives Office
W.J. Rees: *South Wales and the Marches*, 1924
Paul Remfry: *Castles of Radnorshire*, 1996
  'Some Historical Information Concerning Combe Castle', *Herefordshire Archaeological News*, No.65, Spring 1996, p34
  'The Foundation and Fate of Kington and Huntington Castles', *Herefordshire Archaeological News*, No.66, Autumn 1996, pp29-37
Lord Rennell: *Valley on the March*, 1958
J.F.D. Shrewsbury: *The History of Bubonic Plague in England*, 1970
H.M. Taylor: *Anglo-Saxon Architecture*, 1965
F. and C. Thorn (eds): *Domesday Book: 17, Herefordshire*, 1983
  Domesday Book: 25, Shropshire, 1986

Chapter III

Acts of the Privy Council, 1548-53
D. Roy Ll. Adams: *The Parliamentary Representation of Radnorshire*, unpublished MA thesis, University of Wales, 1970
A.T. Bannister: *Diocese of Herefordshire Institutions, 1539-1900*, 1923
John Beddoes' will, PCC 29, Carew
S.T. Bindoff (ed): *The House of Commons, 1509-58*, 1982
John Bradshaw's will, PCC 48, Arundell
E.J.L. Cole: 'Abstract of Radnorshire Wills in the Prerogative Court of Canterbury', *TRS*, Vol. VI, 1936, pp9-10; Vol. XXIII, 1953, p46

'Hereford Probate Records', *TRS*, Vol. XXVI, 1956, pp22-31; Vol. XXVII, 1957, pp2-24

'Nicholas the First', *TRS*, Vol. XXXIII, 1963, pp43-6

J.A. Downie: 'Sir Robert Harley, Sir Rowland Gwynne and the New Radnor Election of 1690', *TRS*, Vol. XLVI, 1976, pp10-20

J.T. Evans: *The Church Plate of Radnorshire*, 1910

M.A. Faraday: 'Mortality in the Diocese of Hereford, 1442-1545', *TWNFC*, Vol. XLIII, Part II, 1980, pp163-174

Ludlow, 1085-1660, 1991

J.K. Gruenfelder: 'Radnorshire Parliamentary Elections', *TRS*, Vol. XLVII, 1977, pp25-31

P.W. Hasler (ed): *The House of Commons, 1558-1603*, 1981

W.H. Howse: *School and Bell*, 1956

Letters, Papers, Domestic and Foreign, Henry VIII, 1535, 1536-37, 1539, 1540-41

John Lloyd (ed): *Radnorshire, Miscellaneous Papers relating to the History of the County, II, Parliamentary Surveys, 1649*, 1900

J.E. Neale: *The Elizabethan House of Commons*, 1950

Philips and Co. Deeds: Powys County Archives Office

Lord Rennell: *Valley on the March*, 1958

John Southwood: *The Meredith Family of Presteigne and Kington, 1391-1940*, 1982

Chapter IV

D. Roy Ll. Adams: *The Parliamentary Representation of Radnorshire, 1536-1832*, unpublished M.A. thesis, University of Wales, 1970

T. Bassett: *A Study of Local Government in Wales under the Commonwealth*, unpublished M.A. thesis, University of Wales, 1941

Ruth Bidgood: 'Families of Llandewi Hall, Pt.I', *TRS*, Vol. XLIV, 1974, pp 7-25

Brampton Bryan Estate Papers Index, Bundles 40, 60 and 85, Hereford and Worcester County Record Office

Calendar of State Papers Domestic, 1635-36, 1636-37, 1638-39, 1644-45, 1645-47, 1648-49, 1651, 1660-61

E.J.L. Cole: 'Court Rolls of Presteigne and Norton', *TRS*, Vol. XXII, 1952, pp37-48

A.W. Davies: 'Illustrations of the Parish Register of Presteign', *Archaeologica Cambrensis*, Vol. XXXVIII, 1864, pp.85-99

D.A. Davies: 'Plague, Death and Disease', *TWNFC*, Vol. XLIII, 1981, pp307-16

Documents relating to the Fire of Presteigne, 1681, Radnorshire Society Library

A.H. Dodd: 'Wales in the Parliaments of Charles I', *Transactions of the Honourable Society of Cymmrodorion*,1946-47, pp59-95

Mrs Everett Green (ed): *Calendar of the Committee for the Advance Money, 1642-56*, 1888

Calendar of the Committee for Compounding with Delinquents, 1643-60, 1889-93

M.A. Faraday: 'The Hearth Tax in Herefordshire', *TWNFC*, Vol. XLI, Part I, 1973, pp77-90
    'The Radnorshire Hearth Tax Returns of 1670, *TRS*, Vol. LIX, 1989, pp29-58
W.H. Howse: 'Contest for a Radnorshire Rectory', *Journal of the Historical Society of the Church in Wales*, Vol. VII, 1957, pp69-79
    'A Presteigne Petition of 1669', *TRS*, Vol. XXV, 1955, pp25-27
    'Presteigne's Great Fire of 1681', *TRS*, Vol. XXV, 1955, pp17-18
    'Crops grown in the parish of Presteigne in 1620', *TRS*, Vol. XXVI, 1956, pp46-49
    'New Light on the Visit of King Charles I to Presteigne', *TRS*, Vol. XXIX, 1959, pp28-30
Evan D. Jones: 'Gleanings from Radnorshire Files of Great Sessions Papers', *TRS*, Vol. XIII, 1943, pp7-3
G.E. McParlin: *The Herefordshire Gentry in County Government, 1625-61*, unpublished Ph.D. thesis, University of Wales, 1981
F.C. Morgan: *Transcript of Corpus Christi MS 206: The Puritan Survey*, Hereford Cathedral Library
R.C.B. Oliver: 'The Hartstonges and Radnorshire, Pt. II', *TRS*, Vol. XLIV, 1974, pp26-36
Philips & Co. Deeds, Powys County Archives Office
J.R. Phillips: *Memorials of the Civil War in Wales*, 2 vols., 1874
Presteigne Parish Register Hereford and Worcester County Record Office
Presteigne Parish Tithe Survey, 1620, Radnorshire Society Library
Paul Slack: *The Impact of Plague in Tudor and Stuart England*, 1985
J.F.D. Shrewsbury: *The History of Bubonic Plague in England*, 1970
State Papers Domestic SP 28/189, SP 28/202, Public Record Office
Margaret R. Toynbee: 'A Royal Journey through Breconshire and Radnorshire in 1645', *TRS*, Vol. XX, 1950, pp3-12; Vol. XXI, 1951, pp4-16
J. Webb: *Memorials of the Civil War ... as it affected Herefordshire*, 2 vols., 1874

Chapter V

D. Roy Ll. Adams: *The Parliamentary Representation of Radnorshire, 1536-1832*, unpublished M.A. thesis, University of Wales, 1970
Brampton Bryan Estate Papers Index, Bundles 40 and 60, Hereford and Worcester County Record Office
1801 Census, printed material
John Clark: *A General View of the Agriculture .... of the County of Radnor*, 1794
    A General View of the Agriculture ... of the County of Hereford, 1797
Mary Clement: *Correspondence and Minutes of the S.P.C.K. relating to Wales, 1699-1740*, 1952
Walter Davies MSS: Notebooks AAB and Bii, National Library of Wales

Walter Davies: *A General View of the Agriculture ... of South Wales*, 2 vols., 1815
D. Stedman Davies: 'Radnorshire Inns', *TRS*, Vol XI, 1941, pp13-18
                'Further Inns',*TRS*, Vol. XIII, 1943, p.47
Sir Frederick Eden: *The State of the Poor*, 1797
Hereford Diocesan Consistory Court Records, 1715-17, Hereford and Worcester County Record Office
W.H. Howse: 'Radnor's Inns', *TRS*, Vol. XV, 1945, pp54-7
          A Welsh Border Town, 1950
          'A Sale Bill of 1814, with new light on the Manors around Presteigne', *TRS*, Vol. XXIII, 1953, pp6-13
          School and Bell, 1956
D. Jones: *Before Rebecca: Popular Protest in Wales, 1793-1835*, 1973
R. Macklin: 'The Presteigne Area, 1750-1850', *TWNFC*, Vol. XL, Part I, 1970, pp137-54
R.C.B. Oliver: 'The Hartstonges and Radnorshire' Part I, *TRS*, Vol. XLIII, 1973, pp34-46
W.K. Parker: 'The Visits of Walter Davies to Radnorshire, 1802-11', *TRS*, Vol.XLVII, 1977, pp52-6
          'John Howard and Radnor County Gaol', *TRS*, Vol. LII, 1982, pp27-34
Parliamentary Papers, Session 1803-04, Vol. XII, Session 1818, Vol. XVI
Radnorshire Turnpike Trust Minute Book, Powys County Archives Office
Radnor Quarter Sessions Order Books Nos. 1 and 2, Powys County Archives Office
G.W. Ridyard: 'Supplementary Notes on the Watermills of Radnorshire', *Melin 9*, p14
A.H. Shorter: 'Paper-mills in Herefordshire', *TWNFC*, Vol. XXXIII, Pt.111, 1951, pp261-2
D. Thomas: *Agriculture in Wales During the Napoleonic Wars*, 1967
D. Vine: 'The Kington Turnpike Trust, 1756-1877', *TWNFC*, Vol. XLV, Pt. III, 1984, pp733-42

Chapter VI
D. Roy Ll. Adams: *The Parliamentary History of Radnorshire, 1526-1832*, unpublished M.A. thesis, University of Wales, 1970
N. Carlisle: *Topographical Dictionary of the Dominion of Wales*, 1811
Censuses 1801-51, printed material
Walter Davies: *A General View of the Agriculture ... of South Wales*, 2 vols., 1815
T.F. Ellis: *Parliamentary Survey of the Borough of Presteigne*, 1832
Hereford Journal
Hereford Times

W.H. Howse: *MSS Notebooks A,G and H*, Radnorshire Society Library
    Presteigne Past and Present, 1945
    Welsh Border Town, 1956
D. Jones: *Before Rebecca: Popular Protest in Wales, 1793-1835*, 1973
D. Macklin: 'The Presteigne Area, 1750-1850', TWNFC, Vol.XL, Part I, 1970, pp137-54
J.Nichols (ed): *Illustrations of the Literary History of the 18th Century*, 3 vols., 1818
W.K. Parker: 'The Great Rebuilding: the renewal of Radnorshire's Civic Buildings', *TRS*, Vol. L, 1980, pp21-33
    'Presteigne Escapes', *Country Quest*, June, 1981
    The Shire Hall, Presteigne, 1982
    'Radnor County Gaol: The Last Decade', *TRS*, Vol. LII, 1982, pp35-46
Parliamentary Papers, Session 1818, Vol. XIX; Session 1822, Vol.V; Session 1826, Vol. III; Session 1830-31, Vol. XI; Session 1834, Vols. XXX, XXXI, XXXII, XXXIII, XXXIV
Patricia Parris: 'The Shire Hall, Presteigne, Some Further Information', *TRS*, Vol. LI, 1981, pp40-44.
    'Mary Morgan: Contemporary Sources', *TRS*, Vol. LIII, 1983, pp57-64
Presteigne Parish Register, Hereford and Worcester County Record Office
Presteigne Poor Law Union Papers, 1836-45, Public Record Office
Radnor Quarter Sessions Order Books, Nos. 4-11, Powys County Archives Office
Radnor Quarter Sessions Records, Powys County Archives Office
Radnorshire Turnpike Trust Minute Book, Powys County Archives Office
Richard Williams: 'Fetters and Freedom', *TRS*, Vol. XXVI, pp56-62

Chapter VII

A.W. Ashton & I.L. Evans: *The Agriculture of Wales and Monmouthshire*, 1944
Censuses 1851-1901, printed material
C.R. Clinker: 'The Railways of West Herefordshire', *TWNFC*, Vol. XXXV, Part III, pp286-92
Report of the Commission of Inquiry into the State of Education in Wales, 1847
G. Drage: *Notes on the Militia*, 193
R.W.D. Fenn: 'Sir Richard Green Price of Norton Manor, 1803-87', *TRS*, Vol. LV, 1985, pp54-67
Hereford Journal
Hereford Times
W.H. Howse: *MSS Notebooks, A,F,G,H,T,W and Z*, Radnorshire Society Library
    Presteigne Past and Present, 1945
    Welsh Border Town, 1956
    School and Bell, 1956

M.A. Hoyer & M.L. Heppell: *The Welsh Border*, 1911
I.G. Jones & D. Williams: *The Religious Census of 1851: A Calendar of Entries Relating to Wales*, 1976
J. Jones: *The History of the Baptists in Radnorshire*, 1891
Kelly's Directory of South Wales, 1890, 1895, 1901 and 1914 editions
G.J. Lewis: 'Geography of religion in the Middle Marches of Wales in 1851', *Transactions of the Honourable Society of the Cymmrodorion*, 1950, pp123-42
W.C. Maddox: *A History of the Radnorshire Constabulary*, 1959
E. Newell: *Press Cuttings Notebook of 1880*, Radnorshire Society Library
E. Newell: *Press Cuttings Notebook, 1881-83*, Radnorshire Society Library
G. Archer Parfitt: 'The Military History of Radnorshire Pt.I', *TRS*, Vol. XXVI, 1956, pp63-88
J. Pigot: *National and Commercial Directory*, 1830 and 1844 editions
Presteigne Assembly Rooms: Schedules and deeds, etc., Powys County Archives Office
Presteigne Parish Agricultural Returns, 1875, 1877-78, 1885-87, 1895-97, 1905-07, PRO
Presteigne Parish Tithe Commutation Schedule, 1845, Hereford and Worcester County Record Office
Presteigne Primitive Methodist Circuit Quarterly Meeting Minute Books, Warden View Methodist Church, Presteigne
Radnor Express
Radnorshire Quarter Sessions Order Books, Nos.9-12, Powys County Archives Office
Radnorshire Society Quarter Sessions Records, Powys Archives County Office
Schools Inquiry Commission, Vol. XX, Monmouthshire and Wales, 1870
J.B. Sinclair & R.W.D. Fenn: *The Faculty of Locomotion*, 1991
Slater's Royal National and Commercial Directory of Gloucestershire ... North and South Wales, 1858, 1868 and 1880 editions

Chapter VIII
A.W. Ashley & I.L. Evans: *The Agriculture of Wales and Monmouthshire*, 1944
Brecon and Radnor Express
Censuses, 1901-71
Hereford Times
W.H. Howse: *Press-cuttings Notebook P2*, Radorshire Society Library
Knighton Poor Law Union: Abstracts of Outdoor Relief/National Assistance Payments, 1922/23-1939/40, Powys County Archives Office
Leominster News
W.C. Maddox: *History of the Radnorshire Civil Defence Scheme, 1935-46*, unpublished typescript, Powys County Archives Office
The LDV and Home Guard in Radnorshire, 1940-55, unpublished typescript, Powys County Archives Office

Norton Parish Meeting Minutes, 1894-1974, Presteigne Museum
G. Archer Parfitt: 'The Military History of Radnorshire Parts II & III', *TRS*, Vol. XXVII, 1957, pp46-61; Vol. XXVII, 1958, pp56-65
W.K. Parker: 'The Presteigne Coal Venture', *TRS*, Vol. LIII, 1983, pp10-27
Presteigne Chamber of Trade Minute Book, 1956-68, Presteigne Museum
Presteigne Platoon LDV, Observation Post Report Book, Presteigne Museum
Presteigne Platoon LDV, Road Patrol Book, Presteigne Museum
Presteigne Civil Parish Agricultural Returns, 1905-07, 1915-17, 1925-27, 1935-37, PRO
Presteigne Urban District Council Minute Books, 1935-39, 1939-46, 46-74, Powys County Archives Office
J. Owen Pryce *et at*: *A Review of Population Changes in Mid-Wales, 1901-51*, 1959
Radnor Express
Radnorshire County Council: *An Analysis of the Development Plan for Radnorshire*, 1951
Radnorshire County Council: *Air Raid Precautions/Civil Defence Committee Minutes*, Powys County Archives Office
Radnorshire County Council: *General Correspondence: Presteigne Elementary School 1924-32*, Powys County Archives Office
Radnorshire County Council: *General Correspondence: Presteigne Grammar School, 1940-55*, Powys County Archives Office
Radnorshire County Council: *Prevention and Relief of Distress in War Time*, Powys County Archives Office
Radnorshire County Council: *Public Assistance Committee Minutes, 1931-40*, Powys County Archives Office
Radnorshire County Council: *Register of Licences (cars and motor cycles) 1903-12*, Powys County Archives Office.
Radnorshire Standard

Chapter IX
Brecon and Radnor Express
Censuses 1971-91
Mid Wales Journal
Presteigne Urban District Minute Book 1953-7
Presteigne and Norton Town Council Minutes, 1974-95
Radnor District Council: *Presteigne Local Plan: Draft Written Statement*, 1985
Radnor District Council: *Presteigne Local Plan: Draft Written Statement*, 1987
Welsh Office: *Public Inquiry Report: Powys County Council, Knighton-Presteigne Road (Presteigne Diversion) Order*, 1980

Index

Aberystwyth 29, 94, 96, 97, 109, 110
Abley, Mrs Elizabeth 142, 172
Ackhill 14, 46, 78, 120
Agriculture 78-82, 89, 90-1, 102, 104, 108, 110, 111, 112, 136, 146-49, 170-1, 176, 184, 185, 187-9, 191-2
Ailesbury, Earl of 117
Amateur Christy Minstrels 204
Andrewes, Master 68
Anglo-Saxons 8-10, 11, 14, 26
April Fair 136
Apple Tree Inn 99, 122, 208
Apple Tree Meadow 220
Apple Tree Orchard 219
Archery Club 168
Arkwright, Mr. J.S. 186
ARP 207, 208, 210, 213, 214
Arsenal F.C. 197
Arthur, Prince 29
Assembly Rooms 113, 141, 142, 143, 161, 162, 164, 166, 167, 172, 175, 186, 204, 213, 215, 216, 221, 227
Assizes 37, 123, 133, 176, 193, 221
Atkins & Paul 203
Automobile Club 206
Ave Maria Lane 217

Back Lane 19, 33, 36, 51, 85, 90, 188, 203
Badminton Club 206
Bailey, PS 207
Baker, John 32, 38, 42
Baker, Richard 24
Ball, John 159
Band of Hope 153
Baptists 149, 152, 153, 156, 164, 167
Barland 16
Barley Mow 89, 99, 136, 138, 139
Barley Mow Field 202, 203
Barnes, James 123, 130
Baskerville, Thomas 84
Bayley, Rev James 86, 87
Beatty, Alexander 159
Beaumont, Thomas 126, 168

Beavan, Capt J. 143, 167
Beavan, Richard 117
Beddoes, John 31-3, 36, 44-7, 59, 62, 79, 86, 155
Beddoes, John, School 44-7, 205, 223, 226, 227, 228
Beddoes View 225
Beebee, Mr 89
Beebee, Thomas 155
Beeston, Rev. Eusebius 87
Beggars Bush 67, 96
Bell (inn) 100
Bell Meadow 45
Bethell, W.J. 194
Bevan, Rev Hugh 63
Birch, Col 69
Birmingham 110, 120
Bishop's Castle 56
Black Lion 100
Blackbourne, Thomas 42
Blackburn, Miss 156
Blackburn, Rev Charles 154
Blayney, John 46
Blayney, Thomas 70, 72
Blayney family 61
Bleddfa 20, 110
Blue Boar 98, 160
Blue Ribbon 153
Bodenham, Mr 130
Bohun, Humphrey 17
Botanical Drugs Ltd 217, 223
Boultibrooke 61, 67, 84, 86, 111, 120, 125, 147, 158, 164, 188
Bowen, Rev. Charles 150
Bowls 168, 206
Boy Scouts 170, 206
Boyd, Sir John 88
Boys' Brigade 170
Boys' Club 172, 212
Bradshaw, John I 47
Bradshaw, John III 24, 60
Bradshaw family 32, 38-41, 42, 43, 53, 60-1, 80
Brampton Bryan 66-7, 73, 84
Braose, Reginald de 16, 17
Braose, William de 16, 17
Brecknock 30
Brecon 17, 67, 215
Bretton, Richard 63

Brickworks 136, 139, 172
Bridge Inn 100
Brilley 63, 147
Brimfield 11
Bristol 159
British Legion 186, 206, 217, 218
British School 154, 156, 202
Britten, T.G. 169
Broad Street 18, 19, 36, 37, 48, 50, 66, 77, 79, 80, 81, 84, 92, 98, 102, 113, 122, 123, 136, 137, 139, 140, 152, 155, 156, 161, 174, 186, 190, 200, 201, 209, 216, 228, 230
Broadaxe Lane 122, 128, 228
Broadaxe Business Park 226
Broadheath 13, 36, 60, 68, 79, 80, 81, 88, 138, 164, 167, 168, 174, 185, 209, 212, 216
Broadheath Common 85
Broadheath House 85
Bromyard 11
Bronze Age 1-2
Brown, Mr 216
Bryce, James 153
Brydges, Lady 156, 158, 174, 188
Bryngwyn 84
Buckton 6
Bull Hotel 100, 113, 153
Bull, John 70
Burfa 2, 5, 6
Burford 86
Burgage, the 48, 138, 143, 160, 203, 217
Bus services 194, 221
Bush Farm 67
Butts, the 91, 138
Byton 1, 8, 14, 26, 63, 73, 86, 87, 90
Byton Farm 85
By-pass 226

Caen Wood 184
Caersws 7
Calloway, Thomas 132
Candlemas Fair 136
Canon's Lane 50, 77
Capital Stores 137

239

Caradoc 6
Cardigan 134
Careless, Mr A.E. 199
Cascob 13, 14, 29, 85, 94, 111, 193, 194
Cascoppe, John 25
Castell Collen 6, 7
Castle (inn) 76, 89, 97, 98, 99, 144, 163, 164
Cat & Fiddle 100
Cattle market 81-2, 146, 188, 222
Chamber of Commerce 193
Chamber of Trade 208, 209, 218, 221, 223, 226, 228, 229
Chandler, Peter 130
Chandler, Sarah 117, 120, 130, 131
Chandler, Thomas 120
Chapel Farm 42
Chapel Terrace 210
Chapman family 40
Charles I 64, 65, 67, 68, 70, 72
Charles Hill & Co 217, 224
Chicken Lane 58
Child, Peter 81
Choral Society 150
Church of St. Andrew 12, 15, 16, 22, 24-8, 42-4, 149-51, 164, 214, 227
Church schools (see also Schools) 165
Church Street 36, 47, 50, 76, 77, 86, 88, 98, 155, 174
Church Way 50, 77
Cinema 172, 204, 216-7
Civil War, the 64-74
Clatterbrook 79, 122
Claterbrune 1, 13, 14, 15, 214, 218, 219, 225
Clayton, William 42
Clement ap Gruffydd 42
Cloth industry 23, 30-6, 50-2, 59, 75, 83, 88, 89, 90, 102, 109, 126, 192
Clothing club 161
Clun 2, 11
Coal club 161
Coal mining 179-181, 184, 195
Coates, Thomas 123
Coates, Miss 184
Cockfighting 160, 168
Cold Oak 85
Cole, Luggar & Young 122

Cole, Thomas 73
Cole's Hill 185
Colebrook Meadow 174
Combe 1, 2, 11, 13, 85, 88, 136
Combes Moor 152
Com. of Enquiry into the State of Education in Wales 150, 153, 155
Conservatives 153, 163, 165, 179, 198
Conservative Club 186
Cooksey, Vincent 127-9
Cooperage 172
Cornewall, Humphrey 60
Cornewall, Thomas 80
Cornewall family 40
Corton 96, 97, 128, 168, 183, 185
Corton hoard 7
Council of Wales & the Marches 29, 37, 38, 40-1, 46, 62
County Ball 162
County Gaol 37, 70, 91-3, 113, 118-20, 127, 128-34, 143, 155
Coxall Knoll 6
Craven Arms 141, 171
Cricket 168, 205, 206
Cricketers' Arms 100, 168, 207
Cripps, Rev W.G. 198
Croft, Sir John 46
Croft, Lord 227
Croft Ambrey 3, 5
Cromwell, Oliver 70, 71
Cromwell, Thomas 30, 40
Crowther, Brian 55, 65
Curfew 45
Cuthbert, Rev. R.H. 150
Cutler, Robert 84
Cycling club 169, 170

Dark Ages 8-10
Dauntsey, John 71
Davies, Edward 43
Davies, Evan 65
Davies, James 120, 122
Davies, Mrs 155
Davies, Philip 174, 200, 201
Davies, William 165
Davyes, Richard 42
Debating & Literary Society 166
Debenham, Dr 173

Debenham, Miss 169
Debenham Mrs 156
Dee, Hugh 47
Dee, John 46
Deerfold Cross 194
Deerfold Forest 42
Development Assn 193
Devereux, Walter, Lord Ferrars 42
Devonshire, Duke of 155
Discoed 2, 6, 10, 11, 13, 14, 22, 26, 36, 48, 59, 73, 88, 90, 96, 109, 136, 152, 164, 225
Dipththeria 175
Disestablishment of Welsh Church 153, 163, 180
Dixon, James 159
Dolau 94
Dolley 46, 78, 124, 152
Dolley Green 219
Doluggan 148
Dolyhir 185
Downton 85
Dramatic Society 167
Drage, Col 182, 186
Drovers' roads 81
Duke's Arms 89, 97, 98, 113, 162, 163, 164, 206
Dyer, John 42

Eadric the Savage 15
Eardisley 215, 216
Eckley, Elenor 77
Eden, Sir Frederick 102, 103, 104, 105
Edith, Queen 12
Ednol 111
Edward the Confessor 12, 14
Edwards, Frank 165
Edwards, John 168
Edwards, Rev 63
Elan Valley 212
Elections 41, 49, 61, 63, 84, 85, 86, 91-2, 118, 123, 126, 141, 198
Electricity supply 203
Enclosure 79-80, 111, 141
Enterprise Park 227
Evans, Rev D. 155
Evans, Sir Geraint 227
Evans, John 131
Evans, Mrs Sophia 142, 151, 156, 159, 166
Eveleyn, F.C. 169

240

Eveleyn, Miss 183, 184, 186, 212
Eveleyn family 168, 169
Evenjobb 29, 64, 67, 85
Eywood 84

Falcon (inn) 98
Farmers' Arms 99
Farr family 45
Female Benefit Society 158
Field Company, the 146
Fire, the 74-77
Fire engine/brigade 176, 221
First World War 182-187
fitz Hugh, Osbern 18
fitz Richard, Osbern 18
fitz Warin, William 19
Folly, the 96
Folly Bank 165, 180, 193
Folly Farm 179, 180
Foot & mouth disease 147-8
Football 168-70, 197
Ford Street 20, 32
Forden 7
Forester, Ann 155
Foresters, the 158, 164, 166, 217
Forestry 184-5, 189, 192
Forge Crossing 144
Fountain (inn) 99
Fowle, Rev. Edward 150
Fowler, Alice 38
Fraxino family 16, 18, 24
Free Schools 156
Free Trade 165
Friendly societies 105, 158, 169-70
Frog Street 36, 50, 88, 89
Fulling mills 88, 109

Gallows Lane 37, 92, 113, 117, 122
Gaol Meadow 216
Garrison House 47, 86, 138, 154
Gas House Row 139
Gas lighting 137-38, 203
George (inn) 89, 100
Girl Guides 170, 206
Gittowe, John 32
Gladestry 29
Gladstone 165
Glasbury 128
Globe Inn 99
Globe Inn Friendly Society 158

Gloucester 66, 96
Glyndwr 6, 22
Godwinson, Harold 15
Godwinson, Swein 14
Golf Club 168, 206
Gomey, Thomas 70
Gommey 78
Gouge, William 62
Gough, Philip 46
Grammar School (see also Schools) 86-8, 153, 155, 193, 223
Great Sessions 37, 41, 70, 77, 91, 98, 113, 118, 120, 122
Great Street 18
Great Western Road 226
Green, Charles 154, 167
Green End 137, 180
Green Price, Dansey 143, 144, 167
Green Price, Richard 138, 140-6, 163, 167
Green Price, Mr Whitmore 207
Green Price family 124, 162, 168, 169
Greenfield 156, 169, 174, 209
Greenfield Road 190, 215
Greenfield Road School 202
Greenhouse, Mr 200
Greenly, John 87
Greycoat Club 126
Griffiths, Aaron 165, 179, 180, 182
Griffiths, Rev Humphrey 87
Griffiths, Isaac 86
Griffiths, John 161
Grove House 85, 89
Grove Inn 100
Grove Meadow 161, 168
Grubb, Rev John 87
Gumma 152
Gwernfael 212
GWR 143, 201
Gwynne, Sir Rowland

Hacklett, Deborah 102
Hall Green 217
Hamer, Miss 183, 184
Hanley family 45, 46
Hardinge, Justice 113-118, 120
Harford House 124, 156
Harley, Auditor 85
Harley, Lady Brilliana 67
Harley, Edward 70, 71, 72

Harley, Sir Robert 58, 61, 62, 63, 65, 66, 71, 73, 78
Harley, Robert (son) 72
Harley family 18, 49, 72, 84, 85
Harley Hill 202, 206
Harley Hill, Battle of 165
Harley's Wood 184
Harp Inn 100
Harpton 6, 8, 10, 84, 118
Harpton Court 37
Harpton House 125
Harper's Lane 19, 36, 51, 89, 137, 152, 217, 224
Hartington, Lord 141
Hatfield, Mr 216
Haverfordwest 134
Hay 17
Haycock, Edward 120,122
Hayes, Miss Elizabeth 156
Heb, Jenkyn 34
Hereford 11, 15, 21, 29, 30, 66, 68, 69, 137, 171
Hereford Assizes 123, 137
Hereford cattle 148
Hereford City Gaol 134
Hereford County Gaol 134
Hereford Street 18, 19, 32, 48, 50, 89, 97, 98, 114, 137, 140, 152, 156, 175, 176, 188, 192, 202, 203, 209, 220, 228
Hereford United F.C. 197
Herefordshire 14, 15, 65, 72, 105, 138, 203
Herefordshire Regiment, TA 182-3
Hergest 21
Herston Cross 2
Herrits, Mrs P.E. 200
Herryson, William 42
High Street 18, 19, 36, 37, 48, 50, 51, 76, 77, 85, 89, 92, 97, 102, 104, 113, 137, 139, 152, 155, 208, 209, 210, 228, 230
Higgins, Andrew 70
Higgins PS, 185, 200
Highlands Farm 85
Hill, Edward 217
Hill Farm 85, 138, 209
Hindwell Brook 1, 3, 6
Hindwell Fort 6, 7
Hoarstone Cottage 2, 13
Hockey clubs 169, 204, 205
Hodges, Mr 216
'Hole' the 160

241

Home Guard 210, 214
Home Farm 2
Hop Ground, the 122
Horticultural Society 158
Horton 117
House of Correction 92, 93, 122, 124, 128, 131
Housing 101, 102, 107-9, 136, 138, 170, 186, 190, 218, 219-21, 225
Howard, John 92, 93
Howarth, Sir Humphrey 84
Howse, W.H. 223
Huck family 45
Hudson, Miss 183
Humet 13-4, 15, 18
Hunting 167
Huntington 16, 17, 19, 23, 63
Hyde, Peter 80

Ice Age 1
Ince, Henry 127-8
Inns 93-100
Irish Home Rule 163
Iron Age 2-6
Iron School, the 156, 157
Isolation Hospital 175, 202

Jacobites 83, 84
James, Edward Lee 124, 154
James, Evan 61
James, Griffith 61
James, Richard 61
Jay Lane Fort 6
Jenkin, John 46
Jenyns, John 46
John, King 16
John ap Owen 46
John, Mr Stanley 195
Jones, Rev. Hugh 87
Jones, Jenkin 72
Jones, Col John 73
Jones, Rev John 74
Jones, Richard 61, 84
Jones, Thomas, 152, 153
Jones, Rev Watkin 202
Jones, William 66
Jones family 61
Jones Brydges, Sir Harford 86, 111, 118, 124, 126, 127, 128, 157, 161
Jones Brydges family 124, 142
Jubilee Boys' Club 151, 169, 197, 205

Junior Imperial League 207

Kaye Alloy Castings 220, 221, 224, 226, 229
Kewley, Rev. H. 150, 153, 156, 167, 169, 174, 180, 183, 186
Kidderminster 194
Kilpeck 113
Kilvert, Francis 150
King's Head 99
King, Tom 130
Kington 10, 16, 21, 29, 59, 63, 75, 82, 96, 97, 109, 110, 112, 136, 143, 171, 176, 194, 203, 221
Kington Bank, the 120
King's Turning 68, 85
Kinnerton 8, 10, 13, 96
Kinsham (see also Lower & Upper) 63, 78, 86, 87
Kinsham Court 179
Kinsham Grange 1
Knighton 10, 20, 22, 29, 49, 59, 68, 69, 74, 82, 91, 97, 104, 110, 112, 120, 128, 136, 140, 143, 165, 171, 176, 194, 210, 215, 223
Knill 1, 6, 14, 21, 63, 86
Knill, John ap 38
Knill, Sir Roger de 16
Knucklas 49, 212
KSLI 183
Kyngley, Philip 43

Labtech Ltd 227, 229
Labour Party 198
Labourers' Revolt, the 124
Ladies College 156
Langdale, Lady 161
Laping, Annette 155
Laundry 177
Lee, Rowland 30, 38, 40
Legge, Thomas 89, 154
Legge, Col William 68
Leintwardine 7, 53, 55, 60
Leisure Centre 227
Leominster 11, 12, 21, 29, 30, 53, 68, 75, 81, 94, 96, 123, 136, 171, 194, 221
Letchmoor 85
Letchmoor Farm 130
Letchmoor Lane 58, 130
Lewis, A. 174
Lewis, Elizabeth 102

Lewis, Capt F.O. 205, 214
Lewis, John 143
Lewis, Thomas 138, 139
Lewis, Thomas Frankland 126
Lewis, Rev Philip 71, 73, 74
Lewis, Robert 152
Lewis family 37, 84, 118, 128
Liberals 141, 153, 163, 165, 179, 198
Libraries 142, 166
Lime kilns etc. 89, 138, 146, 181, 192
Lingen 14, 26, 38, 63, 73, 81, 93, 111
Link Line 228
Lion (inn) 99
Little Brampton 8, 11, 14, 36, 81, 88, 136, 225
Litton 11, 85
Liverpool 211
Llanbadarn Fawr 63
Llandovery 141
Llandeveylocke 63
Llandrindod Wells 135, 136, 142, 156, 165, 170, 175, 177, 194, 221, 229
Llangunllo 29, 63, 81, 143, 148, 212
Llewelyn the Great 16
Llewelyn ap Gruffyd 18
Llewelyn, Gruffydd ap 15
Llewelyn, Lady Delia 218
Lloyd, Bell 84
Lloyd, Hugh 67
Lloyd, Lewis 48
Lloyd, Peter 46, 62
Lloyd's Bank 140
Local Defence Volunteers 208, 213-4
London 94, 96, 97, 109, 117, 172, 173
Lowe, Robert 92
Lower, Dr 183
Lower, Mrs 184
Lower Heath 68, 213
Lower Kinsham 2, 11, 26, 78, 85, 147
Lucas, Rev Richard 73-4, 80
Ludlow 30, 31-2, 38-40, 53, 55, 67, 81
Lugg, River 1-2, 6, 8, 10, 11, 22, 32, 36
Lugg Bridge Mill 88, 89
Lugg View 228

Luker, John 97

Machine House (inn) 99
Mackenzie, James 138
Maddison, Preb C.E. 151
Maelienydd 23, 47, 85
Maes Treylow 59, 78, 90, 96
Maesllwch 84
Maesllwch Castle 113
Magonsaetan 8
Malting 89-90, 105, 110, 111, 137, 138, 146, 148, 171
Mangar Aids 226-7, 229
Manor of Presteigne 47-50, 60, 61, 76, 85
Market Hall 141-3, 150, 172, 176, 209, 210, 221
Market Lane 58
Market Square 112
Mars-Jones, Justice 123
Martha, tollgate keeper 128
Martin, Richard 23
Mary, Queen 43, 44
Masons Arms 99
Matilda, Empress 16
May Fair 103, 128, 130, 135, 158, 159, 162, 200-2
McGregor, Mr J. 195
Memorial Hall 172, 218, 221, 228
Mercia 10, 14
Meredith, John 87
Meredith, Lewis 65
Meredith, Morgan 63
Meredith, Nicholas 46, 49, 70
Meredith, Richard 32, 88
Meredith family 32, 46, 61, 63
Methodists 152, 164
Meyrick, Sir Gelly 37, 41
Michaelchurch 63
Michaelmas Fair 136
Mid Border Community Arts Assn 227
Midland Bank 140
Midland Shires Farmers 226
Milbank, Sir Powlett 161, 163, 165, 175, 188
Miles, Henry 130
Miles, John 49
Militia 84, 90, 91, 138, 170, 175
Mill House 85
Mill Lane 88
Milton 14
Ministry of Labour Training

Camp 195-198, 208
Minton, Susannah 113
Monaughty 63, 96, 148
Monnington, William 71
Monnington family 58
Montgomery 29, 69, 134
Moor Farm 139
Morgan, George 186
Morgan, John 43
Morgan, Lewis 71
Morgan, Mary 113-118
Morgan, Thomas 34
Mories, Adam 43
Morris, H.F. 165
Morris, William 33
Mortimers 16-18, 19, 22, 24
Moryce ap Lellowe 43, 45
Moses, Mr T.G. 223
Mothers Union 170
Motor vehicles 173
Music societies 166-7, 204
Mutual Cattle Insurance Society 148

Nail-making 136, 172
Nantmel 67
Napoleonic War 107, 111
Nash 11, 14, 26, 29, 36, 81, 85, 88, 90, 91, 96, 98, 136, 138, 146, 152, 192, 225
Nash Court 85
Nash Quarry 192, 193, 194
Nash Wood 179, 180, 184, 185
National School (see also Schools) 150, 154, 157, 202
Neild, James 92, 93, 114
Neolithic Age 1-2
New Club 158, 162
New Inn 99
New Mill Orchard 174
New Radnor 20, 21, 29, 31, 37, 40, 43, 49, 58, 67, 74, 96, 97, 109
Newall, Mrs 212
Newark, Miss Georgina 156
Newbery, Rev. Thomas 154
Newchurch 67
Newell's Ironmongers 136, 152
Newell, Mrs Grace 152
Newtown 68
Nicholson, Thomas 142
Nolan, Sir Sidney 227
Northwood 64
Norton 2, 8, 14, 20, 22, 26, 49,

69, 73, 83, 85, 90, 91, 111, 141, 152, 184, 209, 223, 225
Norton Manor 86, 111, 124, 141, 188, 209, 210

Oak Inn 84, 98, 100
Oddfellows 158, 217
Offa's Dyke 9, 10
Old Club 105, 158
Old Radnor 43
Old Radnor Trading Company 146, 185
Oldfield, Mike 45
Orchard Close 225
Orchard Field 203
Ordovices 6
Ormanthwaite, Lord 165
Ormerod, Rev Oliver 149, 150
Otway, Captain 163, 164, 168
Otway, Mrs 161
Owen, Frank 62
Owen, John Downey 127
Owens, Capt J.H. 195
Oxford Arms 97, 99, 100, 206

Painscastle 29, 49, 67
Paradise 85, 168
Paradise Farm 209
Parliamentary Reform 126
Parsons, Cecil 127, 132, 138, 140, 161
Passive Resistance Movement 165
Payne, Wilson 120
Paytoe, Thomas 130, 131
Pembridge 68, 148, 203
Penybont 110
Perry & Co 143
Petty Sessions 199
Phillips, Robert 154
Pilleth 21, 29, 61, 65, 81, 96, 111, 148
Plague 21, 22, 23, 30-1, 36, 53-60, 65, 73, 75, 88, 101
Plant Mat, the 37
Police Force 123, 138, 159
Police Station 155, 170, 185
Polo club 168
Poor Law Commission 124
Poor Law Unions 112, 123, 127, 150
Poor Relief 192, 193
Population 36, 50, 51-2, 54, 59, 75, 83, 98, 101, 102, 105,

107-108, 135-138, 146, 162, 170, 173, 187, 189, 218, 223, 225
Port family 16, 18, 24
Pound Lane 19, 36, 88
POW camp 185, 214-16
Powell, John ap 34
Powell, Vavasour 71, 72, 74
Presteigne Promotion Association 229
Price, Ann 84
Price, Charles 61, 65, 66, 67
Price, Charles H. 114
Price, Edward 84
Price, James 45, 61, 63
Price, John 58
Price, Richard 86, 111, 122, 167
Price, Thomas 155
Price, William 143
Price family 40, 61
Primitive Methodists 149, 150, 152, 153, 154, 160, 167, 180, 198
Primrose Lane 89
Primrose League 163
Prince Regent 120
Private charities 160
Prize fights 158, 168
Pugh, Thomas 151, 161
Pugh, Mr R.A. 165, 180
Pugh, Mr W.A. 156

Quoits 168
Quarrell, Mrs 72
Quarter Sessions 37, 41, 77, 91, 104, 123, 151, 152, 164, 170, 221
Queen's Head 100
Querentune 13

Radio club 207
Radnor, lordship of 17
Radnor Battery RFA 208
Radnor Borough 49, 142, 154
Radnor Coal Syndicate 179-82
Radnor Farm 136, 139
Radnor Forest 29
Radnor Wild Life Trust 228
Radnorshire 8, 10, 15, 30, 40, 58, 61, 64, 65, 66, 67, 69, 74, 83, 106, 114, 134, 135, 160, 165, 193, 212, 223
Radnorshire Arms 49, 61, 97,
99, 126, 127, 162, 166, 168, 206
Radnorshire Bank 140, 152
Radnorshire Co. 146
Ragged School 156
Railways 135, 136, 141, 143-6, 148, 172, 173, 176, 194, 212, 221
Ralf, Count of Vexin 14, 15
'Ranters' 152
Rascoll family 45
Rea, James Thomas 148
Read, John 24, 61
Rebecca Riots 128
Rectory 61-3, 73, 74
Red Cross hospital 183, 184
Red Lion 99
Redfearn, Mr D.E. 223
Religious affairs 149-53
Rendle, Mr A.E. 195
Rennell of Rodd, Lord 221
Rhayader 23, 29, 37, 38, 40, 49, 95, 124, 128, 165
Richards, Frank 66
Richards Castle 15
Ricketts, Thomas 167
Rodd 11, 14, 46, 78, 85, 136, 148, 225
Rodd, the 182
Rodd, Hugh 16
Rodd, John 43
Rodd, William 42, 43
Rodd Court 85
Roddhurst 97, 152
Rode, Walter a 43
Rodney, Lord 86
Rogers, Aaron 148
Rogers, Benjamin 148
Rogers, Charles 179
Rogers, Ald. Coltman 155
Rogers, Edward 122
Rogers, John 148
Rogers, Richard 174
Roman period 6-8
Romilly, Sir Samuel 117
Rose & Crown 97, 99
Ross 55
Rowley 78, 85
Rowley, Benjamin 89
Royal Oak 100
Rushock 21, 29
St Andrews Fair 136
St Andrews Football Club 151, 169, 197, 215
St Antholin's 61, 73
St Davids Street 19, 22, 40, 47, 48, 76, 77, 85, 89, 98, 151, 155, 174, 201, 230
Sandford, Rev S. 86, 87
Sandys, Col Robert 67
Sanitation 102, 174-5, 198, 203, 218, 225
Saw-mill 172
Sawyer, Sir Edmond 48
Scapula 6
Scott, Sir Gilbert 141
Scottleton Street 2, 19, 116, 152, 157, 190, 193, 203
Schools 76, 77, 153-157, 165, 176, 193, 202, 210, 216, 223
Schools Enq. Comm. 153
Scrope, Osbern le 10, 13, 14, 15, 16
Scrope, Richard le 14
Scull, Rev John 62, 63, 73, 74
Seally, William 132
Second World War 207-216
Secondary School 223
Seymour, John 33, 43
Seymour, Sir Thomas 48
Sheep Market 188, 220
Sheep Music Festival 227, 229
Ship Money 64, 65
Shire Hall 37, 50, 77, 92, 113, 118-20, 122-3, 138, 162, 166, 175, 207, 221, 227, 229, 230
Shobdon 1, 40, 96
Shropshire 13, 14
Shurley, John 44
Sibbes, Rachel 62
Silia 165
Silia Meadow 218
Silia Woods 228
Silures 6
Silver Jubilee Committee 203
Skittles 168
Slough Road 184, 195, 199
Smallpox 101-2, 175
Smirke, Charles 120
Smith, A.H. 155
Smith, Mrs 184
Smythe, Robert 98
Society for the Prosecution of Felons 124
Society for the Protection of Game 124, 127
Sparey, H.J. 165, 203

SPCK 86
Spittletree factory 136, 172
Stamford, Earl of 66, 72
Stanage 122
Stansbatch 5, 6, 152
Stapleton 2, 11, 15, 22, 70, 78, 81, 85, 96, 101, 111, 136, 152, 225
Stapleton Castle 18, 26, 85
Station Road 19, 48, 50, 201, 226, 228
Staunton 6
Stephen, King 16
Stephens, W. 99, 140, 163
Still, Ann 155
Stocking Farm 177
Stonewall Hill 6, 68, 96, 209
Strangward 73
Sun (inn) 99
Sunday School 149, 164, 169
Swynderby, William 42

Talbot 98
Talgarth 216
Tanhouse 174
Tannery 110, 137, 171
Tariff Reform 163, 165
Taylor, Nicholas 62, 68, 71, 72, 74, 81, 84
Taylor, Peter 71
Taylor, William 70
Taylor family 61
Taylor's Farm 85
Telegraph system 137
Telephone Exchange 175
Teme, River 1, 2, 8
Temperance meetings/ societies 153, 164, 207
Tennis club 169, 204, 206
Thickens, Thomas 152
Thomas, Mr G. 163
Thomas, Mr W. 186, 198, 202
Thomas, William 42, 48
Threlwall, Thomas 155
Timber yards 110, 137
Titley 14, 63, 84, 96, 97, 112, 136, 143, 221
Toc H 206
Tollgates (see also Turnpike Trusts) 93-98
Town Band 151, 166
Town Council 226, 227, 228
Townend 218, 219
Traders' Association 176-7

Trevor, Sir Thomas 64
Tudge, William 148
Turner, Thomas 62
Turnpike Trusts 93-98, 109, 123, 125, 128
Twelve Men, the 62

UDC 165, 172, 174, 175, 177, 184, 186, 188, 189, 190, 192-5, 194, 198-204, 208-13, 218-23, 226, 227
Unemployment 162, 191-2, 193, 194-7
Upper Broadheath 85
Upper Heath 2
Upper Kinsham 26
Upton-on-Severn 56

Vaughan, Charles 37, 44
Vaughan, Edward 89
Vaughan, John 37
Vaughan, William 41
Vaughan family 40
Verdon, Henry 131, 132
Vicares, Roger 46
Virgo, W.H. 173
Volunteer Hall 162, 186, 206

Wages 102, 103, 105, 111, 184, 191
Wale, J.H. 165
Walford 60
Walker, Dr David 219
Walker, Cllr Lane 210
Walker, Dr R. 194, 217
Walsh, Hon Arthur 167
Walsh, Sir John 118
Walsh, Capt 186
Walsh family 128
Walsham, John 62, 71, 72
Walsham, Richard 48
Walton 2, 8, 10, 29, 96, 98, 194
Warden, the 6, 152, 159, 161, 162, 168, 174, 175, 193, 199-201, 219
Warden Castle 17-8, 19
Warden Close 225
Warden Court 89
Warden Road 89, 96, 210
Warden's Wake 128, 135, 136, 152, 158, 159, 162
Wars of the Roses 23-4
Water supply 174-5, 177, 190, 218-20, 225-6

Watkin, Tudor MP 221
Weatherstone, Letitia 155
Weaver, John 46, 138
Weaver, Peter 43
Weaver, Thomas 62
Wegnall Farm 68
Wegnalls 88
Wellington, Henry 43
Welshpool 123
Went, William 48, 49, 131
Went's Meadow 122
Weobley 68
Wesleyans 151
West, Rev A.W. 150
West Street 19, 51
West Wall 36, 85, 88, 90, 160
Western Avenue 219
Whalley, Rev William 68
Wherby Lane 19
Whigs 118, 124
Whitcombe, Dr William 127-9
White Hart 97, 99
Whitewall Farm 13, 79, 85, 174
Whitmore, Sir William 65
Whitmore, Sir George 65
Whittaker, John 130
Whitton 69, 96, 194
Wigmore 17, 53, 55, 67, 87, 97
Wigmore Abbey 24-6, 40, 42, 44, 47, 62
Wigmore, Thomas 46
Wignore, William 61
Wilkins, Walter MP 113-8
Wilkins, Walter Jnr 113-8, 122, 140, 167
Willey 11, 14, 73, 111, 136, 147, 152, 225
Willey Court 68, 89
Willey Lodge 179
Willets, Thomas 81
Williams, John 120
Williams, Jonathan 84
Williams, Robert 60, 61
Willoughby, Lord 63
Wilson, Mr A.M. 184, 190, 203
Wilson Terrace 190
Wishlade, Benjamin 120, 122
Withybeds 228
Wolseley, Sir Robert 61
Womens Institute 217
Women's Land Army 185, 216
Wood, Miss 156
Woodland Trust 228
Woodward, F.J. 154

Wool trade 22-3
Worcester 56, 68, 94, 97, 109, 159
Worcester, Battle of 70
Working conditions (see also Wages) 102, 104, 160, 191
Working Men's Club 157
Workhouse 104, 105, 128
Wozencroft, Mr 200
Wylly, Hugh 48

Young, Samuel 180
YMCA 197